Computer System Organization

AUTHOR

Dr. Sonal Yadav
Assistant Professor
Dept. of Computer Science & Engineering (CSE)
National Institute of Technology Raipur,
Chhattisgarh

REVIEWER

Prof. Milan Mehta
AProfessor (HAG)
Dept. of Computer Science & Engineering (CSE)
Gujarat Technological University - Ahmedabad,
Sigma Institute of Engineering (648) Bakrol, Vadodara, Gujarat

KHANNA BOOK PUBLISHING CO. (P) Ltd.
4C/4344, Ansari Road, Darya Ganj,
New Delhi, India

All India Council for Technical Education
Nelson Mandela Marg, Vasant Kunj,
New Delhi, India

ISBN: 978-93-55387-71-4
Book Code: DIP451EN

Computer System Organization

by Dr. Sonal Yadav

First Edition: 2025

Originally Published by:
All India Council for Technical Education, Ministry of Education, GOI

Exclusively Published & Distributed by:
Khanna Book Publishing Co. (P) Ltd.
4C/4344, Ansari Road, Daryaganj,
New Delhi (INDIA)

Visit us at: **www.khannabooks.com**
Write us at: **contact@khannabooks.com**

To view complete list of books,
Please scan the QR Code:
KPH

Printed in Bharat.

प्रो. टी. जी. सीताराम
अध्यक्ष
Prof. T. G. Sitharam
Chairman

सत्यमेव जयते

आज़ादी का अमृत महोत्सव

अखिल भारतीय तकनीकी शिक्षा परिषद्
(भारत सरकार का एक सांविधिक निकाय)
(शिक्षा मंत्रालय, भारत सरकार)
नेल्सन मंडेला मार्ग, वसंत कुंज, नई दिल्ली-110070
दूरभाष : 011-26131498
ई-मेल : chairman@aicte-india.org

ALL INDIA COUNCIL FOR TECHNICAL EDUCATION
(A STATUTORY BODY OF THE GOVT. OF INDIA)
(Ministry of Education, Govt. of India)
Nelson Mandela Marg, Vasant Kunj, New Delhi-110070
Phone : 011-26131498
E-mail : chairman@aicte-india.org

FOREWORD

Engineers are the backbone of any modern society. They are the ones responsible for the marvels as well as the improved quality of life across the world. Engineers have driven humanity towards greater heights in a more evolved and unprecedented manner.

The All India Council for Technical Education (AICTE), have spared no efforts towards the strengthening of the technical education in the country. AICTE is always committed towards promoting quality Technical Education to make India a modern developed nation emphasizing on the overall welfare of mankind.

An array of initiatives has been taken by AICTE in last decade which have been accelerated now by the National Education Policy (NEP) 2020. The implementation of NEP under the visionary leadership of Hon'ble Prime Minister of India envisages the provision for education in regional languages to all, thereby ensuring that every graduate becomes competent enough and is in a position to contribute towards the national growth and development through innovation & entrepreneurship.

One of the spheres where AICTE had been relentlessly working since past couple of years is providing high quality original technical contents at Under Graduate & Diploma level prepared and translated by eminent educators in various Indian languages to its aspirants. For students pursuing 2nd year of their Engineering education, AICTE has identified 87 books, which shall be translated into 12 Indian languages - Hindi, Tamil, Gujarati, Odia, Bengali, Kannada, Urdu, Punjabi, Telugu, Marathi, Assamese & Malayalam. In addition to the English medium, books in different Indian Languages are going to support the students to understand the concepts in their respective mother tongue.

On behalf of AICTE, I express sincere gratitude to all distinguished authors, reviewers and translators from the renowned institutions of high repute for their admirable contribution in a record span of time.

AICTE is confident that these outcomes based original contents shall help aspirants to master the subject with comprehension and greater ease.

T. G. Sitharam
(Prof. T. G. Sitharam)

ACKNOWLEDGEMENT

The authors are grateful to the authorities of AICTE, particularly Prof. (Dr.) T G Sitharam, Chairman; Dr. Abhay Jere, Vice-Chairman, Prof. Rajive Kumar, Member-Secretary, Dr. Ramesh Unnikrishnan, Advisor-II and Dr. Sunil Luthra, Director, Training and Learning Bureau for their planning to publish the books on *Computer System Organization*. We sincerely acknowledge the valuable contributions of the reviewer of the book Prof. Milan Mehta, Principle of Sigma Institute of Engineering, Vadodara.

I would like to thank my PhD student Mr. Revya Naik V for his valuable support to complete this book. I express my gratitude to my PhD supervisors, Prof. Manoj Singh Gaur, Director, IIT Jammu, and Prof. Vijay Laxmi, Professor (CSE), MNIT Jaipur, for their continuous inspiration and learning opportunities. I am also thankful to my Postdoc mentor Prof. Hemangee K. Kapoor, Professor (CSE), IIT Guwahati for providing a learning experience.

I sincerely thank my friends, colleagues and family members for their patience while I wrote this book. Finally, a special thanks to my parents Mr. Jai Singh Yadav and Mrs. Rajbala Yadav, for continuously encouraging me to contribute to society.

This book is an outcome of various suggestions of AICTE members, experts and authors who shared their opinion and thought to further develop the engineering education in our country. Acknowledgements are due to the contributors and different workers in this field whose published books, review articles, papers, photographs, footnotes, references and other valuable information enriched us at the time of writing the book.

Dr. Sonal Yadav

PREFACE

The book titled "Computer System Organization" is an outcome of the rich experience of our teaching of basic and advanced courses of computer architecture. The initiation of writing this book is to expose fundamentals of computer system organization to the engineering students, the usage of assembly programming to interact with computer's hardware. Keeping in mind the purpose of wide coverage as well as to provide essential supplementary information, we have included the topics recommended by AICTE, in a very systematic and orderly manner throughout the book. Efforts have been made to explain the fundamental concepts of the subject in the simplest possible way.

During the process of preparation of the book, we have considered the various standard text books and accordingly we have developed sections and a variety of questions like multiple choice, short and long answer, numericals problems and supplementary material. While preparing the different sections emphasis has also been laid on examples, supplementary material and also on comprehensive synopsis of key points for a quick revision of the basic principles. The book covers all types of medium and advanced level problems and these have been presented in a very logical and systematic manner. The gradations of those problems have been tested over many years of teaching to a wide variety of students.

Apart from illustrations and examples as required, we have enriched the book with numerous solved problems in every unit for proper understanding of the related topics. Under the common title "Computer System Organization" there is a set of five chapters covering different aspects and organization of computers in engineering. The first chapter covers Structure of Computers, which is followed by chapters on Microprogrammed Control, Microprocessor Architecture, Assembly Language Programming, Memory, and Digital Interfacing. It is important to note that all chapters have relevant laboratory practicals. In addition, besides some essential information for the users under the heading "Know More" we present notable Indian inventors as well as rich Indian Vedas knowledge and fundamental principles for motivating readers to practice our valuable principles in modern lifestyle.

As far as the present book is concerned, "Computer System Organization" is meant to provide a thorough grounding in computer architecture on the topics covered. This part of the computer system organization book will prepare engineering students to apply the knowledge of computer architecture to tackle 21st century and onward engineering challenges and address the related aroused questions. The subject matters are presented in a constructive manner so that an Engineering degree prepares students to work in different sectors or in national laboratories at the very forefront of technology.

We sincerely hope that the book will inspire the students to learn and discuss the ideas behind basic principles of computer system organization and will surely contribute to the development of a solid foundation of the subject. We would be thankful to all beneficial comments and suggestions which will contribute to the improvement of the future editions of the book. It gives us immense pleasure to place this book in the hands of the teachers and students. It was indeed a big pleasure to work on different aspects covered in the book.

Dr. Sonal Yadav

OUTCOME BASED EDUCATION

For the implementation of an outcome based education the first requirement is to develop an outcome based curriculum and incorporate an outcome based assessment in the education system. By going through outcome based assessments evaluators will be able to evaluate whether the students have achieved the outlined standard, specific and measurable outcomes. With the proper incorporation of outcome based education there will be a definite commitment to achieve a minimum standard for all learners without giving up at any level. At the end of the programme running with the aid of outcome based education, a student will be able to arrive at the following outcomes:

PO1. Basic and Discipline specific knowledge: Apply knowledge of basic mathematics, science and engineering fundamentals and engineering specialization to solve the engineering problems.

PO2. Problem analysis: Identify and analyses well-defined engineering problems using codified standard methods.

PO3. Design/development of solutions: Design solutions for well-defined technical problems and assist with the design of systems components or processes to meet specified needs.

PO4. Engineering Tools, Experimentation and Testing: Apply modern engineering tools and appropriate technique to conduct standard tests and measurements.

PO5. Engineering practices for society, sustainability and environment: Apply appropriate technology in context of society, sustainability, environment and ethical practices.

PO6. Project Management: Use engineering management principles individually, as a team member or a leader to manage projects and effectively communicate about well-defined engineering activities.

PO7. Life-long learning: Ability to analyse individual needs and engage in updating in the context of technological changes.

COURSE OUTCOMES

After completion of the course the students will be able to:

CO-1: Have a good understanding of functioning of computer system

CO-2: Have a good understanding of the functioning of various subcomponents of computers.

CO-3: Student will be able to understand computing requirements for a specific purpose.

CO-4: Analyze performance bottlenecks of the computing device.

CO-5: Choose appropriate computing device for a given use case.

Mapping of Course Outcomes with Programme Outcomes to be done according to the matrix given below:

Course Outcomes	Expected Mapping with Programme Outcomes (1- Weak Correlation; 2- Medium Correlation; 3- Strong Correlation)						
	PO-1	PO-2	PO-3	PO-4	PO-5	PO-6	PO-7
CO-1	3	3	3	3	1	2	3
CO-2	3	3	3	3	1	2	3
CO-3	3	3	3	3	1	2	3
CO-4	3	3	2	3	1	2	3
CO-5	3	3	2	3	1	1	3

GUIDELINES FOR TEACHERS

To implement Outcome Based Education (OBE) knowledge level and skill set of the students should be enhanced. Teachers should take a major responsibility for the proper implementation of OBE. Some of the responsibilities (not limited to) for the teachers in OBE system may be as follows:

- Within reasonable constraint, they should manoeuvre time to the best advantage of all students.
- They should assess the students only upon certain defined criterion without considering any other potential ineligibility to discriminate them.
- They should try to grow the learning abilities of the students to a certain level before they leave the institute.
- They should try to ensure that all the students are equipped with the quality knowledge as well as competence after they finish their education.
- They should always encourage the students to develop their ultimate performance capabilities.
- They should facilitate and encourage group work and team work to consolidate newer approach.
- They should follow Bloom's taxonomy in every part of the assessment.

Bloom's Taxonomy

Level	Teacher should Check	Student should be able to	Possible Mode of Assessment
Create	Students ability to create	Design or Create	Mini project
Evaluate	Students ability to justify	Argue or Defend	Assignment
Analyse	Students ability to justify	Differentiate or Distinguish	Project/Lab Methodology
Apply	Students ability to use information	Operate or Demonstrate	Technical Presentation/ Demonstration
Understand	Students ability to explain the ideas	Explain or Classify	Presentation/Seminar
Remember	Students ability to recall (or remember)	Define or Recall	Quiz

GUIDELINES FOR STUDENTS

Students should take equal responsibility for implementing the OBE. Some of the responsibilities (not limited to) for the students in OBE system are as follows:

- Students should be well aware of each UO before the start of a unit in each and every course.
- Students should be well aware of each CO before the start of the course.
- Students should be well aware of each PO before the start of the programme.
- Students should think critically and reasonably with proper reflection and action.
- Learning of the students should be connected and integrated with practical and real life consequences.
- Students should be well aware of their competency at every level of OBE.

ABBREVIATIONS AND SYMBOLS

List of Abbreviations

General Terms			
Abbreviations	**Full form**	**Abbreviations**	**Full form**
AC	Accumulator Register	IR	Instruction Register
ADC	Analog-to-Digital Conversion	ISA	Instruction Set Architecture
ALSU	Arithmetic Logic Shift Unit	ISZ	Increment and Skip if Zero
ALU	Arithmetic and Logic Unit	LSB	Least-Significant Bit
ASHL	Arithmetic Shift-Left	MAR	Memory Address Register
ASHR	Arithmetic Shift-Right	MDR	Memory Data Register
AX	Accumulator Register	MICR	Magnetic Ink Character Recognition
BHT	Branch History Table	MMU	Memory Management Unit
BIOS	Basic Input/Output System	MSB	Most-Significant Bit
BIU	Bus Interface Unit	NASM	Netwide Assembler
BP	Base Pointer	NOP	No Operation
BSR	Bit Set/Reset	OCR	Optical Character Recognition
BX	Base Register	PC	Program Counter
CAR	Control Address Register	PROM	Programmable Read-Only Memory
CD	Compact Disc	RAM	Random Access Memory
CIL	Circular Shift-Left	RAW	Read After Write
CIR	Circular Shift-Right	RISC	Reduced Instruction Set Computer
CISC	Complex Instruction Set Computer	ROM	Read Only Memory
CPU	Central Processing Unit	RTL	Register Transfer Language
CS	Code Segment	SC	Sequence Counter
CU	Control Unit	SD	Secure Digital
CX	Count Register	SHL	Logical Shift-Left
DAC	Digital-to-Analog Conversion	SHR	Logical Shift-Right
DB	Define Byte	SI	Source Index
DI	Destination Index	SIMD	Single Instruction Stream Multiple Data Stream
DS	Data Segment		
DVD	Digital Versatile Disc	SP	Stack Pointer
DX	Data Register	SS	Stack Segment
ES	Extra Segment	SSD	Solid State Drive
EU	Execution Unit	USB	Universal Serial Bus
FIFO	First-In First-Out	WAR	Write After Read
HDD	Hard Disc Drive	WAW	Write After Write
I/O	Input/Output	WMFC	Wait until Memory Function Completed
IP	Instruction Pointer	ZF	Zero Flag

List of Units

General Terms			
Abbreviations	**Full form**	**Abbreviations**	**Full form**
GB	Gigabytes	NS	Nanoseconds
KB	Kilobytes	TB	Terabytes

List of Symbols

Symbols	Description	Symbols	Description
+	Addition	X	Multiplication
^	AND operation	A'	NOT A
/	Division	v	OR operation
X	Don't Care	–	Subtraction
*	Multiplication	⊕	XOR operation

LIST OF FIGURES

1. Structure of Computers

Fig. 1.1: Computer functional units 3
Fig. 1.2: Input devices 4
Fig. 1.3: Memory Hierarchy: registers, caches, and main memory are volatile memory and solid state drive, mechanical hard drives are non-volatile memory 5
Fig. 1.4: Placement of cache memory 5
Fig. 1.5: Secondary storage 6
Fig. 1.6: Arithmetic logic unit (ALU) 6
Fig. 1.7: The control unit decodes instructions and generates control signals through master clock to synchronize events (IR: Instruction Register) 7
Fig. 1.8: Interconnection networks 8
Fig. 1.9: Output unit 9
Fig. 1.10: Von-nuemann architecture 9
Fig. 1.11: System bus structure is made up of data bus, address bus, and control bus 10
Fig. 1.12: Structure of processor registers and main memory 11
Fig. 1.13: MSB and LSB bits in a 8-bit binary number 12
Fig. 1.14: Representation of +64 and –64 signed numbers in the sign-and-magnitude, 1's complement, and 2's complement number systems 13
Fig. 1.15: Overflow detection on adding two positive numbers +64 and +84 14
Fig. 1.16: Overflow detection on adding two negative numbers –64 and –84 15
Fig. 1.17: Different representation of values in registers 19
Fig. 1.18: Data transfer from registers via bus 19
Fig. 1.19: Arithmetic and logic shift unit microoperations schematic diagram and function table 21
Fig. 1.20: Schematic diagram of logic micro-operations and function table 23
Fig. 1.21: Logical shift (a) left and (b) right micro-operations 26
Fig. 1.22: Arithmetic shift (a) left and (b) right micro-operations 26
Fig. 1.23: Circular shift (a) left and (b) right micro-operations 26

2. Micro Programmed Control

Fig. 2.1: Control memory address selection 38
Fig. 2.2: Control unit block diagram 39
Fig. 2.3: Hardwired control unit 39
Fig. 2.4: Microprogrammed control organization 40
Fig. 2.5: Hardware implementation of addition and subtraction operation for sign-and-magnitude numbers 42
Fig. 2.6: Sign-and-magnitude addition and subtraction operation flowchart 42

Fig. 2.7: Addition and subtraction hardware implementation for 2's complement numbers 43
Fig. 2.8: Flowchart of addition and subtraction for 2's complement numbers 43
Fig. 2.9: Multiplication for sign-and-magnitude numbers 44
Fig. 2.10: Sign-and-magnitude multiplication flowchart 44
Fig. 2.11: Booth's multiplication hardware implementation 46
Fig. 2.12: Booth's multiplication flowchart 46
Fig. 2.13: Restoring division flowchart 47
Fig. 2.14: Non restoring division 49
Fig. 2.15: Registers for floating point arithmetic operations 53
Fig. 2.16: Addition or subtraction of floating point binary numbers 53
Fig. 2.17: Multiplication of floating point binary numbers 54
Fig. 2.18: Magnitudes division 55
Fig. 2.19: Division of floating point binary numbers 55
Fig. 2.20: Pipelined execution of floating-point adder 56
Fig. 2.21: Pipelined execution of instructions 57
Fig. 2.22: Structural or resource hazard 58
Fig. 2.23: Structural/Resource hazard solution 58
Fig. 2.24: Occurrence of Read after Write (RAW) hazard in pipelined execution of the instructions 59
Fig. 2.25: RAW data hazard solution 59
Fig. 2.26: Control hazard situation 61
Fig. 2.27: Control hazard solution 62
Fig. 2.28: State diagram of 1-bit dynamic branch prediction 62
Fig. 2.29: Actual prediction and hardware prediction 63

3. Microprocessor Architecture

Fig. 3.1: Register indirect addressing mode when operand address stored in a register and when address stored in memory 83
Fig. 3.2: Main memory and register contents in index addressing mode 83
Fig. 3.3: Main memory and register contents in base-index and base-index offset addressing mode 84
Fig. 3.4: Modification in register address with autoincrement and autodecrement addressing modes 85
Fig. 3.5: 8086 Microprocessor architecture 86

4. Assembly Language Programming

Fig. 4.1: Assembly language ADD instruction representation in machine language 99

5. Memory and Digital Interfacing

Fig. 5.1: Memory and I/O interfacing 165
Fig. 5.2: Peripheral devices 165

Fig. 5.3: Block diagram of I/O module 166
Fig. 5.4: Classification of semiconductor memories 167
Fig. 5.5: A typical RAM chip with 7 address lines and 8 bidirectional data lines 168
Fig. 5.6: Direct cache block mapping of typically 4096 main memory blocks to 128 cache blocks 169
Fig. 5.7: Associative mapping 171
Fig. 5.8: Set-associative mapping 173
Fig. 5.9: Logical address to physical address mapping using memory management unit 175
Fig. 5.10: A typical ROM chip with 9 address lines and 8 unidirectional data lines 176
Fig. 5.11: Flowchart of programmed I/O 182
Fig. 5.12: Interrupt driven I/O flow 182

LIST OF TABLES

Table 1.1: Positive and negative numbers representation with sign-and-magnitude, 1's complement and 2's complement number representations 12
Table 1.2: Even and odd parity code representations 17
Table 1.3: Symbolic representation of registers in register transfer 19
Table 1.4: Arithmetic Micro-operations 22
Table 2.1: Sign-and-magnitude numbers multiplication example (–6 × 3) 45
Table 2.2: Booth multiplication example (–5 × –4) 47
Table 2.3: Restoring division algorithm example 48
Table 2.4: Non restoring division example 50
Table 4.1: Difference between procedure and macro 111
Table 4.2: List of arithmetic operations 113
Table 4.3: List of logical operations 147
Table 5.1: Difference between SRAM and DRAM 168
Table 5.2: Address lines bit values for port selection 179
Table 5.3: Control register format for BSR mode 179
Table 5.4: Pin selection of port C 180

CONTENTS

Foreword *iii*
Acknowledgement *v*
Preface *vii*
Outcome Based Education *ix*
Course Outcomes *x*
Guidelines for Teachers *xi*
Guidelines for Students *xii*
Abbreviations and Symbols *xiii*
List of Figures *xv*
List of Tables *xviii*

1. Structure of Computers.. 1–34
Unit specifics 1
Rationale 1
Pre-requisites 2
Unit outcomes 2
1.1 Digital Computers 2
1.2 Computer Functional Units 3
1.2.1 Input Units 3
1.2.2 Memory 4
1.2.3 Arithmetic Logic Unit 6
1.2.4 Control Unit 7
1.2.5 Interconnection 8
1.2.6 Output Unit 9
1.3 Von-Neumann Architecture 9
1.4 Bus Structures 10
1.5 Basic Operational Concepts 10
1.6 Data Representation 12
1.6.1 Fixed Point Integer Representation 12
1.6.2 Floating Point Number Representation 16
1.7 Error Detection Code 17

1.8 Register Transfer And Micro Operations 18

1.8.1 Register Transfer 18

1.8.2 Bus and Memory Transfers 20

1.8.3 Arithmetic Logic Shift Unit 21

Unit summary 27

Exercises 28

Practical 32

Know more 33

References and suggested readings 34

2. Micro Programmed Control 35–73

Unit specifics 35

Rationale 35

Pre-requisites 36

Unit outcomes 36

2.1 Control Memory 36

2.2 Address Sequencing 37

2.3 Control Unit Design 38

2.3.1 Hardwired Control Unit 39

2.3.2 Microprogrammed Control Unit 40

2.4 Computer Arithmetic 41

2.4.1 Addition and subtraction for sign-and-magnitude numbers 41

2.4.2 Addition and subtraction for 2's complement numbers 43

2.4.3 Integer Multiplication 44

2.4.4 Integer Division 47

2.5 Fraction Number Representation 50

2.5.1 Fixed point representation 50

2.5.2 Floating point representation 51

2.5.3 Floating point arithmetic operations 52

2.6 Arithmetic Pipeline 55

2.7 Instruction Pipeline 57

2.7.1 Resource or Structural Hazards 57

2.7.2 Data Hazards 59

2.7.3 Control Hazards 61

2.8 RISC Pipeline 64
2.9 Vector Processing 64
2.10 Array Processors 64
Unit summary 65
Exercises 66
Practical 70
Know more 71
References and suggested readings 73

3. Microprocessor Architecture 74–97
Unit specifics 74
Rationale 74
Pre-requisites 75
Unit outcomes 75
3.1 Introduction 75
3.2 Instruction Set Architecture 78
3.2.1 CISC Characteristics 78
3.2.2 RISC Characteristics 79
3.3 Design Principles From Programmer Perspective 79
3.3.1 Instruction Format 79
3.3.2 Addressing Modes 80
3.4 Architecture Of 8086 Microprocessor 85
3.4.1 8086 microprocessor functional units 85
3.4.2 Instruction Types in 8086 88
Unit summary 90
Exercises 91
Practical 95
Know more 96
References and suggested readings 97

4. Assembly Language Programming 98-129
Unit specifics 98
Rationale 98
Pre-requisites 99
Unit outcomes 99

4.1 Introduction 99
4.2 Assembly Language Programs 101
4.2.1 First Assembly Program with NASM 102
4.3 Assembler Directives 107
4.4 Procedures and Macros 108
4.4.1 Procedures 109
4.4.2 Macros 110
4.5 Assembly Programs 112
4.5.1 Simple Programs 112
4.5.2 Arithmetic Programs 113
4.5.3 Logical Instructions 115
4.5.4 Branch Instructions 116
4.5.5 Evaluation of Arithmetic Expressions 118
4.5.6 String Manipulation 119
4.5.7 Sorting 121
Unit summary 124
Exercises 125
Practical 128
Know more 128
References and suggested readings 129

5. Memory and Digital Interfacing 130-154

Unit specifics 130
Rationale 130
Pre-requisites 131
Unit outcomes 131
5.1 Introduction 131
5.2 Memory Types and Characteristics 133
5.2.1 Types of Memory 133
5.2.2 Random access memory (RAM) 133
5.2.3 Cache Memory Mapping Techniques 134
5.2.4 Read Only Memory (ROM) 141
5.3 Secondary Memory 141

5.4 Programmable Peripheral Interface 142
5.4.1 Operational modes of 8255 143
5.4.2 Interfacing To Processor 144
5.4.3 Interfacing keyboard and display devices 145
Unit summary 146
Exercises 147
Practical 150
Know more 151
References and suggested readings 153
References for Further Learning **155**
CO and PO Attainment Table **157**
Index **159-160**

1 Structure of Computers

UNIT SPECIFICS

The following aspects are discussed in this unit:

- Basic structure of computer functional units;
- Von neumann and harvard architectures;
- Bus structure and types of buses;
- Processor basic operational concept;
- Numeric and floating point numbers representation and arithmetic operations;
- Error detection methods;
- Working of the ALU for arithmetic, logic, and shift micro-operations.

The practical applications of the topics are presented for the purpose of fostering greater curiosity and creativity and enhancing problem-solving skills. In addition to a large number of multiple-choice questions and short- and long-answer questions marked in two categories according to the lower and higher levels of Bloom's taxonomy, the unit provides practice assignments in the form of numerical problems, a list of references, and suggested readings. It is crucial to note that several QR codes, which may be scanned for further information on various topics of interest, have been included in different parts and can be used to obtain necessary supporting data.

The related practical based on the content is followed by a "Know More" section on the topic. This section has been carefully constructed such that the supplementary information it contains is valuable to the book's readers. This section discusses Indian innovators' contributions to computer system organization and Indian vedic knowledge's impact in contemporary digital computers.

RATIONALE

This fundamental unit contains information about the functional components and subcomponents of a computer system. The features, performance, and application of these components are discussed thoroughly. Buses enable these components to transmit and receive signals, address, and data with each other as well as with memory. The basic bus structure and types of buses are also covered. The design of conventional von neumann architecture based on the "stored program concept" is compared to the design of contemporary harvard architecture. The representation of signed and unsigned integer and floating point numbers, as well as associated arithmetic operations, explains how digital computers store and execute various operations with these numbers.

Noise interference during data transmission causes errors in the data. The techniques for identifying errors are also explained. In addition, students learn about the architecture of an arithmetic logic shift unit, which is necessary for understanding arithmetic, logic, and shift microoperations. This unit makes it easier to identify hardware components of digital computers and understand how they work together. This unit provides the foundation for understanding the subsequent units in this book.

PRE-REQUISITE

Mathematics: Arithmetic operations with integer and floating point numbers (Class X)

Digital Electronics: Number systems and digital logic gates (Polytechnic Engineering)

UNIT OUTCOMES

List of outcomes of this unit is as follows:

U1-O1: Describe basic structure of computer functional units

U1-O2: Describe the integer and floating point numbers system

U1-O3: Apply error detection code to identify bitstream errors occured due to data transmission

U1-O4: Explain bus and memory transfer

U1-O5: Realize the role of arithmetic logic shift unit for implementing micro-operations

Unit-1 Outcomes	EXPECTED MAPPING WITH COURSE OUTCOMES (1- Weak Correlation; 2- Medium Correlation; 3- Strong Correlation)				
	CO-1	CO-2	CO-3	CO-4	CO-5
U1-O1	3	3	3	2	2
U1-O2	3	3	2	3	2
U1-O3	2	1	3	1	2
U1-O4	3	3	2	1	1
U1-O5	3	3	3	1	3

1.1 DIGITAL COMPUTERS

Digital computers are organised through a series of micro-operations performed on stored data in registers. The digital computers are capable of performing a variety of microoperations and can also be programmed to perform a specific sequence of operations. A computer user can control the activities via a program.

A **computer program** specifies the operations, operands, and processing order through a sequence of instructions. A computer's instructions and data are encoded as binary digits, 0 or 1, known as bits. To change the data processing task, either a new program with new instructions or the same instructions with new data can be given.

for computer history and types of computers

A **computer instruction** is encoded as a piece of binary digits to specify a series of microoperations for a computer. Memory stores instruction codes as well as data. Each instruction is read from memory and stored in a processor register. The controller interprets the instruction's binary code and executes it by issuing a series of microoperations [1]. Each computer has its own set of instructions. The ability of a general-purpose computer to store and execute instructions, is known as the stored program concept. Various functional components of the computer execute given tasks in collaboration.

1.2 COMPUTER FUNCTIONAL UNITS

A computer is made up of the input unit, memory unit, arithmetic logic unit (ALU), output unit, and control unit as shown in **Fig 1.1**. The input unit accepts coded information from keyboards or digital communication lines. The received data is stored in the memory for later use or immediate processing by the ALU. Memory-stored programs specify processing steps. The output unit sends the results outside. Control unit coordinates all actions. These functional units can exchange the information via interconnection networks.

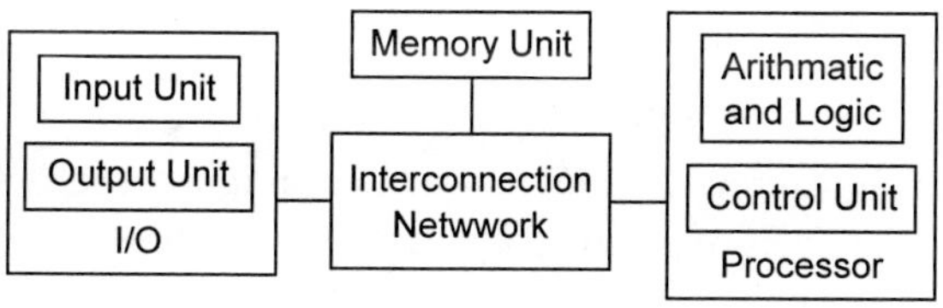

Fig. 1.1: Computer functional units

The processor/CPU is composed of the arithmetic logic units, and the control units [2]. The I/O (input/output) refers to both input and output devices. A computer user sends explicit commands (either instructions or data) that

- govern the transfer of information to processor by loading required program in memory.
- enable the interaction between the user and processor via I/O devices.
- specify the ALU operations that will be executed via processor.

The processor follows the program's instructions and completes the essential tasks in a sequential manner. Except for possible external interruptions by user or I/O devices connected to it, the computer is controlled by the stored program. Data is also kept in the memory. Data are numbers and characters that are used by instructions as operands. Each functional unit is dedicated for a specific task [3].

for understanding interrupts and their types

1.2.1 Input Units

Input units allow computers to receive data. The keyboard is the fundamental input device. When a key is pressed, the letter or digit corresponding to the key is converted into its corresponding binary digit and sent to the processor.

There are a wide variety of input devices for human computer interaction that can be used as depicted in Fig 1.2. Some examples of these devices are the OCR (Optical Character Recognition), mouse, barcode reader, joystick, touch panel, touchpad, MICR (Magnetic Ink Character Recognition), trackball, and scanner. These are frequently used in conjunction with displays to function as graphical input devices. Audio input can be captured using microphones, and once that has been done, it is sampled and converted into digital codes so that it can be stored and processed.

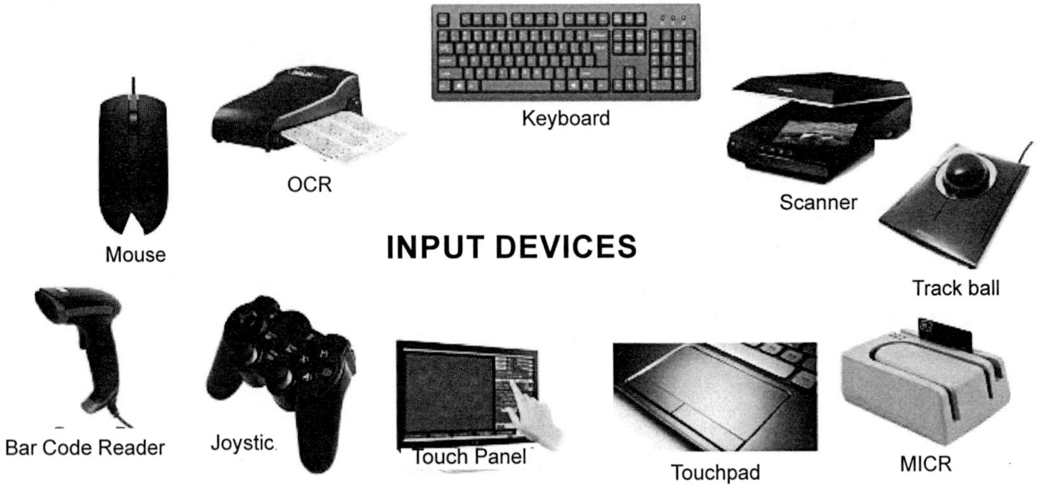

Fig. 1.2: Input devices

Likewise, video input can be captured through the use of cameras. Computers can also take input not only from other computers but also from database servers via using the internet's digital communication facility.

1.2.2 Memory

The memory unit stores data and programs. There are two storage categories known as primary and secondary storage.

- **Primary memory:** Primary memory refers to the primary physical memory. It is utilised for the storage of both data and programming. One bit of information can be stored in each of the numerous semiconductor storage cells that it contains. These cells are organised into groups of a predetermined size that are referred to as words. Memory is structured to store or retrieve a single word within a single operation. Word length refers to the number of bits in each computer word, which is typically 16, 32, or 64 bits. A unique address is assigned to each word location in the memory to facilitate access to any word in memory.

  for understanding the utility of various types of memory

  Memory addresses start with zero. In order to access a particular word, you must first identify its address and then issue a control instruction to the memory in order to begin the process of storing or retrieving the word. Memory stores and retrieves instructions and data under CPU control. After being addressed, each word can be retrieved in a predetermined amount of time. The term "random-access memory" (RAM) refers to this primary memory. Memory access time refers to the amount of time required to retrieve a single word from memory. The positioning of the word is irrelevant at this point in time. As shown in Figure 1.3, contemporary RAM devices have latencies ranging from a few nanoseconds (ns) to 100 ns. Data access speed can be affected by the memory type. Memory capacity ranges from KB (Kilobyte) to GB (Gigabyte). Registers are the smallest and fastest type of memory. Conversely, secondary storage is the largest and slowest memory type. Logic of the processor is typically faster than main memory access time. Primarily, the processing speed is limited by the speed of main memory.

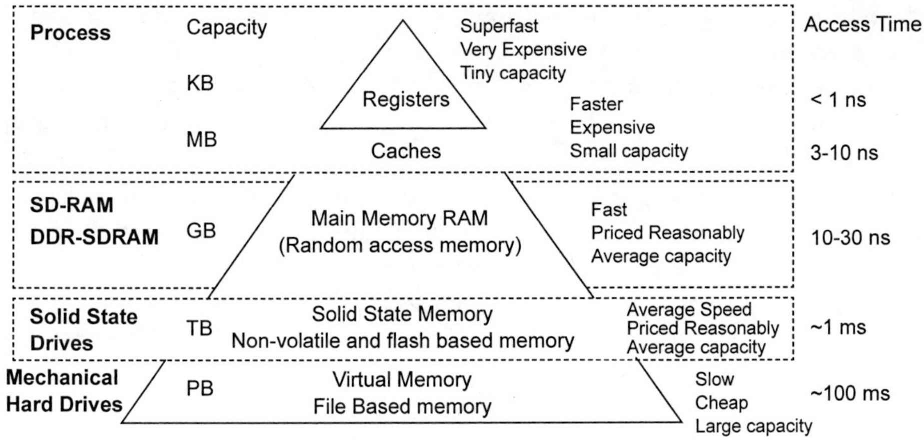

Fig. 1.3: Memory Hierarchy: registers, caches, and main memory are volatile memory and solid state drive, mechanical hard drives are non-volatile memory.

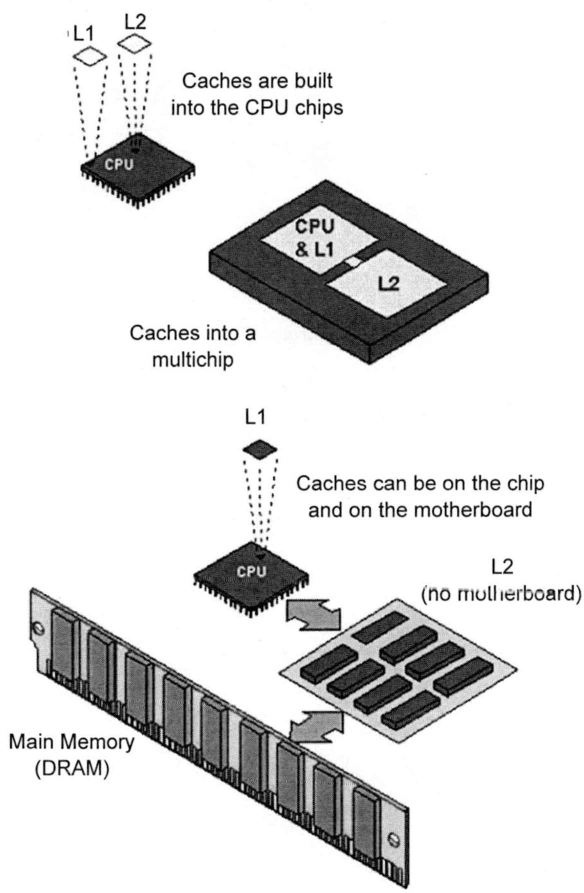

Fig. 1.4: Placement of cache memory

Cache memory can overcome the speed mismatch between the access time to main memory and the execution speed of the processor. A small, fast cache is located between the processor and main memory as depicted in Fig 1.4. A compact, fast cache is put between the processor and RAM to speed up data access as demonstrated in Fig. 1.4. Cache memory stores frequently used data and code during processing.

Modern Processors have two or three levels of cache memories. The L1 cache is placed on a chip near to the processor, while the L2 cache may be situated anywhere between the processor and memory. Alternatively, both the L1, L2 caches could be integrated on the same chip. Chip designers make this selection based on how much they concern about performance, power, and cost of the chip. The access time of L1 cache is nearly comparable to the processor logic clock cycle time.

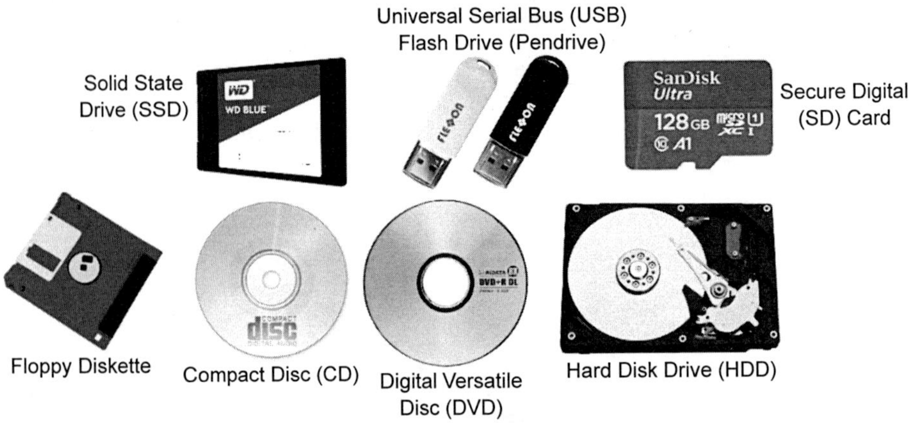

Fig. 1.5: Secondary storage

- **Secondary Storage:** When the power is switched off, the primary memory loses all stored data. Whereas the secondary storage permanently stores data and programs. Secondary storage has longer access times than primary memory. The numerous secondary storage options available such as SSD (Solid State Drive), pendrive (USB flash drive), SD (Secure Digital) card, floppy diskette, Magnetic discs, optical discs (DVD and CD), and hard disk drive as illustrated in Fig 1.5.

to comprehend how the processor perform fetch, decode, and execute instructions

1.2.3 Arithmetic Logic Unit

The arithmetic logic unit (ALU) executes arithmetic and logic operations such as addition, subtraction, multiplication, division, and number comparison. When the processor receives the required operands,

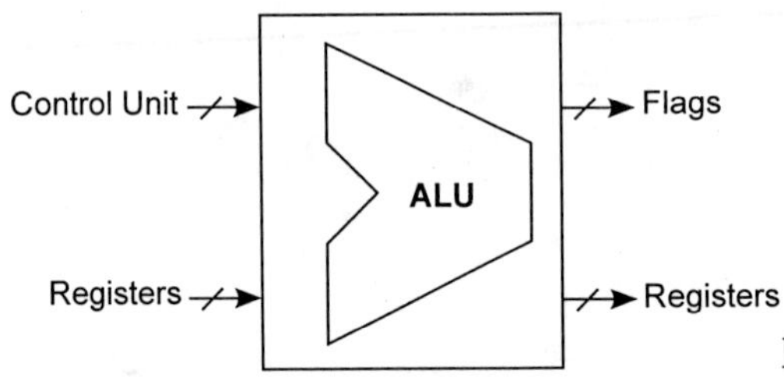

k

Fig. 1.6: Arithmetic logic unit (ALU)

they are stored in processor registers. Each register can hold a single word of data. The ALU then begins its execution.

Consider the addition of two numbers; this operation can be carried out simply retrieving the numbers from memory. Then the control units notify ALU to add up the numbers. The sum can be stored in memory or the processor can store in general purpose registers for immediate use.

1.2.4 Control Unit

The control unit supervises the operation of the processor. The control unit retrieves program instruction from main memory and stores it in the instruction register (IR). The control signals instruct the ALU to execute the same instruction. When the execution is finished, the control unit notifies the output unit to display the results to the user. The control unit coordinates the actions of the memory, ALU, and I/O units. The control unit tasks can be categorized as follows:

1. Its primary function is to manage how information enters, leaves, and is transferred inside a computer's processing units.
2. It determines which devices and processes need to be controlled and how to activate them, as well as retrieving and decoding instructions from main memory.
3. It controls the processing of data within the chip.
4. It takes instructions or commands from the outside and translates them into a set of control signals.
5. It manages the processor's multiple execution units (the ALU, data buffers, and registers).
6. Timer signals of the control unit monitor the exchange of information between the processor and memory.
7. It deals with the instruction fetching, decoding, executing, and storing results.

for understanding interaction of control unit with other functional units

The control circuitry is spread physically throughout the computer. The signals are carried by a set of control lines (wires). The events of all units are synchronised by timing signals from the control circuits as shown in Fig 1.7.

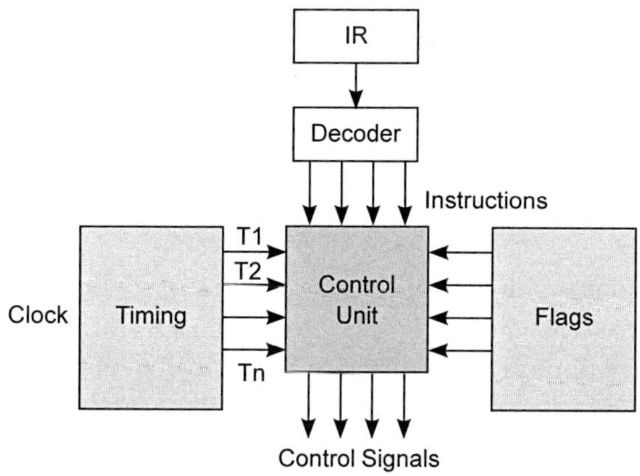

Fig. 1.7: The control unit decodes instructions and generates control signals through master clock to synchronize events (IR: Instruction Register)

A control unit generates a sequence of signals that are synchronized to the master clock and operates the associated processing units. The control unit's main responsibilities include interpreting instructions and organising their execution. The control unit sends instructions to the ALU about what operations to perform and what timing parameters to use for those activities. The control unit's timing signals regulate the speed at which data travels between the processor, memory, and other components.

The program counter (PC) register keeps track of the current instruction number in the instruction sequence. The current instruction being run is stored in the IR. The control unit uses the information in IR to determine the timing signals it generates. The signals help in regulating the several pieces of processing hardware required to execute the instructions.

1.2.5 Interconnection

for detailed structure of interconnects

A programmable system that transfers data between the processor, memory, and I/O devices is known as an interconnection network. As demonstrated in Fig 1.8, multiprocessor systems communicate with other processors via buses. The bus allows the four processors P0, P1, P2, P3, and P4 to communicate with one another. Buses, on the other hand, have limited bandwidth. Other interconnection networks, including rings, mesh, tree, hypercube, and crossbar, are utilised to connect additional processors. Fig 1.8 depicts the design of these interconnects.

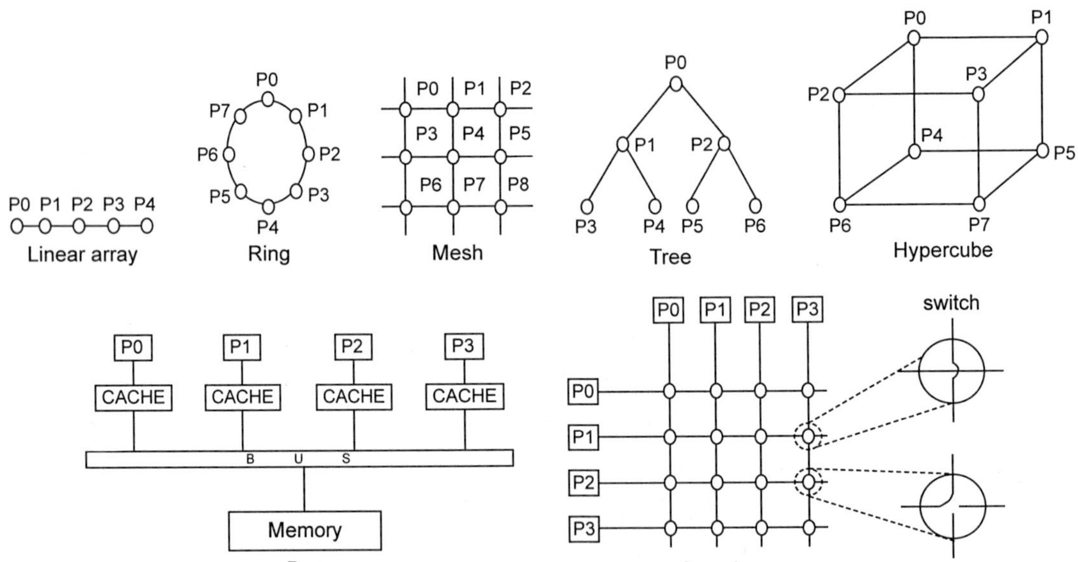

Fig. 1.8: Interconnection networks

A well-designed interconnection network makes the best use of limited communication resources. It is possible to communicate across many hardware components while maintaining high bandwidth and low latency. Traditional interconnects, in addition to buses, include linear arrays, rings, and crossbars. The mesh, tree, and hypercube interconnects are used to connect more processors, as shown in Fig 1.8. Interconnection networks are often straightforward to suit the needs of a certain application due to their simple design principles.

1.2.6 Output Unit

The output unit sends the results of processing to the outside world. Fig. 1.9 displays a few examples of output devices, including a monitor, printer, speaker, headphone, and projector. Printers, among these output devices, are mechanical devices. They are slower than processors, which are constructed of electronic components. The majority of printers either use streams of ink or photocopying, like laser printers. These printers can print at speeds of 20 pages or more per minute.

for understanding the purpose of different output devices

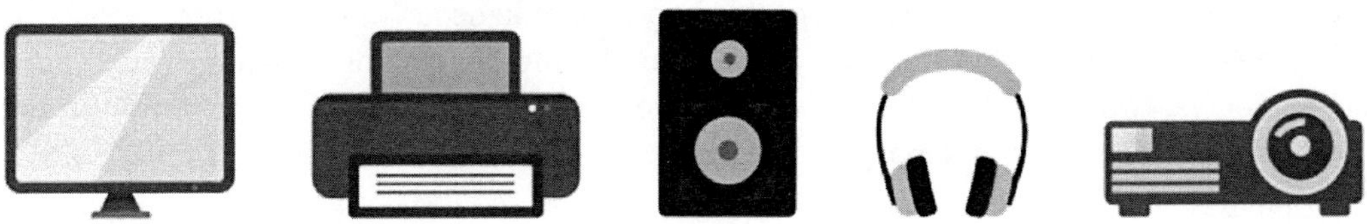

Fig. 1.9: Output unit

Some units, like graphic displays, can both show text and pictures and take information from the user by having a touchscreen. Because these units do both input and output, they are often called input/output (I/O) units.

1.3 VON-NEUMANN ARCHITECTURE

In Princeton, Von Neumann and his colleagues invented a "stored-program computer" in 1946. Von Neumann's stored-program concept is the foundation of modern digital computers. Von Neumann architecture was made up of a control unit, an arithmetic logic unit (ALU), a memory unit, registers, and input/output as shown in Fig 1.10.

to understand the difference between von-neumann and harvard architectures

A single shared memory is used for storing programs and data in von neumann architecture, and a single bus is used for memory access by the processor. The processor retrieves and executes instructions in a sequential manner.

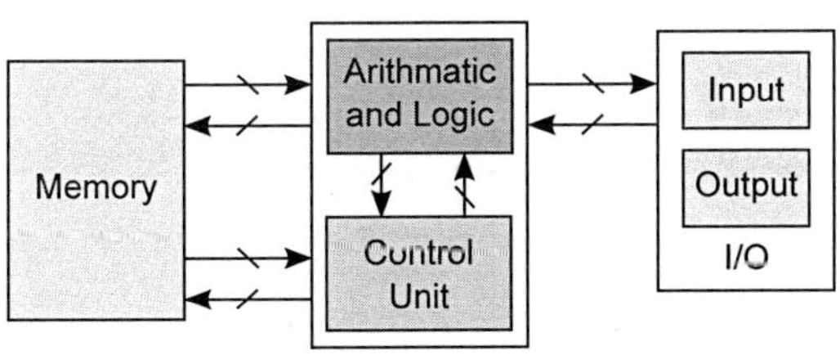

Fig. 1.10: Von-nuemann architecture

Harvard architecture was designed to overcome von-neumann architecture's bottleneck. It uses two separate memories for program code/instructions and data. processor can access program code and data concurrently using separate dedicated buses for each memory segment. The processor can fetch data and instructions at the same time, which speeds up execution.

The modified Harvard design is commonly used in contemporary processors. Data and instructions are stored in two different caches on the chip. Both X86 and ARM processors have this feature.

1.4 BUS STRUCTURES

Binary digits are transported from one register/unit to the other units/registers via a network of physical wires called a bus. Buses connect all of the primary internal components to the CPU/processor and memory, and they transfer data between them. Single bus, double buses, and multiple buses are the most common configurations.

to compare different bus structures

In a single-bus system, all units are connected to a single bus, which serves as the only means of connectivity. Single-bus interconnect designs are simple and cost-effective. Nonetheless, only two units can communicate simultaneously. This feature limits the network's speed. This limitation is overcome by the double bus structure, which provides communication via two buses. In harvard design, a processor can simultaneously retrieve instructions from memory and write data to memory.

Multiple buses are utilised by the majority of commercial processors to provide multiple internal paths for the transfer of information such as instructions, data, addresses, signals, etc. Fig. 1.11 depicts a three-bus structure connecting the CPU (processor), memory, and I/O units. The data bus has bits of width, the address bus has bits of width, and the control bus can transport bits of signals between the CPU (processor), memory, and I/O devices. These buses are collectively referred to as a system bus.

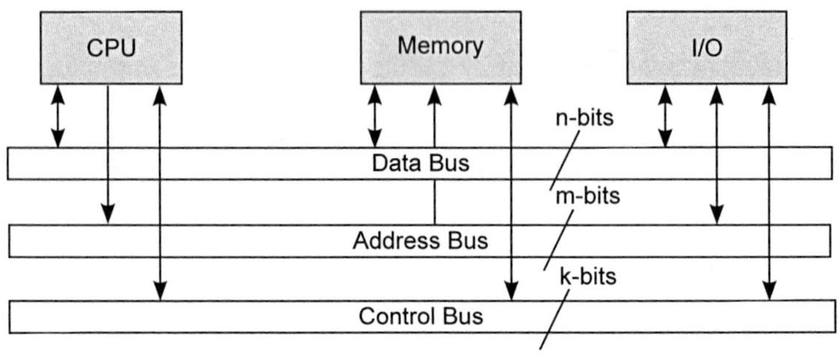

Fig. 1.11: System bus structure is made up of data bus, address bus, and control bus

These buses transfer–

- data via a data bus between the memory unit, input/output devices, and the processor/CPU.
- address through address bus between all linked devices.
- control signals that are sent through the control bus to monitor and coordinate all activities of these units.

During a particular data transmission, control signals determine which unit/register the bus selects. Dedicated data-carrying buses on multiple buses speed up the information-processing. Computers also utilise peripheral bus (I/O bus), local bus, and high-speed buses in addition to the system bus to communicate with various devices.

1.5 BASIC OPERATIONAL CONCEPTS

for detailed information about types of buses

Computers accomplish numerous operations by integrating efforts of several devices/ units. The processor contains a number of registers in addition to the ALU and the control circuitry used for several different purposes. Fig. 1.12 demonstrates the arrangement of processor registers, memory structure and system bus interconnection. The following registers are used to temporarily store specific types of information required by processor:

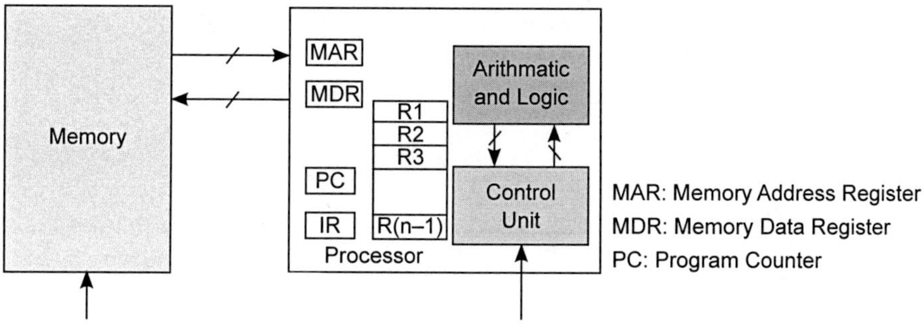

Fig. 1.12: Structure of processor registers and main memory

- Data is retrieved or stored from the processor's memory address register (MAR).The address of the memory location to be accessed is stored in MAR.
- The program counter (PC) stores the memory address of the next instruction to be fetched and executed.
- The currently executed instruction is saved in instruction register (IR). The execution of ALU instructions is initiated by timing signals from the control unit.
- Processor registers (R_0 – R_{n-1}) are general-purpose. They are used for a variety of purposes such as temporarily load/store data from/to memory.

Prior to being run, programmes transfer their contents from secondary storage into main memory. When the PC navigates to the first instruction, the program execution will begin. A read control signal is sent to the memory to retrieve the instruction. The memory-fetched word, which is also the initial instruction of the programme, is saved into register IR. Now it is possible to interpret and execute the instructions given. After execution, it is sent to the processor register. The control unit sends the address, word, and write control signal to memory to write a word.

The PC counter is increased throughout instruction execution to point to the next instruction. Thus, the CPU fetches a new instruction after executing the existing one. Data is sent between memory and processor, input devices, and output devices by the computer. Instructions also control I/O transfers.

When a device requires urgent service, normal program execution may be halted. A monitoring device in a computer-controlled industrial process may detect a potentially hazardous condition, for instance. In order to respond immediately, it is required to pause the present program's execution. To achieve this, the device sends an interrupt signal to the processor, which is a service request.

The CPU will execute an interrupt service routine in response to a service request. Because of these variations, it is necessary to save the current state of the CPU in memory before carrying out the interrupt request. The PC, general-purpose register, and control data are usually stored. After the interrupt-service routine, RAM restores processor state so the interrupted programme may resume.

1.6 DATA REPRESENTATION

A computer system stores binary numbers (either 0 or 1) as a string of bits. In the real world, integer numbers can be represented as decimal, octal, and hexadecimal numbers. The decimal numbers are converted to binary numbers in computers. In binary numbers, the leftmost bit is known as the most significant bit (MSB) and the rightmost bit is known as least significant bit (LSB) [7].

for binary number conversion to decimal, octal, and hexadecimal numbers

MSB — R1 — LSB

0	1	0	1	0	1	1	1
b7	b6	b5	b4	b3	b2	b1	b0

Fig. 1.13: MSB and LSB bits in a 8-bit binary number

The example is shown in Fig. 1.13, where bit b_0 is LSB and bit b_7 is MSB for the binary number stored in 8-bit register R1.

1.6.1 Fixed Point Integer Representation

Integer numbers can be signed or unsigned. Unless the sign of the number is specified, integers are assumed to be unsigned. A negative number is denoted by a minus sign and a positive number by a plus sign in standard arithmetic. Due to hardware constraints, computers must represent everything, including the number sign, using only 1s and 0s. The sign is represented by a bit in the leftmost position of the number. Typically, the sign bit is set to 0 for positive numbers and 1 for negative numbers.

Signed Number Representation

The sign bit of positive and negative binary integers is represented by 0 and 1, respectively.

The remaining bits are expressed by one of the number systems listed below:

1. Sign-and-magnitude
2. 1's complement
3. 2's complement

Table 1.1: Positive and negative numbers representation with sign-and-magnitude, 1's complement and 2's complement number representations

$b_3b_2b_1b_0$	Sign and Magnitude	1's complement	2's complement
0 1 1 1	+7	+7	+7
0 1 1 0	+6	+6	+6
0 1 0 1	+5	+5	+5
0 1 0 0	+4	+4	+4
0 0 1 1	+3	+3	+3
0 0 1 0	+2	+2	+2
0 0 0 1	+1	+1	+1
0 0 0 0	+0	+0	+0

$b_3b_2b_1b_0$	Sign and Magnitude	1's complement	2's complement
1 0 0 0	–0	–7	–8
1 0 0 1	–1	–6	–7
1 0 1 0	–2	–5	–6
1 0 1 1	–3	–4	–5
1 1 0 0	–4	–3	–4
1 1 0 1	–5	–2	–3
1 1 1 0	–6	–1	–2
1 1 1 1	–7	–0	–1

The positive numbers representation is the same in sign-and-magnitude, 1's complement, and 2's complement representation as shown in Table 1.1. Whereas, a negative number's sign-and-magnitude form consists of the magnitude (binary representation of the number) and place 1 at MSB for a negative sign. The negative number is either the 1's or 2's complement of its positive value.

Example 1.1: How are the +64 and –64 signed numbers represented in the sign-and-magnitude, 1's complement, and 2's complement number systems?

Solution: There is only one way to represent +64 with eight bits, although there are three different ways to express –64 as shown in Fig. 1.14. Sign-and-magnitude is represented as 11000000, 1's complement as 10111111, and 2's complement as 11000000.

MSB R1 = + 64

0	1	0	0	0	0	0	0
b7	b6	b5	b4	b3	b2	b1	b0

0 1 0 0 0 0 0 0

For positive numbers, the sign and magnitude, 1's complement, and 2's complement representation is same.

–64 sign and magnitude	1	1	0	0	0	0	0	0
+64	0	1	0	0	0	0	0	0
1's complement	1	0	1	1	1	1	1	1
+	0	0	0	0	0	0	0	1
2's complement representation of –64	1	1	0	0	0	0	0	0

R1 = 64

2's complement representation of –64	1	1	0	0	0	0	0	0
	b7	b6	b5	b4	b3	b2	b1	b0

Fig. 1.14: Representation of +64 and –64 signed numbers in the sign-and-magnitude, 1's complement, and 2's complement number systems

The sign-and-magnitude representation of –64 is obtained from +64 by doing the complement of simply the sign bit. The 1's complement of –64 is derived by complement of all the bits of +64, including the sign bit. The 2's complement is computed by adding one (00000001) to the +64's 1's complement, resulting in 10111111.

The sign-and-magnitude and 1's complement have two representations of 0 (+0 and –0). Therefore, the 2's complement of negative numbers are used in computers to avoid complications in micro operations.

Overflow Detection in arithmetic additions

An overflow occurs when the sum of n digit integers contains n + 1 digits. Registers in digital computers have a finite width. The n + 1 bits of results cannot fit in a standard n-bit register. Therefore, all computers will detect an overflow, and an overflow flag will be set when this occurs. The overflow detection mechanism depends on whether the integers are signed or unsigned.

- An overflow arises on adding unsigned numbers when the result has a carry out of 1 from the MSB.
- Addition of signed numbers involves adding the sign bit together with the original numbers. A 2's complement form is used for the negative numbers. In this case, the end carry value does not point to an overflow. A 2's complement representation allows the n bits to store values from -2^{n-1} to $+2^{n-1} - 1$. For instance, from −8 to +7 is the range that can be represented by 4 bits. When the actual result of an operation exceeds the range that may be represented, overflow occurs.
- An overflow condition cannot arise when one of the numbers is positive and another is negative, since the sum of the two numbers is always less than the greater of the two numbers.
- If both numbers being added are positive or negative, then an overflow may occur.

Example 1.2: Perform the addition of two signed numbers R1 = +64 and R2 = +84 using 2's complement number systems. The size of each register is 8-bit.

Solution: The size of each register is 8-bit. So they can accommodate -2^{8-1} to $+2^{8-1} - 1$ or −128 to +127 binary numbers. On performing decimal addition of both the numbers, we can directly check whether overflow is there or not. The sum of the (+64) + (+84) = +148. In a positive direction, the result can not exceed to +127 to avoid the overflow. Since +148 > +127, So overflow occurs on adding both the numbers.

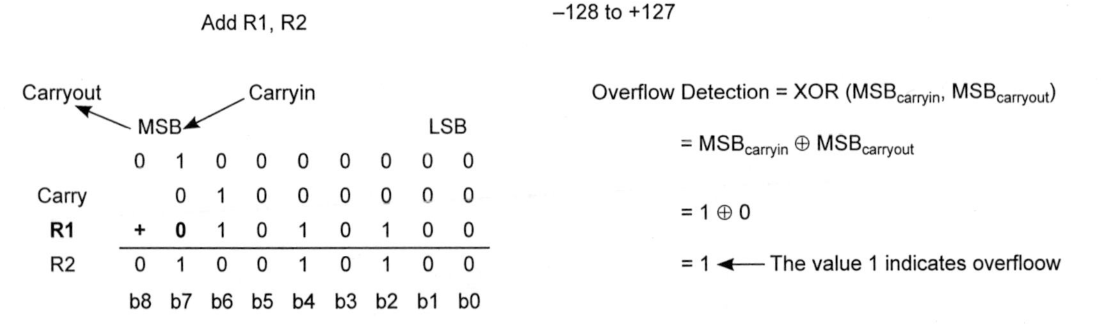

Fig. 1.15: Overflow detection on adding two positive numbers +64 and +84

Fig 1.15 shows how to check for overflow while doing signed binary number arithmetic addition. If the carry out exceeds the capacity of the 8-bit register, this does not always imply overflow. Carryout sometimes can be ignored. Overflow can definitely be recognised by conducting an XOR operation on the carry in and carry out of the MSB bit position. Overflow happens when the output of the XOR operation is 1.

Due to overflow, the supposed positive 8-bit result has a negative sign bit. However, if the carry out of the sign bit position is used as the result's sign bit, the 9-bit answer obtained will be correct. Therefore, addition of +64 and +84 gives an inaccurate result owing to overflow since the result cannot be accommodated inside 8 bits.

A carry in and carry out of the sign bit position (MSB) indicate overflow. If these two carry have different values, overflow will occur. When both carries are fed into an exclusive-OR gate, the gate's output is equal to 1, indicating an overflow.

Example 1.3: Perform the addition of two signed numbers –64 and –84 that are stored in two 8-bit registers R1 and R2, respectively, using 2's complement number system?

Solution: The range of acceptable numbers for each 8-bit register is –128 to +127. The result of adding –64 and –84 is (–64) + (–84) = –148. The maximum negative number that can be stored in an 8-bit register is –128, hence this value exceeds its storage limit.

The arithmetic addition of –64 and –84 is shown in Fig. 1.16. Both integers are negative, hence in registers R1 and R2 they are represented using 2's complement number system. The carry in and carry out of the MSB are fed through an XOR gate during arithmetic addition in order to identify overflows. Overflow is detected because the XOR gate's output is 1.

The resulting 8-bit value should have been negative. However, the b_7 bit indicates that the result is a positive number. The 9-bit answer obtained, however, will be correct if the carry out of the sign bit position is utilised as the result's sign bit. Because the answer cannot be handled in 8 bits, overflow occurs.

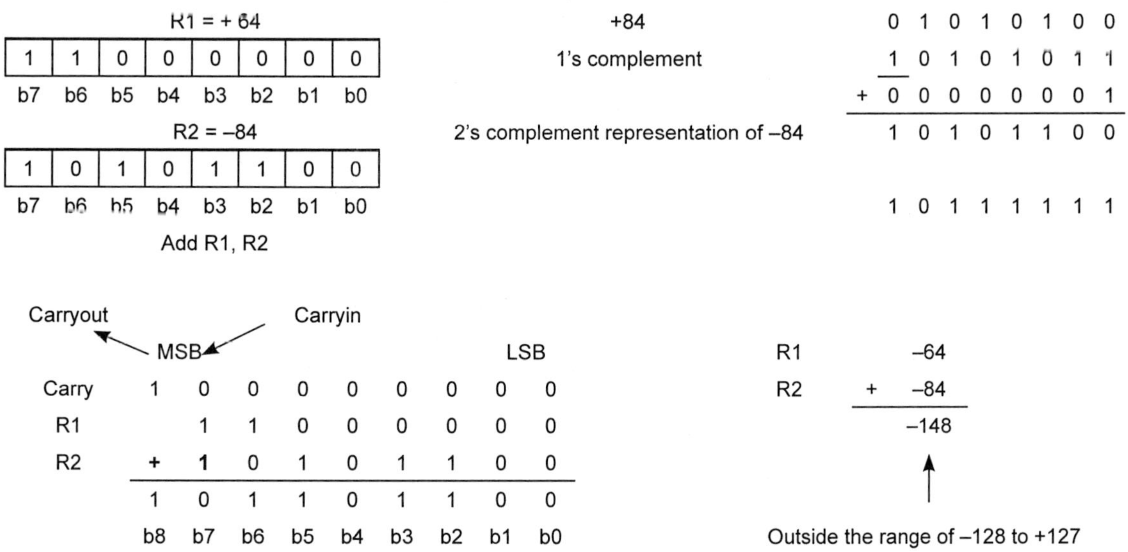

Overflow Detection = XOR ($MSB_{carryin}$, $MSB_{carryout}$)

$= MSB_{carryin} \oplus MSB_{carryout}$

$= 0 \oplus 1$

= 1 ← The value 1 indicates overfloow

carryin	carryout	XOR_{output}
0	0	0
0	1	1
1	0	1
1	1	0

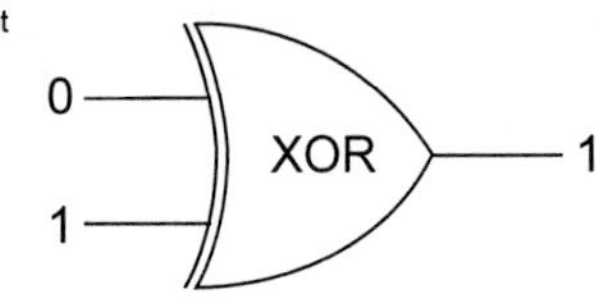

Fig. 1.16: Overflow detection on adding two negative numbers –64 and –84

1.6.2 Floating Point Number Representation

There is an assumed binary point exactly after bit b_0 at the right end of the integer. To represent a signed integer in 2's complement on a computer with a 32-bit word length, the numbers -2^{31} to $+2^{31} - 1$ are used.

to know more about single precision and double precision floating point numbers

The fraction point is supposed to be close to the right of the sign bit—between bits b_{31} and b_{30}. The fraction range lies between -1 and $+1 - 2^{-31}$. The lowest fraction representable is 10^{-10}.

The fixed-point number format imposes restrictions on calculations used in the sciences and the technological fields. For the sake of convenience, binary numbers may represent both large integers and very small fractions.

A computer has the ability to deal with numbers and represent them in such a way that the binary point location may be changed and is automatically updated while computation takes place. When the binary point moves around them, the usage of floating-point integers is required.

The binary point as a floating point shows its location. In decimal scientific notation, integers are expressed as 8.0247×10^{24}, 3.927×10^{-37}, -1.0431×10^{4}, -6.8000×10^{-18}, etc. They have five significant digits of precision. The placement of the decimal point in relation to the significant digits may be determined using the scale factors 10^{24}, 10^{-37}, 10^{4}, and 10^{-18} respectively.

The sign, the mantissa, and the exponent are the three parts that make up a floating-point number. Mantissas are either fractions or integers that are fixed-point in nature. The decimal point, often known as the binary point, is represented by the exponent. The number +51185.987 is written as a fraction followed by an exponent in floating-point format as follows:

Fraction	Exponent
+0.51185987	+05

According to the exponent's value, the fraction's actual decimal point is five digits to the right of where it is represented. This notation is the same as that used in the scientific notation $+ 0.51185987 \times 10^{+5}$.

In order to achieve the most accurate representation of binary floating-point data on a computer, the scaling factor should be set to 2. Representing the base is unnecessary as it is fixed. Positive and negative exponents exist.

The MSB represents the sign bit, where 0 represents a positive number and 1 represents a negative number. There is a biased exponent component and a significant component, which is represented as follows:

$$m \times r^{s}$$

Where m is mantissa and e is the exponent. The register stores their binary numbers, including signs. Always assume radix r and mantissa radix-point position. These two assumptions ensure proper computational outputs. The exponent of a floating-point binary integer is base 2. The binary number +1101.01 has an 8-bit fraction and 6-bit exponent:

Fraction	Exponent
01101010	000100

A 0 in the fraction's leftmost place implies a positive sign. The binary number +4 is represented by the exponent value 000100. Mantissa and exponent may both be written as

$$m \times r^s = +(.01101010) \times 2^{+4}$$

Making the mantissa MSB digit nonzero normalizes a floating-point value. Unlike 000350, 350 is normalized. The number is normalized only if its leftmost digit is nonzero, regardless of the mantissa's radix point.

To normalize 00011110, shift it three places to the left and remove the leading 0's to get 11110000. The number is multiplied by 2^3, which is equal to eight. Subtracting 3 from the exponent keeps the floating-point number the same. Normalized values maximise floating-point accuracy. Zeroes cannot be normalized because they do not have nonzero digits. The mantissa and exponent are all 0's in floating point.

Arithmetic operations using floating-point numbers need more complicated hardware and take longer to execute than operations with fixed-point values. However, due to the scaling issues associated with fixed-point calculations, floating-point representation is required for scientific computations. Modern computers have the ability to do floating-point arithmetic computations.

An IEEE standard for encoding 32-bit floating-point integers uses a sign bit, 23 significant bits, and 8 bits for a signed exponent of the scaling factor [8] with a base of 2. This is enough for the majority of the calculations used in science and engineering. A 64-bit format that adheres to the same IEEE standard provides an increased degree of precision in addition to a greater scope of possible values. This format also includes additional significant bits and signed exponent bits. The chapter 2 discusses the representation of floating-point numbers as well as floating-point arithmetic.

1.7 ERROR DETECTION CODE

Bits 0 and 1 correspond to two distinct analog signal or voltage ranges. These signals may change during the transmission of binary data from one system to another due to noise interference. The noise may change the signal and cause the errors in the data received by the other system. An error occurs if the information received by the receiver does not match to the information sent by the sender. The change in single bit is considered a single-bit error or change in more than one bit is called a bitstream error.

For instance, the sender transmits I_S = 00101111 data. During transmission, MSB bit of I_S is changed from 0 to 1 and the receiver receives I_R = 10101111. This is a **single-bit error.** If more than one bit is changed, lets say, bits b_0, b_1 and b_4 of I_S are changed then receiver receives I_R = 00111100 due to **bitstream error.**

Table 1.2: Even and odd parity code representations

Binary code	Even Parity Bit	Even Parity Code	Odd Parity Bit	Odd Parity Code
000	0	0000	1	0001
001	1	0011	0	0010

Binary code	Even Parity Bit	Even Parity Code	Odd Parity Bit	Odd Parity Code
010	1	0101	0	0100
011	0	0110	1	0111
100	1	1001	0	1000
101	0	1010	1	1011
110	0	1100	1	1101
111	1	1111	0	1110

These errors can be detected with error detection code. Parity and Hamming codes are two such examples. These codes identify errors that occurred during the transmission of the original data bitstream. A parity bit is added to the original bit stream either to the left of the most significant bit (MSB) or to the right of the least significant bit (LSB). This parity bit can be selected as

1. **Even Parity Code:** If the binary code has even ones, the even parity bit should be 0. If not, it should be 1. Here, the even parity codes consist of 4 bits. The possible even number of ones in these even parity codes are 0, 2, and 4.
2. **Odd Parity Code:** If there are odd ones in the binary code, the odd parity bit should be 0. If not, it should be 1. The odd parity codes are similarly made up of 4 bits. The odd number of ones in these odd parity codes may be either 1 or 3.

for hardware implementation of even parity and odd parity codes

If the other system gets the specified number of ones in parity codes according to used even or odd parity codes, its data is correct. Otherwise, data is incorrect.

The representation of both coding schemes are explained in Table 1.2. As per the definitions, the one-bit value of even and odd parity bit is computed in column 2 and column 4 respectively. The binary data contains three bits of information, with one bit of even or odd parity put at the rightmost place of the binary code.

Column 3 and column 5 lists the even and odd parity codes, respectively. The parity bit can detect a single error but cannot correct it. Hamming code can detect one-bit and two-bit errors, or correct one-bit errors. It uses multiple parity bits.

1.8 REGISTER TRANSFER AND MICRO OPERATIONS

Micro-operations are elementary operations performed on register data. The operation's output can either be overwritten in the same register or be moved to a different register. The operations for example, shift, count, clear, and load are micro-operations. Low-level instructions are micro-operations that are used to implement complex machine instructions.

A register transfer language (RTL) represents the micro-operation sequences among the registers of a digital module in symbolic form. It concisely describes the internal organisation of digital computers. It not only expresses the movement of the results of micro-operations between registers, but it also shows the transfer of data between registers and memory.

1.8.1 Register Transfer

Register transfers are facilitated by hardware logic circuits that carry out specific micro-operations and transfer the results to the same or a different register. The register transfer is symbolically represented by the replacement operator (←). The statement $R_2 \leftarrow R_1$, for example, defines the transfer of content from register R_1 to register R_2.

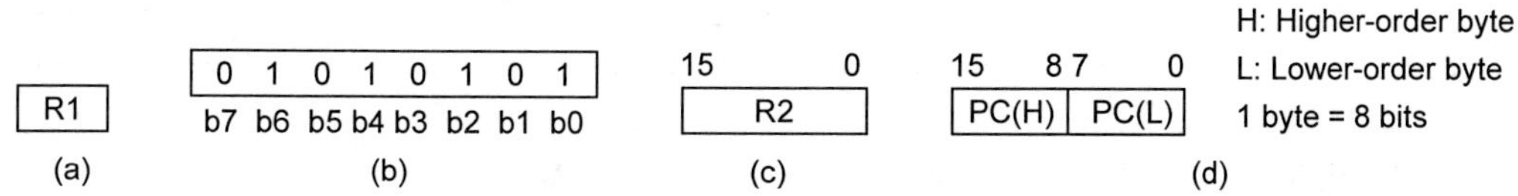

Fig. 1.17: Different representation of values in registers

The register transfer can be defined in different ways:

Table 1.3: Symbolic representation of registers in register transfer

Symbol	Description	Example
Letters and Numbers	Denotes a Register	R1, R2, MAR
() or []	Denotes a part of register	$R_2(8)$ or $R_2[8]$, $R_2(0-7)$ or $R_2[0-7]$
←	Denotes a transfer of information	$R_2 \leftarrow R_1$
:	Denotes conditional operations	$C : R_2 \leftarrow R_1$ if $C = 1$

- A register is generally represented by the name of the register enclosed in a rectangular box or parenthesis , as shown in Table 1.3.
- Additionally, specific bits can be highlighted by enclosing them in parenthesis. For example, in Fig. 1.17(b), R2(8) indicates bit b_8, or PC(8 – 15) indicates bitstream b_8 to b_{15} in Fig. 1.17(c) and Fig. 1.17(d).
- The registers are numbered from R0 to R(n – 1) or R_0 to $R_{(n-1)}$ as shown in Fig. 1.17(a).
- The bit numbering in a register can be indicated on the top of the box, as shown in Fig. 1.17(c) and Fig. 1.17(d).

for bus and memory transfer hardware circuit

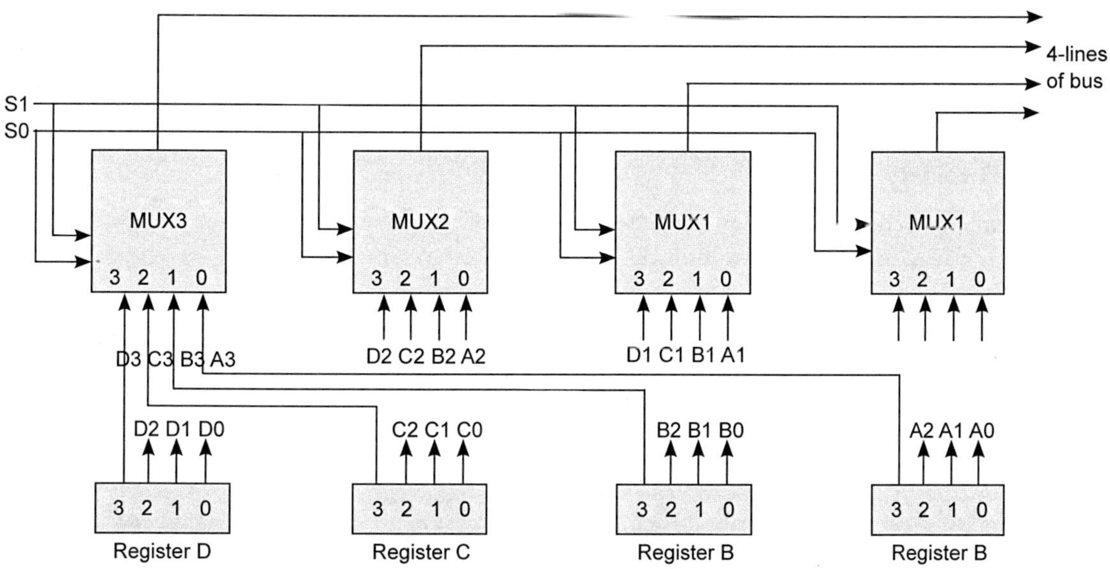

Fig. 1.18: Data transfer from registers via bus

- Bits (0 to 7) of a 16-bit register PC are assigned lower bytes of a 16-bit address, while bits (8 to 15) are assigned higher bytes of a 16-bit address, as shown in Fig. 1.17(d).

Table 1.3 shows different symbolic representations of registers used during register transfer. Furthermore, the conditional register transfer can also be represented. For example, the expression C: $R_2 \leftarrow R_1$ defines a data transfer from register R_1 to register R_2 under a specific control function (C).

If (C = 1), then data of register R_1 transferred to register R_2 ($R_2 \leftarrow R_1$). Because C = 1 indicates that the control unit generates a control signal to activate such data transfer between these registers. By separating the control variables from the register transfer operation, it is easier to specify a control function (C).

1.8.2 Bus and Memory Transfers

In a digital computer, each bit or value is stored in a register. If individual wires are used to connect each register to every other register, the resulting wire complexity will be severe. Data between registers are sent through a shared bus. To carry binary data from one register to another, a bus structure uses a series of lines or wires, one for each bit. During each register transfer, the bus chooses the destination register based on the control signals.

Through multiplexers, the registers whose data may be transmitted to a common bus are connected to the bus. Each register contains n bits, which are numbered 0 through n – 1. The bus is made up of n multiplexers, each multiplexer has n data inputs (0 through n – 1) and $n = 2^m$, resulting in m selection lines.

The bits in each register, which all have the same significant position, are connected to the data inputs of one multiplexer to form one bus line. Similarly, connect each register's bits b_0 through b_{n-1} to the appropriate multiplexer. All multiplexers' selection inputs are connected to the m selection lines.

When n = 4 and m = 2, for example, four bits are selected from a register and transmitted to a four-line shared bus. Because n = 4, a total of four multiplexers (MUX) are needed. Four separate registers, i.e., registers A, B, C, and D are linked to the bus through four multiplexers in this case. When $S_1S_0 = 00$, the bus outputs are drawn from the initial data inputs of all multiplexers, i.e. for register A, bits A_0, A_1, A_2, and A_3 that are the first inputs of MUX0, MUX1, MUX2, and MUX3. Each MUX's output is a bus line. As a result, all four bits are transmitted to the target register through the bus. If S_1S_0 is a 01, the data from the second register (register B) is sent across the bus. Similarly, data from registers C and D is sent when $S_1S_0 = 10$ and 11, respectively as shown in Fig 1.18.

Memory Transfer

Memory Transfer describes read and write operations that are persuaded by other components. It is referred to as a read operation when information is moved from a memory unit to the end user of the system. A write operation refers to the process of storing new information to the memory.

The information can be accessed in two ways either by providing the register name or memory address where it is stored. Load and Store instructions handle read and write operations, respectively from/to memory. These instructions commence data transmission from memory to the processor by first providing the target memory address, let's say ADR, to memory during read operation and then activating the associated control signal. In the subsequent phase, the information is read from memory. Similarly, when writing to memory, the address of a word must be communicated to memory. For example, the current ADD instruction is read from memory.

to know processor addressing modes

Add R3, R1, R2

The control unit then decodes it in order to determine the operation to be performed. During decoding, it is found that data from memory locations ADR and ADR1 need to be loaded into registers R1 and R2, respectively.

Load R1, ADR

Load R2, ADR1

By using the Load instruction, the contents of memory locations ADR and ADR1 are read and loaded into processor registers R1 and R2, respectively. After loading the operands, the control units send the arithmetic add operation signals to the ALU.

The Add instruction performs addition of the values of registers R1 and register R2 and saves the result in register R3. Using the store instruction, Register R3 value can be written to memory.

Store ADR, R3

By executing store instruction, the data in register R3 is written to the memory address ADR. The value of register R3 is written over the contents of location ADR.

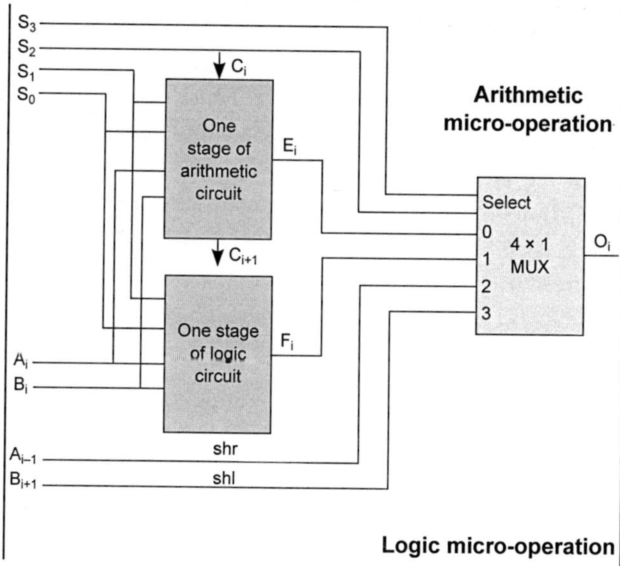

(a) Arithmetic and Logic Shift Unit (ALSU) Schematic Diagram

	S_3	S_2	S_1	S_0	C_i	Micro-operation	Function (O)
Arithmetic micro-operation	0	0	0	0	0	Add	E = A + B
	0	0	0	0	1	Add with carry	E = A + B + 1
	0	0	0	1	0	Subtract	E = A + B'
	0	0	0	1	1	Subtract with carry	E = A + B' + 1
	0	0	1	0	0	Increment	E = A + 1
	0	0	1	0	1	Decrement	E = A – 1
	0	0	1	1	x	Transfer	E = A
Logic micro-operation	0	0	0	0	0	AND	F = A ^ B
	0	0	0	0	1	OR	F = A v B
	0	0	0	1	0	XOR	F = A ⊕ B
	0	0	0	1	1	NOT	F = A'
	0	0	1	0	0	NAND	F = (A ^ B)'
	0	0	1	0	1	NOR	F = (A v B)'
	0	0	1	1	x	XNOR	F = (A ⊕ B)'
	0					SET	1
Shift micro-operation	1	0	x	x	x	Shr	O = Shr A
	1	1	x	x	x	Shl	O = Shl A

(b) Function Table

Fig. 1.19: Arithmetic and logic shift unit microoperations schematic diagram and function table

1.8.3 Arithmetic Logic Shift Unit

A digital computer's microoperations include arithmetic, logic, and shift operations. All of these microoperations are carried out on digital circuits. Arithmetic Logic Shift Unit (ALSU) integrates all microoperations into a single circuit. Several storage registers in computer systems are connected to ALU.

The ALU can perform operations in a single clock pulse, then transfers the results to the destination register. The Arithmetic Logic Shift Unit is created when shift micro-operations are integrated into the ALU. Therefore, the ALSU is a part of the ALU.

ALSU's primary function is to perform all logical, arithmetic, and shift operations that combine into a single ALU with shared selection variables. Arithmetic unit performs addition, subtraction, multiplication, and division. Logical operation refers to operations on numbers and special characters and connects two or more information phrases (expressions). Shift micro-operations are serial information transfer operations.

Fig 1.19(a) shows a diagram of a single stage of ALSU. The subscript indicates a standard stage. The range of the i for a n-bit number is 0 to n – 1 stages. With the S_1 and S_0 inputs, a specific microoperation is selected. A 4 × 1 multiplexer selects between an arithmetic output, logic output, shift right, and shift left outputs. Inputs S_3 and S_2 in a multiplexer select the data. Other two data inputs of the multiplexer receive A_{i-1} for the shift-right operation (shr) and A_{i+1} for the shift-left operation (shl).

A n-bit ALU must repeat the circuit. The carry in C_i of one arithmetic step must be connected to its carry out C_{i+1}. The initial stage receives the carry in via arithmetic variable C_i.

The one-stage circuit depicted in the preceding diagram performs seven arithmetic, eight logical, and two shift operations. The variables S_3, S_2, S_1, S_0, and C_i are used to select each operation. Here, C_i is used exclusively for an arithmetic operation.

In Fig. 1.19(b), the table shows the Arithmetic Logic Shift Unit's function table. There are seven ALU operations, eight logical operations, and two shift operations. The initial seven are arithmetic operations (S_3S_2 = 00). The next S_3S_2 = 01 is used to choose eight logical operations. The S_3S_2 = 10 and S_3S_2 = 11 are used to select shift operations as the final two operations. The remaining three inputs have no effect on the shift. The arithmetic, logic and shift micro-operations are discussed more in coming subsections.

Arithmetic Micro-operations

Arithmetic micro-operations are classified in various categories as listed in Table 1.4. The basic Arithmetic Micro-operations are addition, subtraction, 1's complement, 2's complement, increment, and decrement. In addition, two numbers stored in registers R1 and R2 are added using ALU and the result is stored in any register, let's say in register R3. For subtract operation, the 2's complement of the second number is added to the first number. So ALU can perform both these operations easily with a combinational circuit.

to understand arithmetic micro-operation

A binary up-down counter is used to implement micro-operations that conduct plus one (increment) and minus one (decrement) operations, respectively.

Arithmetic and shift micro-operations are used to conduct the multiply and division arithmetic operations. Most computers perform multiplication by a series of add and shift microoperations. A series of subtract and shift micro-operations are used to divide. Specifying the hardware in this scenario demands a series of micro-operations of add, subtract, and shift.

Table 1.4: Arithmetic Micro-operations

Arithmetic Operation	Sumbolic Representation	Description
Addition	$R_3 \leftarrow R_1 + R_2$	The contents of R1 plus contents of R2 are stored in register R3.

Subtraction	$R_3 \leftarrow R_1 = R_2$	The contents of R1 minus contents of R2 are transferred to register R3.
1's complement	R2 ← R2'	Complement the contents of register R2.
2's complement	R2 ← R2' + 1	Take 2's complement of the contents of register R2.
Substraction	R3 ← R1 + R2' + 1	Perform addition of contents of R1 and the 2's complement of R2. This is another way of doing subtraction.
Increment	R1 ← R1 + 1	The contents of R1 is incremented by one.
Decrement	R1 ← R1 – 1	The contents of R1 is decremented by one.

Logic Micro-operations

Logic microoperations can manipulate individual bits. These operations can modify, delete, and insert bit values. Fig 1.20(a) illustrates nine logic gates connected to a 9 × 1 multiplexer. The output of the gates become the inputs of the multiplexer. According to the value of selection inputs S_3, S_2, S_1, and S_0, the output of the logic gate is transmitted to the multiplexer output. The figure depicts one common stage with subscript i. For every bit of n bits inputs, it is repeated n times.

for applications of logic micro-operations

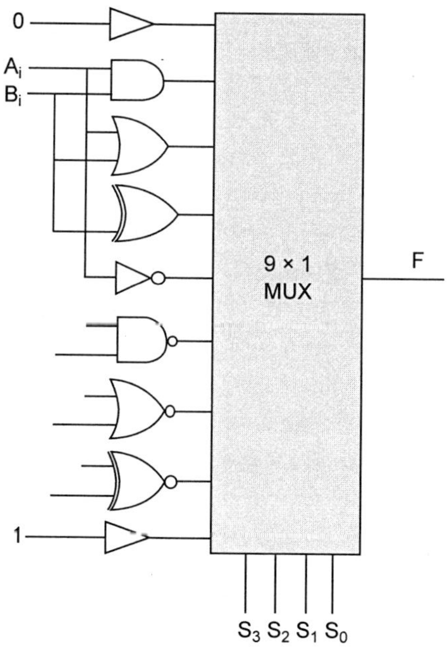

(a) Logic Diagram

S_3	S_2	S_1	S_0	Logic micro-operation	Function (F)
0	0	0	0	CLEAR	0
0	0	0	1	AND	A ^ B
0	0	1	0	OR	A v B
0	0	1	1	XOR	A ⊕ B
0	1	0	0	NOT	A'
0	1	0	1	NAND	(A ^ B)'
0	1	1	0	NOR	(A v B)'
0	1	1	1	XNOR	(A ⊕ B)'
1	0	0	0	SET	1

(b) Function Table

Fig. 1.20: Schematic diagram of logic micro-operations and function table

The selection lines are connected with all stages. Table in Fig. 1.20(b) shows the logic microoperations that can be performed on binary data of registers. Each bit is treated separately. Here, A and B are the registers in which the data is stored and F saves the output after performing selected logic micro-operations. Each micro-operation is discussed below with their truth tables in subsequent order:

1. **Clear:** The Clear logic micro-operation is used to clear the register or set the bits of the register to 0. To use this micro-operation, we need to feed 0 to the register.

2. **AND:** The AND logic micro-operation logically ANDs the bits of data contained in the two registers. The logical AND is represented by the symbol ^.
If both registers A and B are true, the outcome of the AND operation is 1; otherwise, it is 0. The F ← A ^ B specifies that registers A and B will be referred to an AND micro-operation, with the outcome placed in register F. The outcome of the AND logic micro-operation is shown in the truth table based on the input values of registers A and B.

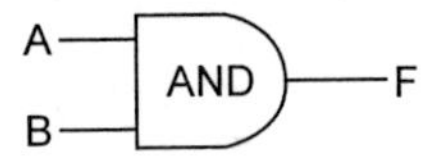

A	B	F
0	0	0
0	1	0
1	0	0
1	1	1

3. **OR:** The OR logic micro-operation performs a logical OR between the bits of two registers. The symbol for the logical OR is v.
If either the value of A register is true and B register is false, or the value of register A is false and register B is true, or both the values of A and B registers are true, then the result of the OR operation is 1, else it is 0. The operation F ← A v B specifies that the values in registers A and B will be subjected to an OR micro-operation, with the output stored in register F. The truth table displays the outputs based on the register A and B input values.

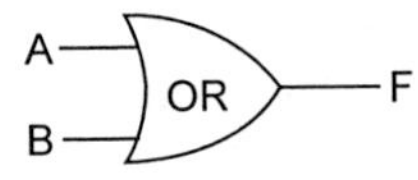

A	B	F
0	0	0
0	1	1
1	0	1
1	1	1

4. **Exclusive OR:** This logic micro-operation, also known as XOR, conducts a logical XOR between bits of two registers. The logical XOR implies that either A or B must be true, but not both. Exclusive OR is represented by the symbol The F ← A B indicates that the values in registers A and B will be subjected to an XOR micro-operation, with the output stored in register F. The truth table shows that when A = 1 and B = 0, or when A = 0 and B = 1, the output is 1.

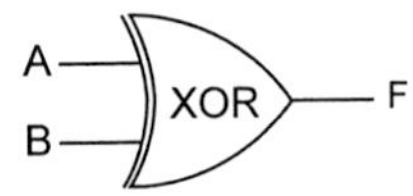

A	B	F
0	0	0
0	1	1
1	0	1
1	1	0

5. **Complement or NOT:** The Complement A logic micro-operation transfers the complemented contents of input register A to the output register F. First, the content of the register is complemented and then moved to the desired register. The truth table, F ← A' represents the complemented value of register A, which is moved to register F. So the truth table is just the opposite of the taken values of the A register.

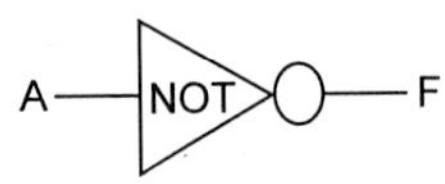

A	F
0	1
1	0

6. **NAND:** The NAND logic micro-operation is the opposite of AND logic micro-operation. As the name suggests, it is Not AND. In contrast to AND, in NAND, the output is 0 when the value of both A register and B register is true, and it is 1 when either A is false, or B is false, or both are false as shown in truth table F ← (A ^ B)'.

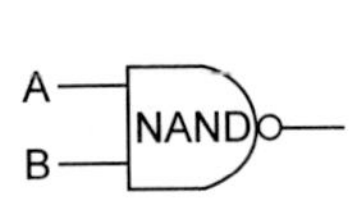

A	B	F
0	0	1
0	1	1
1	0	1
1	1	0

7. **NOR:** The NOR logic micro-operation is Not OR. In contrast to OR, in NOR, the output is 0 when the value of either A register or B register or both A and B registers are true, and it is 1 when both A and B registers are false. The expression F ← (A v B)' represents the truth table of NOR logic micro-operation for different values of input A and B registers.

A	B	F
0	0	1
0	1	0
1	0	0
1	1	0

8. **Exclusive NOR:** The Exclusive NOR (XNOR) micro-operation sets the output 1 when the values of both the registers A and B are the same. They can be true or false, but they have to be the same.

   The truth table of XNOR logic micro-operation F ← (A ⊕ B)' shows that the output will be 1 when either A = 0 and B = 0 or A = 1 and B = 1.

A	B	F
0	0	1
0	1	0
1	0	0
1	1	1

9. **Set to all 1's:** The set to all 1's logic micro-operations is used to set all the register bits to 1.

   For example, F ← 1 means the value of the register F is set to 1. The previous value of register F will be removed.

10. **Transfer A:** The Transfer A logic micro-operation transfers the data of register A to the output register F.

    Truth table of 'Transfer A' logic micro-operation shows that there is a transfer of data from the register A to the output register in this micro-operation, its truth table is the same as the taken values of the register A. If A is 0 then F is 0, if A is 1 then F is 1.

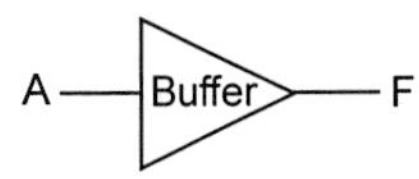

A	F
0	0
1	1

Shift Micro-operations

Information is transferred serially using shift micro-operations. Shift micro-operations are available in three distinct ways:

1. **Logical:** The serial input transfers zero. The symbols "shl" and "shr" are used for logical shifts left and right, respectively.
   - **Logical Shift-Left:** This shift left operation moves each bit one place left. In Fig. 1.21(a), the MSB is discarded and the LSB is filled with zero (the serial input).
   - **Right Logical Shift:** This results in a shift to the right of each bit as shown in Fig. 1.21(b), the removal of the LSB, and the addition of zero to the empty MSB position.

for shift left and shift right hardware implementation circuit design

R1

b7	b6	b5	b4	b3	b2	b1	b0

R1

b7	b6	b5	b4	b3	b2	b1	b0

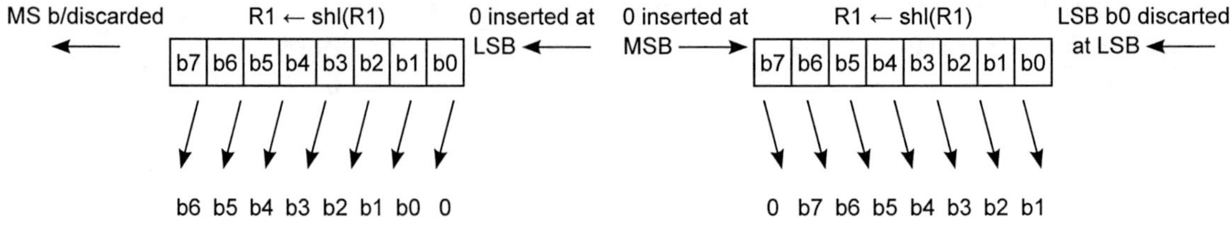

(a) R1 after shift-left (b) R1 after shift-right

Fig. 1.21: Logical shift (a) left and (b) right micro-operations

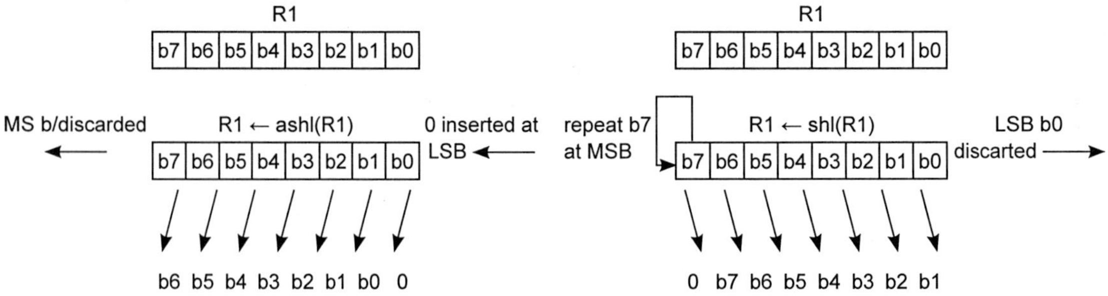

(a) R1 after arithmetic shift-left (b) R1 after arithmetic shift-right

Fig. 1.22: Arithmetic shift (a) left and (b) right micro-operations

2. **Arithmetic:** The shift left and shift right are referred to as arithmetic shift left and shift right micro-operations when they are applied to signed binary values. A signed binary integer is multiplied by 2 when the shift is left. The number is divided by 2 when the shift is right.
   - **Arithmetic shift left:** Each bit is shifted to the left one at a time. The MSB is discarded, and the empty LSB is set to zero. This is identical to the logical shift to the left as shown in Fig. 1.22(a).
   - **Arithmetic shift right:** The LSB is discarded, the empty MSB is filled with the value of the previous MSB, and each bit is moved to the right one at a time. This is known as the right arithmetic shift depicted in Fig. 1.22(b).
3. **Circular:** The circular shift recirculates the register's bit sequence around both ends without losing any information.

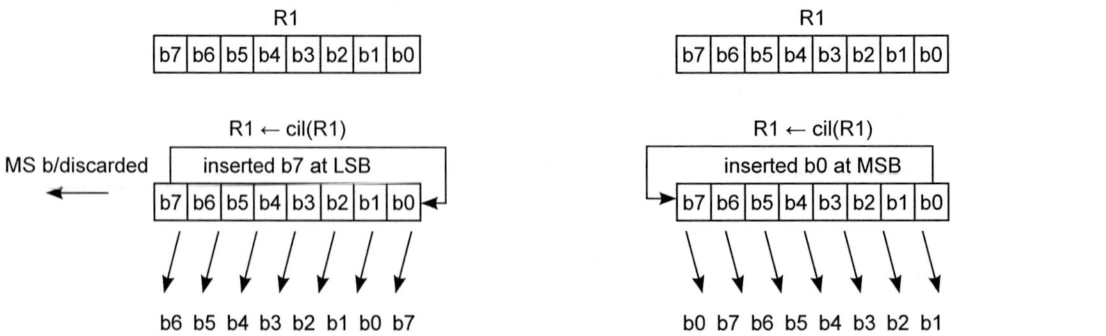

(a) R1 after circular shift-left (b) R1 after circular shift-right

Fig. 1.23: Circular shift (a) left and (b) right micro-operations

- **Left Circular Shift:** The MSB bit is moved to the first position while shifting all other bits to the next position as illustrated in Fig. 1.23(a).
- **Right Circular Shift:** The LSB is moved to the MSB, or the last position, while all of the other bits are shifted to the previous position as represented in Fig. 1.23(b).

UNIT SUMMARY

- A computer is made up of the input unit, output unit, arithmetic logic unit (ALU), memory unit, and control unit.
- Digital computers have a single shared memory for storing programs and data in von neumann architecture, and a single bus is used for memory access by the processor.
- Binary digits are transported from one register/unit to the other units/registers via a network of physical wires called a bus.
- The MAR, MDR, PC, IR, and general purpose registers store specific types of information required by the processor.
- A computer system stores binary numbers (either 0 or 1) as a string of bits.
- Integer numbers can be signed or unsigned. The signed numbers are classified into sign-and-magnitude, 1's complement, and 2's complement number systems.
- Computers use the 2's complement representation (values from -2^{n-1} to $+2^{n-1} - 1$) for signed integers to prevent problems in micro-operations since there are two representations of 0 (+0 and -0) in sign-and-magnitude and 1's complement.
- An overflow occurs when the sum of n digit integers contains n+1 digits.
- Computers use fixed point and floating point number representations.
- Error occurs if the information received by the receiver does not match to the information sent by the sender. The change in single bit is considered a single-bit error or change in more than one bit is called a bitstream error. These errors can be detected with even parity code or odd parity code error detection methods.
- Micro-operations are elementary operations performed on register data.
- Data between registers are sent through a shared bus that uses a series of lines or wires, one wire for each bit.
- Bus chooses the destination register based on the control signals during each register transfer.
- Register transfers are facilitated by hardware logic circuits to carry out specific micro-operations.
- Memory Transfer is referred to as a read operation when information is moved from a memory unit to the end user and a write operation refers to the process of storing new information to the memory.
- Arithmetic Logic Shift Unit (ALSU) integrates arithmetic, logic, and shift operations into a single circuit.
- Arithmetic Micro-operations are addition, subtraction, 1's complement, 2's complement, increment, and decrement.

- Logic microoperations can manipulate individual bits. These operations can modify, delete, and insert bit values. These micro-operations are implemented using digital logic gates such as AND, OR, XOR, NOT, etc.
- Shift micro-operations transfer information serially. These micro-operations are classified as logical, arithmetic, and circular shift operations.
- Arithmetic and shift micro-operations are used to conduct the multiply and division arithmetic operations.

EXERCISES

Multiple Choice Questions

1. The decimal number 485 is the binary equivalent of
   (a) 111100101 (b) 111110111 (c) 101111111 (d) 101110111
2. How many bits are equal to two bytes?
   (a) 4 (b) 8 (c) 12 (d) 16
3. Which memory unit is the fastest?
   (a) register (b) cache (c) harddisk (d) RAM
4. How does the value of PC changes
   (a) value of current instruction (b) previous instruction
   (c) next instruction address (d) none of these
5. The memory address of the instruction to be fetched is transferred from the program counter to the RAM through __________ during a fetch-decode-execute cycle.
   (a) control bus (b) address bus (c) data bus (d) either (a) or (b)
6. Choose the correct order to fill up the empty spaces. The __________ contains the memory address of the data that the CPU must access. The __________ holds the data that the CPU is transferring to or from the memory location. The memory address of the next instruction to be executed is stored in the __________. The result of a calculation performed by the arithmetic/logic unit is stored in the __________.
   (a) ACC, PC, MDR, MAR (b) MAR , PC, MDR, ACC
   (c) PC, ACC, MDR, MAR (d) MAR, MDR, PC, ACC
7. Assuming the last operation on an 8-bit word computer was a subtraction (A-B) with A = 11110000 and B = 00010100 as the operands, what would be the value of Overflow, Sign, Carry, Zero, and Even Parity flags?

   [Hints: Use 2's complement subtraction method, Zero flag: when the result of an arithmetic operation is zero, the zero flag is set to 1, Even Parity Flag: this flag is set if the number of 1's in the result is even].

   (a) 1, 0, 0, 0, 1 (b) 0, 0, 0, 1, 1
   (c) 0, 0, 0, 0, 1 (d) 0, 1, 1, 0, 0

8. Assuming a 4-bit ALU performs the 5 + (–5) operation for signed numbers, what are the values of the Carry, Overflow, Zero, Negative, and Even Parity flags?

[Hint: Use 2's complement arithmetic; Negative flag: the negative flag is set to 1 if the result is negative, Even Parity Flag: this flag is set if the number of 1's in the result is even]

(a) 1, 1, 0, 1, 0 (b) 1, 0, 1, 0, 1 (c) 1, 1, 1, 0, 1 (d) 1, 0, 1, 1, 1

9. Which of the following gates gives output 1 if and only if at least one of its inputs is 1?

(a) NOR (b) AND (c) XOR (d) OR

10. How many NAND gates with two inputs are required to provide the same effect as an OR gate with two inputs?

(a) four (b) three (c) two (d) one

11. A shift register appropriately can be described as the register that can shift information bits

(a) either to the right or to the left (b) to the left only
(c) to the right only (d) to another register

12. Let X stands for the distinct number representation of 8-bit integers in 2's complement form. Let Y be the distinct number representation of 8-bit integers in sign-and-magnitude representation. So, X – Y = ?

(a) 1 (b) 0 (c) 2 (d) None of these

13. A multiplexer

1. chooses one of numerous inputs and sends it to a single output..
2. data is routed from a single input to one of multiple outputs.
3. converts to serial data from parallel data.
4. is a combinational circuit.

Determine which of the following options is true?

(a) 1, 2, 4 (b) 2, 3, 4 (c) 1, 3, 4 (d) 1, 2, 3

14. Choose the option that most accurately defines correct statements.

1. the carry out bit value from the MSB does not indicate overflow.
2. overflow is only possible if both summands have the same sign.
3. overflow can't occur when adding integers with opposite signs.
4. if XOR of carry in and carry out at MSB is equal to 1 then overflow is there.

Determine which of the following options is true?

(a) 1, 2, 4 (b) 2, 3, 4 (c) 1, 3, 4 (d) all are correct

15. What is the memory access time?

(a) ~100 ms (b) ~1 ms (c) 10 – 30 ns (d) 3 – 10 ns

ANSWERS															
1.	(a)	2.	(d)	3.	(a)	4.	(c)	5.	(b)	6.	(d)	7.	(d)	8.	(b)
9.	(d)	10.	(b)	11.	(a)	12.	(a)	13.	(c)	14.	(d)	15.	(c)		

Short and Long Answer Type Questions

Category-I

1. What are the various parts and pieces that make up a computer?
2. What distinguishes computer organisation from computer architecture?
3. How does the value of the programme counter change when an interrupt occurs?
4. Differentiate between caches, primary memory, and secondary storage.
5. Describe the features of the von neumann architecture.
6. Which interconnect do you consider is the most efficient in terms of increasing the number of processors on chip?
7. What is the function of control lines?
8. What are the names of the five major input devices?
9. List five different types of output devices.
10. What specifically are bus and memory transfers?
11. What is the condition of the overflow detection?
12. What is the IEEE 754 standard for representing floating point numbers?
13. What are the logic micro-operations? List three uses of logic operations in the real world.
14. What are the different kinds of micro-operations? When should shift micro-operations be performed?

Category-II

15. Construct a digital circuit to perform logic operations such as XOR, exclusive-NOR, NOR, and NAND all at the same time. It is necessary to make use of two selection variables in order to obtain the output of a certain gate on the output line. Show the logic diagram to demonstrate.
16. Prove that the function $X = \alpha \oplus \beta \oplus \lambda \oplus \omega$, a XOR function, is an odd function. Show that there are only odd numbers of ones in and α, β, λ and ω, if and only if $X = 1$. [**Hint:** First create truth tables for $Y = \alpha \oplus \beta$ and for $Z = \lambda \oplus \omega$, and then you have to build the truth table for $X = Y \oplus Z$]
17. Create the digital circuit for a 3-bit parity generator and a 4-bit parity checker that uses an odd-parity bit.
18. Why do computers require floating point number representation? How do computers represent these numbers? What is the definition of floating point number normalisation? Why is normalisation significant? Describe the various standards for floating point representation.

Numerical Problems

19. Convert the binary values $(101110)_2$, $(1110101)_2$, and $(110110100)_2$ to decimal.

[**Ans:** 46, 117, 436]

20. The following are 8-digit binary numbers; find their 1's and 2's complements: 00000000; 00000001; 10101110; 10000000; and 10000001. [**Ans:** 1's complement: 11111111, 11111110, 01010001, 01111111, 01111110; 2's complement: 00000000, 11111111, 01010010, 10000000, 01111111]

21. Perform subtraction on the following unsigned binary values by subtracting the 2's complement of the subtrahend.

(i) 100 – 110000 (ii) 11010 – 1101

(iii) 11010 – 10000 (iv) 1010100 – 1010100

[**Ans:** (i) 010100, (ii) 01101, (iii) 01010, (iv) 0000000]

22. Register A contains the binary digits 11011001. Compute the B operand and the required logic micro-operation to change the value of A to:

(i) 11111101 (ii) 01101101 [**Ans:** B = 11111101, OR (ii) B = 10110100, XOR]

23. How do you compute the signed numbers below using the 2's complement number system?

(i) (+70) + (+80) (ii) (–70) + (–80) (iii) (+42) + (–13) (iv) (–42) – (–13)

Each number has eight bits to store the binary value along with its sign. What will the outcome of arithmetic operations be? Is there an overflow?[**Ans:** Overflow occurs only in the first two cases, (i) 10010110; (ii) 01101010; (iii) 00011101; (iv) 11100011]

24. The initial values of the 8-bit registers R1, R2, R3, and R4 are as follows: R1 = 11110010, R2 = 11111111, R3 = 10111001, and R4 = 11101010.

Determine the eight bit results in each register once the following sequence of micro-operations has been performed.

R1 ← R1 + R2 Add R2 to R1 R2 ← R2 + 1 Increment R2

R3 ← R3 ^ R4 AND R4 to R3 R1 ← R1 – R3 Subtract R3 from R1

[**Ans:** R1 = 01001001; R2 = 00000000; R3 = 10101000; R4 = 11101010]

25. The binary value 10011100 is stored in an 8-bit register. Assuming an arithmetic shift right, what is the new value in the register? From the starting value of 10011100, find the value of the register after an arithmetic shift left, and indicate whether or not there is an overflow.

[**Ans:** arithmetic shift-right: 11001110, arithmetic shift-left: 00111000, overflow detected]

26. Find the sequence of binary values in register R following a logical shift-right, a circular shift right, a logical shift left, and a circular shift left, starting from R = 11111111.

[**Ans:** Logical shift right: 01111111, Circular shift right: 10111111, Logical shift left: 01111110, Circular shift left: 11111100]

27. An exponent of 8 bits plus a sign bit and a mantissa of 26 bits plus a sign bit make up a 36-bit floating-point binary integer. The mantissa is normalised. Sign-and-magnitudes are used for both the mantissa and exponent. If zero is ignored, what are the largest and smallest positive integers that may be written? [**Ans:** Largest: $(1 - 2^{-26}) \times 2^{+255}$, Smallest: $-(1 - 2^{-26}) \times 2 + 255$]

28. What is the 24-bit binary floating point representation of +46.5? The mantissa is normalised, and the mantissa and exponent are represented by 16 and 8 bits, respectively. [**Ans:** Binary representation: $(101110.1)_2$, Sign: 0, Mantissa: 1000010000000000, Exponent: 01111010]

PRACTICAL

Aim: Draw the logic diagram of the arithmetic logic shift unit using verilog hardware description language.

Tools: Xilinx ISE Design Suite [4]

Theory: Verilog modules are the basic descriptive unit. Module declares it, and endmodule always terminates it. Modules have names and ports. Module name should be meaningfully. Alphabetic, alphanumeric and underscore names are case sensitive. The first character of a name must be either an alphabetic character or an underscore. There is no way to begin a name with a number.

to know installation steps of Xillinx ISE design suite

Port lists interface modules to their environments. Ports are the circuit's inputs and outputs. The environment determines a circuit's input logic values, while the circuit's output logic values are determined by the inputs.

The port list is enclosed in parenthesis that are separated by commas. Sentences are followed by semicolons, but endmodules are not. Commas are used to demarcate each variable. Only use lowercase for the keywords. Following that, input and output will refer to the input and output ports respectively. Internal connections are represented by the presence of wires.

to learn verilog for digital circuits

The building of the circuit is specified by a list of descriptive primitive gates such as "and," "not," "or," and so on. Gate instances are the list's elements. Each gate instantiation begins with an optional name (Gate1, Gate2, etc.) and the gate output and inputs, separated by commas and wrapped in parenthesis. A basic gate's inputs follow its output.

A primitive's output must be mentioned first, while a module's inputs and outputs can be specified in any order. The description of the module concludes with the term endmodule.

Procedure:

1. First, look into the circuit's number of inputs and outputs. Choose a good name for your circuit. Fill up the blanks with the code **module** circuit_name (list of input and output ports separated by comma) (verilog program here) **endmodule**
2. Declare the input variables as input variable names;
3. Declare the outputs as the output port names;
4. Designate a wire as the intermediate output that will become the input of another circuit.
5. A list of defined fundamental gates, each of which is characterised by a keyword, is used to define the circuit design such as **and, not, or,** etc.
6. Each component of the list is a gate instance.
7. Each instance of a gate begins with a name or label such as Gate1, Gate2, etc. After that, the output and inputs of the gate are subsequently described using commas and parenthesis.
8. The primitive gate's output is always mentioned first, followed by the inputs.
9. Create a testbench for circuit verification. Mention all potential input and output combinations.
10. Run Isim in Xilinx to see the outputs and check the circuit's operation.

to learn testbench creation and running ISim in Xilinx

KNOW MORE

Innovations by Indian: Indians frequently demonstrate the ability to alter the world or at least make it a better place to live. USB (Universal Serial Bus) is an integral element of our daily lives. This compact data storage device was co-invented by Ajay Bhatt, an Indian-American computer architect. However, he did not earn any money with this invention. He did not do this for financial gain, but rather to bring change in technology. According to him, the opportunity to accomplish such a significant transformation is rare. Every year on May 11, India celebrates Indian Technology Day and awards young inventors [5].

to know more about Ajay Bhatt

Indian Vedic Science: Vedic education contains immense treasures of human knowledge that have been with us for millennia. India's vedic sciences, which exist in oral traditions as well as 4+ million manuscripts recorded in dozens of Indian scripts and languages, can provide us with a firm platform on which to improve our computing skills. Texts from the shastra, for example, are significantly better suited to machine processing than modern language texts. As a result, applying vedic notions of learning to today's powerful computing technologies yields a rich treasury of knowledge that blends the best of both worlds.

The idea of zero, binary number system, algebraic transformations, hashing, recursion, formal grammars, mathematical logic, and high level language description all originated in India. Atharvaveda, widely known as the Veda of 'magical formulas' has simplified mathematics. The binary scheme that is utilised in all current computers derives from the Atharvaveda. With the use of vedic mathematics, calculations that took hours could be completed in a matter of minutes.

We unknowingly use vedic sutras. The 'EkadhikinaPurvena' and 'EkanyunenaPurvena' Sutras are used in software methods when $i \leftarrow i + 1$ and $i \leftarrow i - 1$ are used, respectively. Similarly, numerous vedic sutras are used in computer multiplier units [6]. It will produce speedier results, which is essential in many applications such as cryptography methods and image processing applications.

It is feasible to establish a much broader and more comprehensive perspective of computer sciences by including ancient vedic knowledge herein. Vedic concepts are derived from natural law, which is adequately expressed in the Rigveda. The vedic seers saw this law as the true governing power of the cosmos, and even the vedic gods are seen to be either subject to or protectors of this law. Natural phenomena such as river flow, the occurrence of night and morning are described in terms of this natural rule. It is now established that there existed a conception of natural law with regard to god among the Babylonia.

There are four such vast collections of vedas, namely (i) the Rigveda, the book of strophes or hymns and prayers (mantras) to be recited during sacrifices and rituals, (ii) the Samaveda, the book of melodies (samans) to which the strophes are to be sung, (iii) the Yajurveda, the book of sacrificial formulas, and (iv) the Atharvaveda, the book of magical formulas [7].

REFERENCES AND SUGGESTED READINGS

1. M. Morris Mano, Computer system architecture. Prentice-Hall, Inc., Third edition. https://poojavaishnav.files.wordpress.com/2015/05/mano-m-m-computer-system-architecture.pdf (last accessed: Aug 15, 2022)
2. Carl Hamacher, Zvonko Vranesic, Safwat Zaky, and Naraig Manjikian, Computer organization and embedded systems. McGraw-Hill Higher Education, 2011.
3. NPTEL Course by Prof. Indranil Sengupta and Prof. Kamalika Datta, Computer Architecture and Organization, IIT Kharagpur, 2017. https://archive.nptel.ac.in/courses/106/105/106105163/ (last accessed: Aug 15, 2022)
4. Xilinx ISE design suite. https://www.xilinx.com/support/download/index.html/content/xilinx/en/downloadNav/vivado-design-tools/archive-ise.html (last accessed: Sept. 20, 2022)
5. About National Technology Day Celebration. https://economictimes.indiatimes.com/news/how-to/national-technology-day-why-is-it-celebrated-history-behind-it/articleshow/100171949.cms (last accessed: Aug 15, 2022)
6. S. Jain and V.S. Jagtap, Vedic mathematics in computer: a survey. International Journal of Computer Science and Information Technologies, 5(6), pp.7458-7459, 2014.
7. A Concise History of Science in India, ed. D M Bose, S N Sen and B V Subbarayappa, 1971.
8. NPTEL Course by Jatindra Kumar Deka, Arnab Sarkar, and Santosh Biswas, Computer Organization and Architecture: A Pedagogical Aspect, IIT Guwahati, 2017. https://archive.nptel.ac.in/courses/106/103/106103180/ (last accessed: Aug 15, 2022)

2 Micro Programmed Control

UNIT SPECIFICS

The following aspects are discussed in this unit:

- Control memory and address sequencing of control unit;
- Basic structure of control unit;
- Signed integer numbers arithmetic operations;
- Different methods for multiplication and division;
- Arithmetic operations for floating point numbers, i.e., addition, subtraction, multiplication, division;
- Arithmetic and Instruction pipeline, hazards and their solutions;
- RISC pipeline and vector processing;
- Array processors.

The practical applications of the topics are presented for the purpose of fostering greater curiosity and creativity and enhancing problem-solving skills. In addition to a large number of multiple-choice questions and short- and long-answer questions marked in two categories according to the lower and higher levels of Bloom's taxonomy, the unit provides practice assignments in the form of numerical problems, a list of references, and suggested readings. It is crucial to note that several QR codes, which may be scanned for further information on various topics of interest, have been included in different parts and can be used to obtain necessary supporting data.

The related practical based on the content is followed by a "Know More" section on the topic. This section has been carefully constructed such that the supplementary information it contains is valuable to the book's readers. This section discusses Indian innovators' contributions to computer system organization and Indian vedic knowledge's impact in contemporary digital computers.

RATIONALE

A control unit coordinates the processor's actions. It directs the ALU to execute instructions and coordinates the actions of other components. This chapter examines the fundamental structure of the control unit and demonstrates how program instructions are fetched, decoded, and executed. The processing unit is referred to as CPU (central processing unit). Multiple processing units exist in modern computers. Therefore, the term processor is more appropriate than CPU. Computer arithmetic introduces a number of interesting logic design aspects.

This chapter examines the various techniques of computer arithmetic operations, such as addition, subtraction, multiplication, and division, for sign-and-magnitude and the 2's complement number system. The floating-point number representation as per IEEE standards and the methods for conducting floating point numbers' arithmetic operations are analysed. The methods for adding, subtracting, multiplying, and dividing floating point numbers are discussed. Processor organisation has changed with technological advancements to deliver high performance. Many functional units operate in parallel to obtain high performance. Such processors feature a pipelined structure in which an instruction is executed before the previous instruction is finished. This chapter provides a comprehensive look at the pipelined structure, possible hazards, and proposed solutions.

PRE-REQUISITE

Mathematics: Arithmetic operations with integer and floating point numbers (Class X)

Digital Electronics: Number systems and digital logic gates (Polytechnic Engineering)

UNIT OUTCOMES

List of outcomes of this unit is as follows:

U1-O1: Describe role of control memory and address sequencing in control unit design

U2-O2: Describe various methods of addition, subtraction, multiplication, division for integer numbers

U2-O3: Explain IEEE standards and arithmetic operations for floating point numbers

U2-O4: Explain arithmetic and instruction pipeline, data and control hazards and their solutions

U2-O5: Explain RISC pipeline, vector processing and array processors

Unit-2 Outcomes	EXPECTED MAPPING WITH COURSE OUTCOMES (1- Weak Correlation; 2- Medium Correlation; 3- Strong Correlation)				
	CO-1	CO-2	CO-3	CO-4	CO-5
U2-O1	3	3	2	3	3
U2-O2	3	2	3	3	2
U2-O3	3	3	2	2	1
U2-O4	3	3	2	3	3
U2-O5	3	2	3	2	1

2.1 CONTROL MEMORY

The control unit initiates sequences of microoperations in the computer. The functionality of the control unit can be implemented with any one approach either hardwired or microprogramming. Hardwired approach generates the control signals using hardware. Whereas, microprogramming is another method for controlling the microoperation sequences in a digital computer.

A microprogrammed control unit stores the microprogram. Each micro-program has a sequence of microinstructions or control words. These control words are represented by binary values, which are strings of 1s and 0s. Each microinstruction or control word comprises a unique bit pattern. Each binary state of the control unit specifies a microoperation, and control signals are generated in consequence. As a result, the control words may be programmed to conduct different actions on the system components. A micro-routine is made up of a series of microinstructions.

Once the control unit is operational, there is no requirement for further microprogram updates because the control memory is ROM. When the hardware is being manufactured, ROM words are made permanent. The words in ROM stand for microinstructions. Control memories are contained within control units. The control memory is not the same as the main memory. The programme changes in main memory, unlike control memory.

Machine instructions start control memory micro-instructions. These micro-instructions generate control signals for micro-operations like fetching the instruction from main memory, evaluating the effective address, executing the operation, and returning to the fetch phase to repeat the cycle for the next instruction.

Through the use of dynamic microprogramming, a micro-program is able to load data from auxiliary memory, such as a magnetic disk. Dynamic microprogramming uses writable control memory. This memory is usually used for reading but may modify the micro-program.

2.2 ADDRESS SEQUENCING

The control memory is kept the collections of micro-instructions, and each collection defines a certain routine. The computer relies on a dedicated micro-program routine stored in the control memory to produce the micro-operations necessary to execute an instruction. The hardware that manages the control memory's address sequence must be able to sequence micro-instructions inside a routine and perform branching between routines.

The control address register of a computer is "initialised" when it is first powered on. The microinstruction sequence that initiates instruction fetch usually begins here. The microinstructions that make up the fetch routine are sequenced when the control address register is incremented. The instruction is then delivered to the computer's instruction register following the fetching step.

A control memory routine determines the operand's effective address. Computer instructions can define indirect address and index register modes. A branch microinstruction can access the control memory effective address computation routine based on mode bits. The memory address register will store the operand's address after effective address computation.

Generate the microoperations that execute the memory-fetched instruction. Operation code determines processor register microoperation stages. Each instruction has a microprogram stored in control memory. Instruction code bits are mapped into control memory where the routine exists. After reaching the needed routine, incrementing the control address register may sequence the microinstructions that execute the instruction, although processor register status bits can also affect microoperation sequencing.

Subroutine-based microprograms must store return addresses in external register. Since the device cannot write return addresses to ROM. After the instruction has been completely executed, control must return to the fetch routine. Execute a microinstruction that performs an unconditional branch to the fetch routine's initial address.

Figure 2.1 shows the microinstruction address circuitry. Control memory microinstructions start computer register microoperations and define how to get the next address. The image shows four ways the control address register (CAR) gets the address. The incrementer selects the next microinstruction by incrementing the control address register. The microinstruction's field defines the branch address. Conditional branching is enabled by selecting a status bit from the microinstruction. Mapping logic circuits relocate external addresses to control memory. The microprogram uses a specific register to exit a subroutine using its return address.

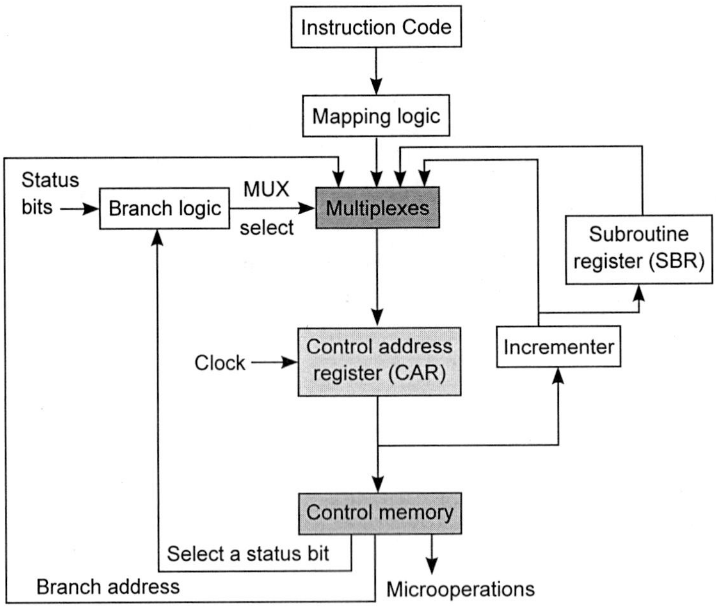

Fig. 2.1: Control memory address selection

2.3 CONTROL UNIT DESIGN

Control unit generates the control signals to activate various components in the processor like registers, internal bus, ALU and paths between various components as shown in Fig 2.2. Inputs for the control unit are condition codes, instruction registers, operation codes, external inputs and clock. These inputs convey the various information as follows.

1. Instruction Register (IR) loads the instruction to be executed from memory data register (MDR). The MDR contains a copy of the value in the memory location specified by the memory address register. After the instruction decode, processor knows which operation has to perform. These operation bits are input for the control unit.
2. Condition codes (flags) bits are inputs for the control unit. Condition codes give the status of previous instruction operation. For example, in Increment and Skip if Zero (ISZ) instruction effective address is incremented by one and compared with zero if equal then Zero Flag (ZF) set to 1, and the processor skips the next instruction execution.
3. External Inputs are such control signals that are provided from the system bus like wait until memory function completed (WMFC), these control signals are generated from main memory. From input devices, interrupt request signals are also generated to the control unit.
4. Clock: In processor, a number of micro-operations are performed in a single clock cycle simultaneously.

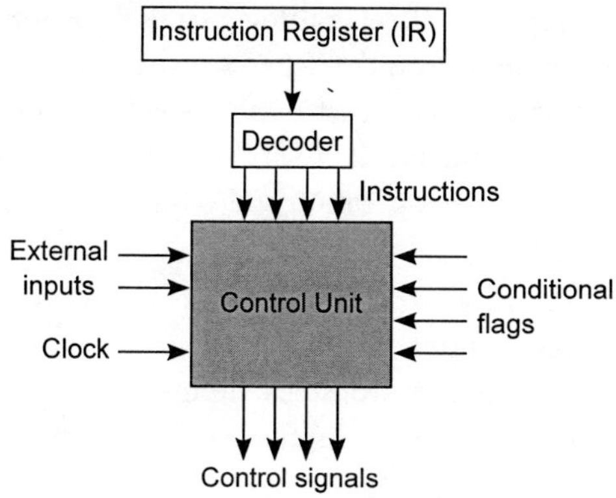

Fig. 2.2: Control unit block diagram

2.3.1 Hardwired Control Unit

The logic gates, flip-flops, decoders, and other digital circuits implement control logic in the Hardwired Control structure. RISC-based computers require hardwired control. A block diagram of a Hardwired Control structure is shown in Fig 2.3.

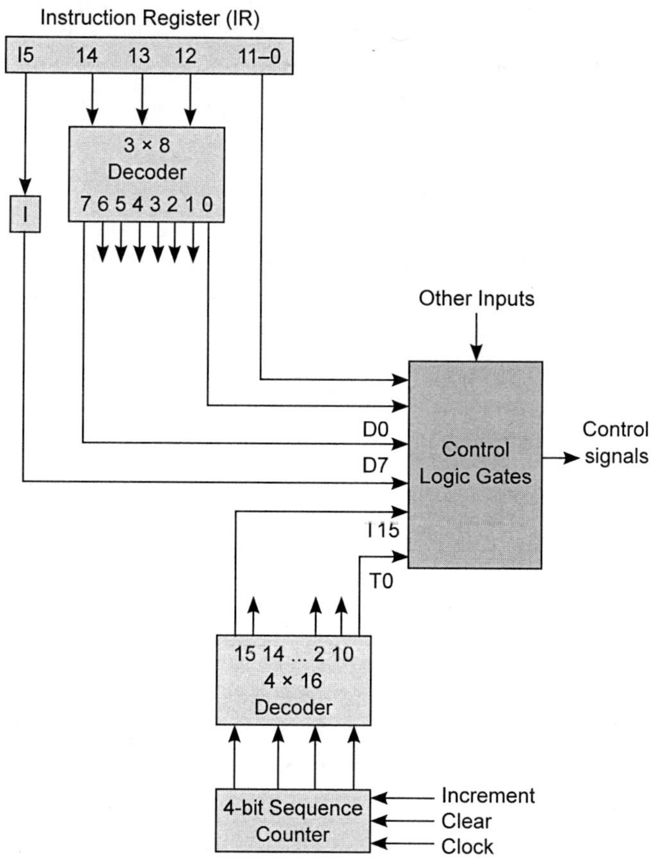

Fig. 2.3: Hardwired control unit

Two decoders, a sequence counter, and several logic gates constitute a Hardwired Control. The instruction register (IR) contains a memory-unit's fetched instruction. The I bit, the operation code, and bits 0 – 11 are the components that make up the instruction register. A 3 × 8 decoder encodes operation code bits 12 – 14. The decoder has outputs labelled D0 through D7. The bit 15 operation code is read into the I-flip-flops. Control logic gates use operation codes 0 – 11. The binary Sequence counter (SC) counts 0 – 15.

The processor has to generate control signals in the proper sequence for executing instructions. For Hardwired control design, hardware components like AND gates, OR gates, encoder and decoder are used. A counter is used to keep track of the control steps. Inputs for the hardwired control unit are clock, instruction register, condition codes and external inputs like WMFC and interrupts.

Each step takes one clock cycle. Step decoders have signal lines for each control sequence time unit. Instruction register opcode bits inputs for IR decoder. The instruction decoder outputs one line per machine instruction. For any instruction loaded in the IR register, one output line from IR [0-11] is set to 1 and all other lines are set to 0 (not active). The encoder combines all the input signals and generates separate control signals. Hardwired control unit generates control signal to limited instructions.

2.3.2 Microprogrammed Control Unit

Microprogrammed control unit generates a sequence of control signals for instruction execution. It is used to design complex instruction set computer (CISC) style processors. The program that generates control signals is known as "Microprogrammed." These microprograms are stored in a specific control memory.

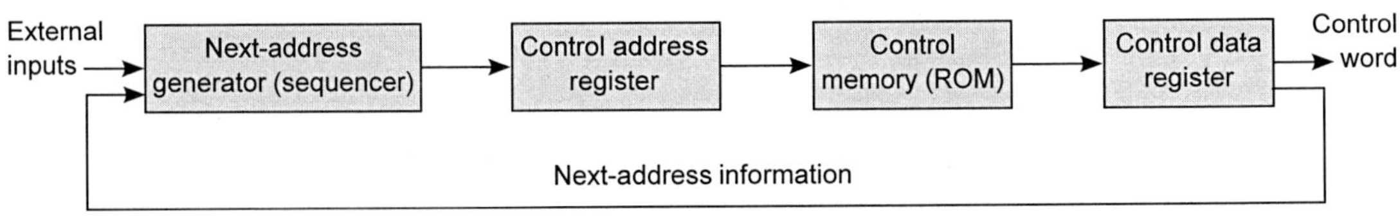

Fig. 2.4: Microprogrammed control organization

Figure 2.4 demonstrates the working of a microprogrammed control unit. ROM memory holds control data permanently. The control data register has the memory-read microinstruction, whereas the control memory address register specifies its address.

A control word in the microinstruction defines one or more microoperations. Control will choose the next address when these tasks have been completed. The next microinstruction could be in sequence or in control memory. As a result, some bits of the present microinstruction must have an impact on the address of the next one. External inputs may alter the next address. The next address generator circuit calculates and sends the control address register to read the next microinstruction during microoperations.

Microinstructions start microoperations and set control memory address sequences. The next address generator determines the address sequence received from control memory and is often termed as microprogram sequencer. Microprogram sequencers increments control address registers by one. Control operations begin with an address from control memory, an external address, or an initial address.

The control data register stores the currently active microinstruction until the next address is computed and read from memory. Data registers are also known as pipeline registers. The control word's microoperations can be executed while the next microinstruction is generated simultaneously.

A combinational ROM circuit reads the address value and outputs the word. The output wires contain the ROM word's content as long as its address value is in the address register. Like random access memory, no read signal is required. Each clock pulse executes control word microoperations and transfers a new address to the control address register.

The microprogrammed control unit allows to specify a different microprogram residing in control memory. It can further classify into two categories:

- **Horizontal Microprogrammed control unit:** In horizontal microprogrammed control unit
    1. n bits in control word, all n bits will generate n control signals.
    2. Some bits for external inputs, some bits for functional codes like conditional jump, some bits for condition codes (flags) and some bits for next instruction address.
    3. In this control unit, control word has more number of bits (longer).
- **Vertical Microprogrammed control unit:** In vertical microprogrammed control unit
    1. For n bits control words, only control signals are generated. Suppose there are 64 bits for functional codes, only 6 control signals shall be generated for all 64 bit functional codes.
    2. Control word has less number of bits (shorter).

On comparing both types of control unit, the following advantages/disadvantages can be faced with microprogrammed control unit over hardwired control unit:

1. Microprogram Control Unit is less costly as compared to hardwired control unit because it is implemented with a program.
2. Microprogram Control Unit is easy to modify compared with hardwired control units. If the instructions are changed then microprograms are also modified but the hardwired control unit is difficult to modify because it has array logic gates (AND, OR) and a lot of wiring.
3. Microprogrammed control unit is slower compared to hardwired control because it generates control signals for many instructions.
4. Hardwired control is used by RISC architecture and microprogrammed control unit is used by CISC architecture.

2.4 COMPUTER ARITHMETIC

Arithmetic operations, i.e., addition, subtraction, multiplication, and division can be done on both unsigned and signed integers. The hardware implementation techniques of arithmetic operations for sign-and-magnitude and 2's complement numbers' operations are explained in this section.

2.4.1 Addition and subtraction for sign-and-magnitude numbers

The sign-and-magnitude numbers are stored in A and B registers. The flip-flops As and Bs hold the sign bit value. Either As or Bs flip-flop holds only one bit information 0 or 1. The addition overflow register (AVF) holds one bit information, and its value indicates whether or not overflow occurred after addition. If the result of addition exceeds the register storage capacity, overflow occurs. This overflow information is stored in AVF.

The values of the B register and A register are added using a parallel adder circuit for the addition operation. When the M (mode control) bit is set to 0 for addition, the complementer circuit transmits the value of the B register without complementing. The result of adding the values of registers A and B is stored in registers A and As. For subtraction operation, M (mode control) bit value set to 1 signifies a complementer circuit complements B register value and transfers to a parallel adder circuit. The parallel adder circuit adds the value of the B register, the value of the A register, and the input carry, and stores the result in the A and As registers, as seen in Fig. 2.5.

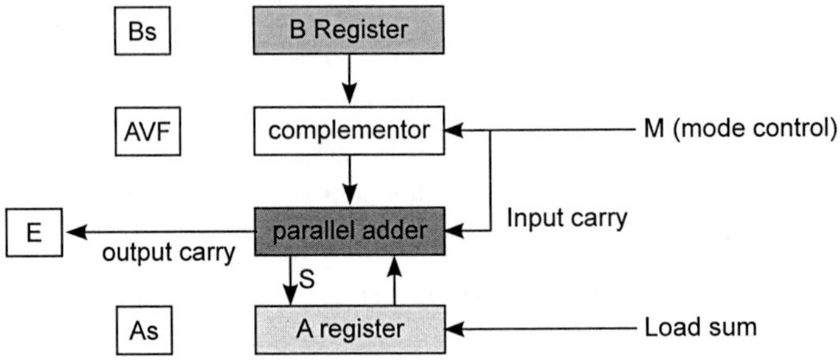

Fig. 2.5: Hardware implementation of addition and subtraction operation for sign-and-magnitude numbers

Using a flowchart, Fig. 2.6 illustrates the subtraction and addition operations for sign-and-magnitude numbers. For subtraction, the register values A and B store the minuend in A and the subtrahend in B. For addition, the values are stored as augend in register A and addend in register B. Prior to either addition or subtraction, the sign bits are compared using the XOR operation, and if the XOR result is 1, it indicates that the signs are distinct. If the output of XOR is 0, both signs are the same.

The result of the addition operation is saved in EA if the XOR output is 0. In this operation EA ← A + B, the output carry is placed in E and the result is stored in A. If an overflow occurs after an addition operation, it is saved in the AVF. If the signs are different (XOR output is 1), a subtraction operation (EA ← A – B) is performed. The outcome is saved in the A register, whereas the output carry is saved in the E register. In a subtraction operation, there will be no overflow, AVF is set to zero.

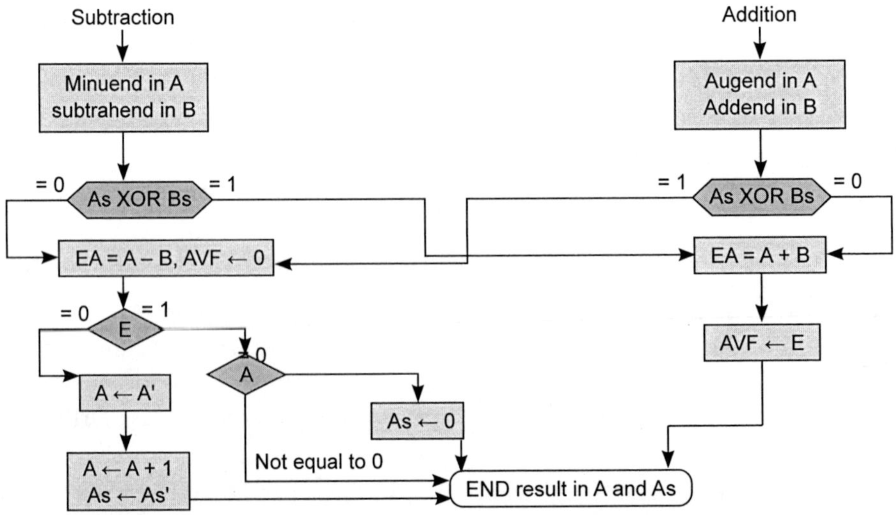

Fig. 2.6: Sign-and-magnitude addition and subtraction operation flowchart

Before doing subtraction, the sign bits of magnitudes are compared using the XOR operation. If the XOR output is 1, the signs are different, the operation is subtraction, and two magnitudes are added. If the XOR output is zero, it indicates that both magnitude signs are identical and that the operation is subtraction. The subtraction operation's output is stored in the E and A registers. Output carry E compared with 0 and 1. If E value is 1 means A > = B, it signifies that magnitude A is greater or equal to magnitude of B. A's (result) value is compared to the value 0, if equal then the magnitude A is equal to magnitude B. The As sign is set to 0 and the result is saved in A and As. If E is 0, magnitude A is less than magnitude B, then the result is the complement of 2 saved in A register and the complement of As sign bit 1 saved in As flip-flop.

2.4.2 Addition and subtraction for 2's complement numbers

The sign bits of integers are not separated in 2's complement addition and subtraction operations. Numbers, including sign bits, are kept in the AC (accumulator register) and the BR (base register). Overflow may occur in complementer and parallel adder circuits. When an overflow occurs, the overflow status register V is set to 1, as illustrated in Fig. 2.7. The output carry is discarded.

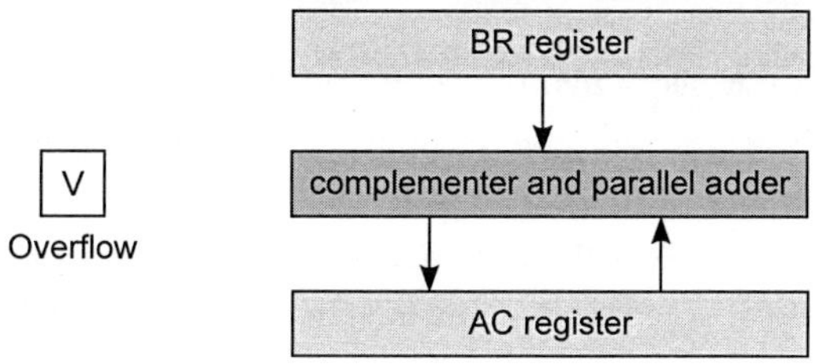

Fig. 2.7: Addition and subtraction hardware implementation for 2's complement numbers

The method for addition and subtraction of binary integers of 2's complement numbers is shown in Fig. 2.8. Accumulator register (AC) binary value containing sign bits and base register (BR) binary value are added. If the exclusive OR of the final two bits contains a 1, the overflow V is set to 1; otherwise, it is set to 0. AC register value is added to the 2-bit complement of BR register value during subtraction operations, and vice versa.

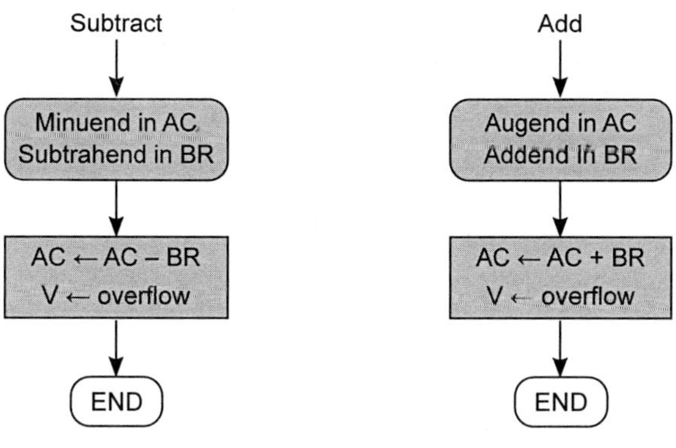

Fig. 2.8: Flowchart of addition and subtraction for 2's complement numbers

2.4.3 Integer Multiplication

For example, of sign-and-magnitude numbers multiplication

There are a variety of techniques for multiplying signed integers. In this section, different multiplication methods for sign-and-magnitude and the 2's complement number system are discussed.

1. **Multiplication for sign-and-magnitude numbers:** For sign-and-magnitude multiplication operation, hardware components are registers A, B and Q, sequence counter register (SC), complementer and parallel adder circuit and As, Qs, Bs, Qi flip-flops.

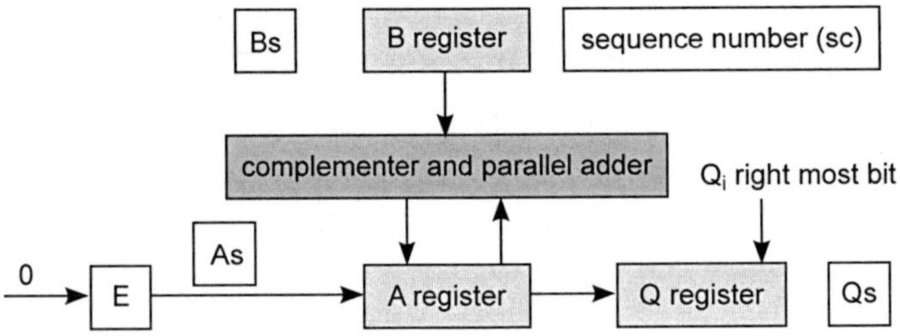

Fig. 2.9: Multiplication for sign-and-magnitude numbers

Registers, hardware, and steps required to multiply two sign-and-magnitude integers are shown in Fig. 2.9. The multiplicand stores in register B, whereas the multiplier stores in register Q. The initial value of Register A is 0. After performing multiplication of the values of A and B registers, partial product is stored in register A. The sequence counter is set to n (number of bits in multiplier excluding s).

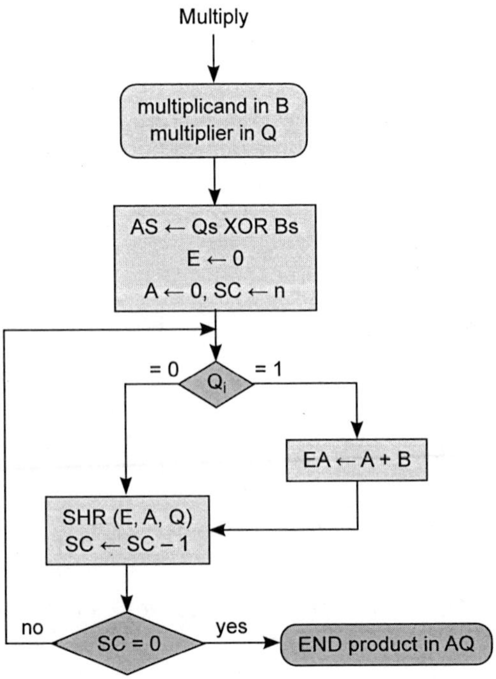

Fig. 2.10: Sign-and-magnitude multiplication flowchart

Registers A and E are initialised to 0 in Fig. 2.10. The XOR operation is executed using the multiplicand sign bit and the multiplier sign bit, with the result bit being stored in the As flip-flop. If the rightmost bit Qi of the register Q is 0, a shift-right operation is done on E, A, and Q, and the SC counter is decremented by one. If Qi is 1, the values of registers A and B are added using a parallel adder circuit, and a partial product stored in register A. This procedure is continued until the sequence counter (SC) approaches 0 and the result is placed in the A, Q registers.

Example 2.1: Compute the multiplication of –6 and 3 using the sign-and-magnitude method.

Solution: The multiplicand is the number –6, while the multiplier is the number 3. The multiplicand –6 is stored in register B in the following way. The value of flip-flop Bs is 1, since the multiplicand is negative and the magnitude 0110 is stored in B.

The multiplier 3 is stored in the Q register with the binary value 0011, and Qs is set to 0. The As flip-flop holds the sign of the product; when the XOR operation is performed on Qs (that is, 0) and Bs (that is, 1), the As is set to 1. The E and A registers are initialized with 0 and SC is initialized with the total number of bits, i.e. 4, in the multiplier. Final result is stored in A and Q; AQ = 00010010, or 18 in decimal. Since As is 1, so the final product is -18 (AQ = 10010010). Table 2.1 displays the computations and intermediate register values for multiplication.

Table 2.1: Sign-and-magnitude numbers multiplication example (–6 × 3)

Multiplicand in B = 0110	E	A	Q	SC
Multiplier in Q	0	0000	0011	4
Qi = 1; and B to A	–	0110	–	–
First partial product in A	0	0110	0011	–
Shift right (EAQ)	0	0011	0001	3
Qi = 1; add B to partial product A	–	0110	–	–
Partial product in A	0	1001	0001	–
Shift right (EAQ)	0	0100	1000	2
Qi = 0; shift right (EAQ)	0	0010	0100	1
Qi = 0; shift right (EAQ)	0	0001	0010	0
As = 1; set As = 1 in A for final product (AQ)	0	1001	0010	–

2. **Booth's multiplication for 2's complement numbers:** In Booth's approach for doing multiplication, the registers AC (accumulator), BR (base register), QR (quotient), SC (sequence counter), and complementer and parallel adder circuits are used.

   Flip-flop Q_i is the rightmost bit in the multiplier, whereas Q_{i-1} is a flip-flop. In this multiplication operation, the multiplicand is stored in the BR register, the multiplier is stored in the QR register, the initial value of the AC register is zero, and the SC value is the number of bits in the multiplier, including the sign bit.

   The hardware implementation of Booth's multiplication is shown in Fig. 2.11. The starting value of the Q_{i-1} flip-flop is zero, and Q_i is the rightmost bit in the multiplier. Depending on the values of Qi Q_{i-1}, either addition or subtraction is done. If Qi Q_{i-1} is 00 or 11, arithmetic right shift is performed on the binary values of AC, QR, and Q_{i-1}, and SC is decremented by one. When Qi Q_{i-1} equals 01, addition is performed.

The arithmetic right shift on AC, QR, Q_{i-1}, and SC is decremented by one after addition. If Q_i Q_{i-1} is equal to 10, subtraction is done. The right shift on AC, QR, Q_{i-1}, and SC is decreased by one after subtraction. As illustrated in Fig. 2.12, these procedures are continued until the sequence counter (SC) reaches 0.

For more example on booth's multiplication

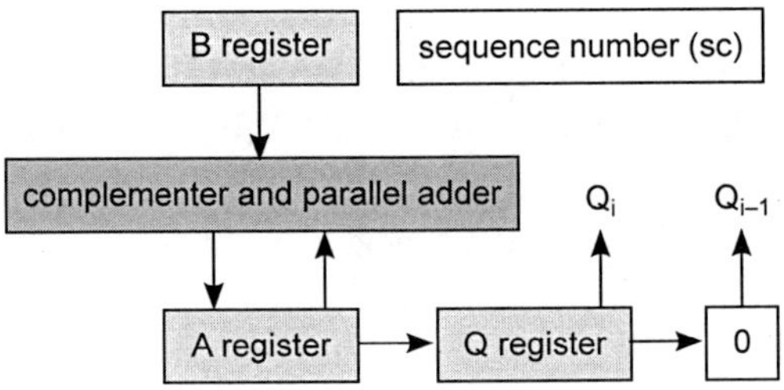

Fig. 2.11: Booth's multiplication hardware implementation

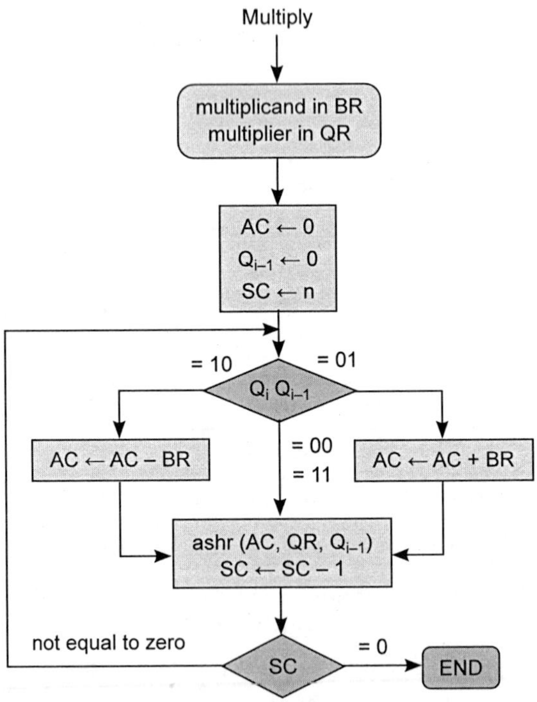

Fig. 2.12: Booth's multiplication flowchart

Example 2.2: How do you multiply the numbers –5 and –4 using the booth multiplication method?

Solution: The BR register contains the 2's complement of the multiplicand –5, which is 1011. The 2's complement of multiplier –4 is 1100, which is kept in the QR register. The initial value of the AC register is 0000, and SC is set to 4 since the multiplier has four bits.

Table 2.2: Booth multiplication example (–5 × –4)

Q_i Q_{i-1}	BR = 1011 2's comp of BR - 0101	AC	QR	Q_{i-1}	SC
	Initial	0000	1100	0	4
0 0	ashr (AC, QR, Q_{i-1})	0000	0110	0	3
0 0	ashr (AC, QR, Q_{i-1})	0000	0011	0	2
10	subtract BR	0101	–	–	–
		0101	–	–	–
	ashr (AC, QR, Q_{i-1})	0010	1001	1	1
1 1	ashr (AC, QR, Q_{i-1})	0001	0100	1	0

Depending on the values of Q_i Q_{i-1}, an addition or subtraction operation is performed, followed by an arithmetic shift right. In this scenario, arithmetic shift right is done if Q_i Q_{i-1} is 00 or 11. This procedure is continued until the SC value reaches 0. AC and QR registers are used to store the final product. In Table 2.2, the register and flip-flop values for each step are given in detail.

2.4.4 Integer Division

There are two approaches for doing division: the restoring method and the non-restoring method.

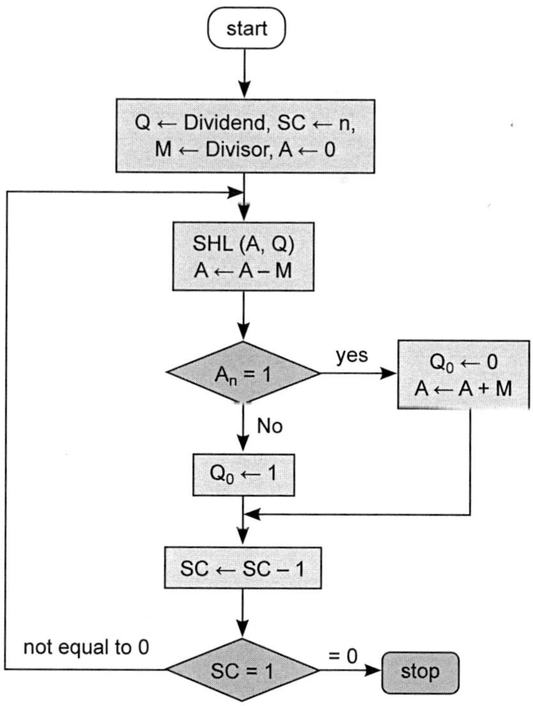

Fig. 2.13: Restoring division flowchart

1. **Restoring method:** Initial values are assigned to the registers A, Q, M, and SC (sequence counter). Register M stores the positive divisor of the n-bit binary value, whereas register Q stores the positive dividend. Register A has n + 1 bits, all of which are set to 0. The sequence counter is initialised to n.

   Fig. 2.13 demonstrates the flowchart for restoring division. The first operation executed on the (A,Q) register value is a shift left. Afterwards, the value of register M is subtracted from the value of register A, and the resulting value is stored in register A. The sign bit of register A, represented by A_n, is now compared to zero. If A_n is 1, Q_0 is set to 0 and A is restored by adding M; otherwise, Q_0 is set to 1. The value of SC is decremented by one upon completion of these stages. The procedure is continued until the SC value reaches 0.

Example 2.3: How do you divide 7/3 using the restoring division method?

Solution: Register Q has the value 0111 (dividend), register A has the value 00000, and register M has the divisor binary value 00011. The 2's complement of M is 11101, which is added to register A during the subtraction operation. The sequence counter's steps are shown in Table 2.3.

Table 2.3: Restoring division algorithm example

Steps	A	Q	SC
Initial	00000	0111	4
Shift left (A, Q)	00000	1110	
$A \leftarrow A - M$	11101	–	
$A_4 = 1$, so $Q_0 \leftarrow 0$	11101	1110	
M	00011	–	
$A \leftarrow A + M$	00000	1110	3
Shift left (A, Q)	00001	1100	
$A \leftarrow A - M$	11101	–	
$A_4 = 1$, so $Q_0 \leftarrow 0$	11110	1100	
M	00011	–	
$A \leftarrow A + M$	00001	1100	2
Shift left (A, Q)	00011	1000	
$A \leftarrow A - M$	11101–		
Carry is discarded	00000	–	
$A_4 = 0$; $Q_0 \leftarrow 1$	00000	1001	1
Shift left (A, Q)	00001	0010	
$A \leftarrow A - M$	11101	–	
$A_4 = 1$, so $Q_0 \leftarrow 0$	11110	0010	
M	00011	–	
$A \leftarrow A + M$	00001	0010	0

In Table 2.3, the value of register A after a 7/3 division operation is the remainder (0001), and the value of register Q is the quotient (0010). The accuracy of the result may be confirmed by performing integer division on 7/3, which yields quotient value 2 and remainder value 1.

2. **Non restoring division:** The non-restoring division technique restores partial remainder at the end of the division operation rather than at intermediate phases. The division process requires the use of registers A, M, Q, and SC. When the division process is finished, the value of register A is the remainder, and the value of register Q is the quotient. The initial value of register A is 0, and the number of bits in the divisor is assigned to SC.

   Fig. 2.14 demonstrates the steps needed to execute division using non-restoring techniques. If A_n is 1, then add M to A and set Q_0 to 0; otherwise, subtract M from A and set Q_0 to 1. The sequence counter SC value is then decremented by one. This process is continued until the SC value approaches zero. When the division operation is finished, the sign bit of register A is examined; if A_n is 1, the value of register M is added to register A (partial remainder added with divisor). Otherwise, the division process is terminated, and the value of register A is the remainder and the value of register Q is the quotient.

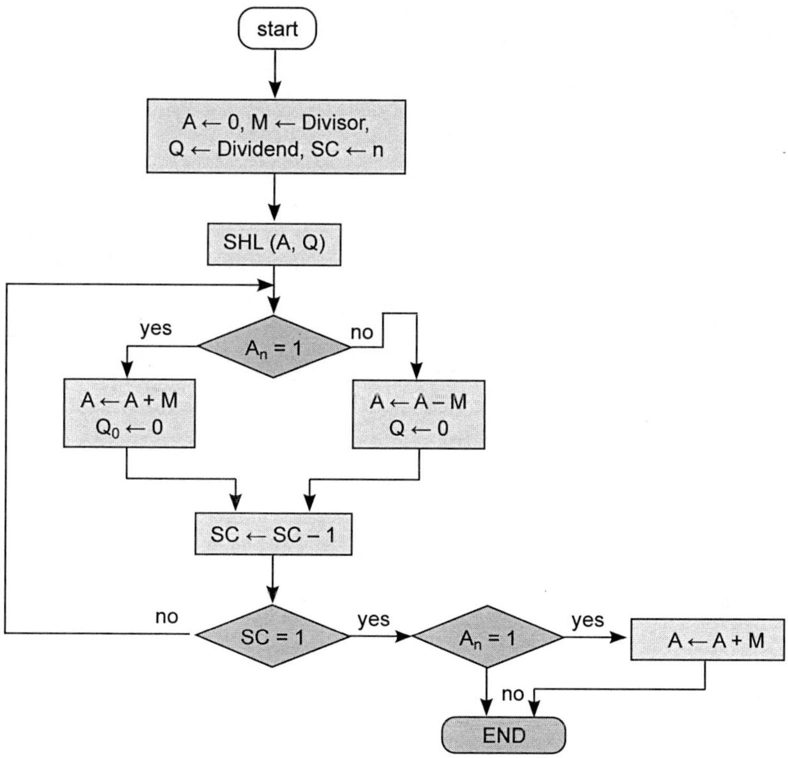

Fig. 2.14: Non restoring division

Example 2.4: How do you perform a 7/3 division using the non-restoring division method?

Solution: The register values are specified as follows. Register Q has been set to 0111 (dividend), whereas register A has been set to 0. Because register A contains bits, all five bits are set to zero, i.e., 00000. The value of register M is 00011 (divisor). M's 2's complement is 11101.

During the subtraction operation, the 2's complement of M is added to register A. Table 2.4 displays the sequence counter steps and actions done on each register value.

Table 2.4: Non restoring division example

Steps	A	Q	SC
Initial	00000	0111	4
Shift left (A,Q)	00000	1110	
Subtract M ($A \leftarrow A-M$)	11101	–	
	11101	–	
$A_4=1$; $Q_0 \leftarrow 0$	11101	1110	3
Shift left (A,Q)	11011	1100	
Add M ($A \leftarrow A+M$)	00011	–	
$A_4=1$; $Q_0 \leftarrow 0$	11110	1100	2
Shift left (A,Q)	11101	1000	
Add M ($A \leftarrow A+M$)	00011	–	
	00000	–	
$A_4=0$; $Q_0 \leftarrow 1$	00000	1001	1
Shift left (A,Q)	00001	0010	
Subtract M ($A \leftarrow A-M$)	11101	–	
$A_4=1$; $Q_0 \leftarrow 0$	11110	0010	0
If SC=1 and $A_4=1$; add M ($A \leftarrow A+M$)	00011	–	
	00001	0010	

There are no straightforward techniques for doing direct division on signed operands. In division, the operands may be transformed into positive values using preprocessing. For signed numbers division, the quotient and remainder signs may be modified after using either restoring or non-restoring division methods.

2.5 FRACTION NUMBER REPRESENTATION

Fraction numbers are represented in two forms, fixed point representation and floating point representation.

2.5.1 Fixed point representation

The decimal point does not move in fixed-point notation. The decimal point in a converted binary number is located in the same place as it is in the original decimal value.

For example, the given decimal number 41.6875 has a fixed decimal point. Thus, digits before the decimal point are represented in binary format, and digits after the decimal point are converted to binary format. If a complete number is represented in 25 bits of binary, then 16 bits represent the number before the decimal point, 8 bits represent the digits after the decimal point, and 1 bit represents the sign.

----------25 bits----------		
1 bit for sign	16 bits for before decimal digits	8 bits for after decimal digits

2.5.2 Floating point representation

In floating point representation, the decimal point either goes to the left or to the right. Based on the movement of the decimal point, the exponent is either increased or decreased. Fixed-point representation cannot represent very large or small fractional numbers, which is a drawback. Using a floating point representation, however, both small and large numbers may be represented. IEEE 754 format is used to represent floating point numbers [4].

1. **IEEE 754 single precision representation:** In a single precision representation, the first bit indicates whether a floating-point value is positive or negative. With an 8-bit exponent, the range of unsigned integers is 0 to 255, although 0 and 255 are reserved for specific uses. Except for these two integers, the range of biased exponents is between 1 and 254.

----------32 bits----------		
Sign	Exponent	Mantissa
----------1 bit----------	----------8 bits----------	----------23 bits----------

actual exponent = biased exponent – excess 127

Where, excess 127 = $(2^{8-1} - 1)$ for single precision representation, the actual exponent ranges from –126 (1 – 127) to 127 (254 – 127). To get the actual exponent from the biased exponent, excess 127 is subtracted.

Example 2.5: In single precision format, how do you express –14.25?

Solution: The single precision representation can be computed as follows:

- The binary value of 14.25 is 1110.01 and this binary number with exponent is 1110.01 $\times 2^0$.
- Normalization format is $1.M \times 2^{(\text{exponent} - 127)}$, the given number can be represented in normalized form as 1.11001×2^3. Here, the actual exponent is 3, however it will be expressed in 8-bit biased exponent format.
- Biased exponent = actual exponent + excess 127.
- Here, biased exponent = 3 + 127 = 130. So the biased exponent is stored in 8 bit binary format 10000010, and the sign bit is 1.
- Therefore, the given number –14.25 is represented in IEEE 754 single precision format as 1 10000010 11001000000000000000000.

2. **IEEE 754 Double precision representation:** IEEE 754 double precision floating point representation uses 64-bit systems. The first bit represents the sign bit, followed by 11 bits representing the exponent and 52 bits representing the mantissa.

----------64 bits----------		
Sign	Exponent	Mantissa
----------1 bit----------	----------11 bits----------	----------52 bits----------

Biased exponent = actual exponent + excess 1023

Here, excess 1023 = $2^{11-1} - 1$. Unsigned range for biased exponents is 0 to 2048, however 0 and 2048 are reserved for specific purposes. If excess value 1023 is subtracted, the remaining range is −1022 to 1023.

2.5.3 Floating point arithmetic operations

The most common floating point operations are addition, subtraction, multiplication, and division. For simplicity, these operations are demonstrated on decimal numbers. However, same procedures may also be performed on binary numbers.

1. **Addition or subtraction:** For floating-point arithmetic addition or subtraction, it is necessary to determine whether both exponents are equivalent. If not equal, the decimal point in mantissa is moved to the right or left to align it.

   For example, the addition of the following two floating point numbers can be performed as follows.

$$0.5372400 \times 10^{2}$$
$$0.1580000 \times 10^{-1}$$

   The exponents of two numbers, 2 and −1, are not equivalent. It may be aligned by moving either the first/second number's mantissa to the right/left. The second number is shifted three positions towards right. On moving either first or second number mantissa to the left, the most important digits are lost. When shifting right to the first integer, the least significant bits are discarded. In this instance, the second number moved three places to the right.

$$\begin{array}{r} 0.5372400 \times 10^{2} \\ +\ 0.0001580 \times 10^{2} \\ \hline 0.5373980 \times 10^{2} \end{array}$$

   The AC register stores the results of addition or subtraction operations performed on floating point numbers stored in the AC and BR registers as shown in Fig. 2.15. Addition or subtraction can be performed in four steps.

   S1: Check for zeros.

   S2: Align mantissas.

   S3: Perform addition or subtraction on mantissas.

   S4: Result normalization

   The registers AC, BR, and QR contain one floating-point number, which consists of three components: sign, mantissa, and exponent. As represents the floating point number sign in the AC register, A1 represents the most significant bit in the mantissa, and a represents the exponents of floating point numbers. The registers AC and BR are used in addition or subtraction as shown in Fig. 2.16. The QR register is used in multiplication of floating point numbers as can be seen in Fig. 2.17.

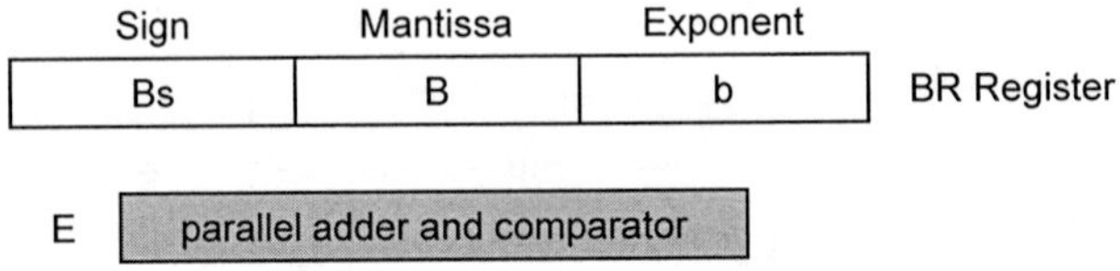

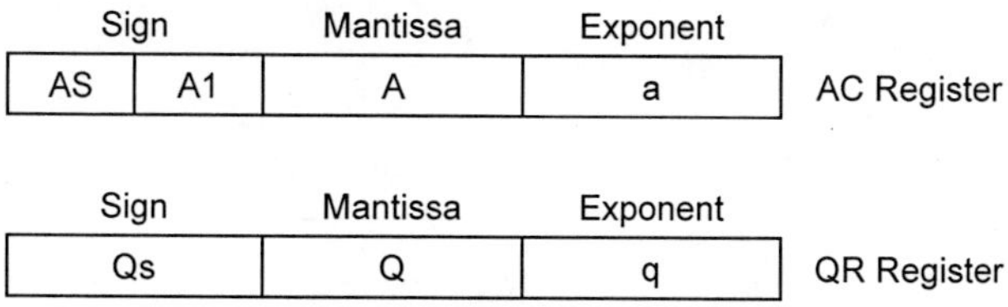

Fig. 2.15: Registers for floating point arithmetic operations

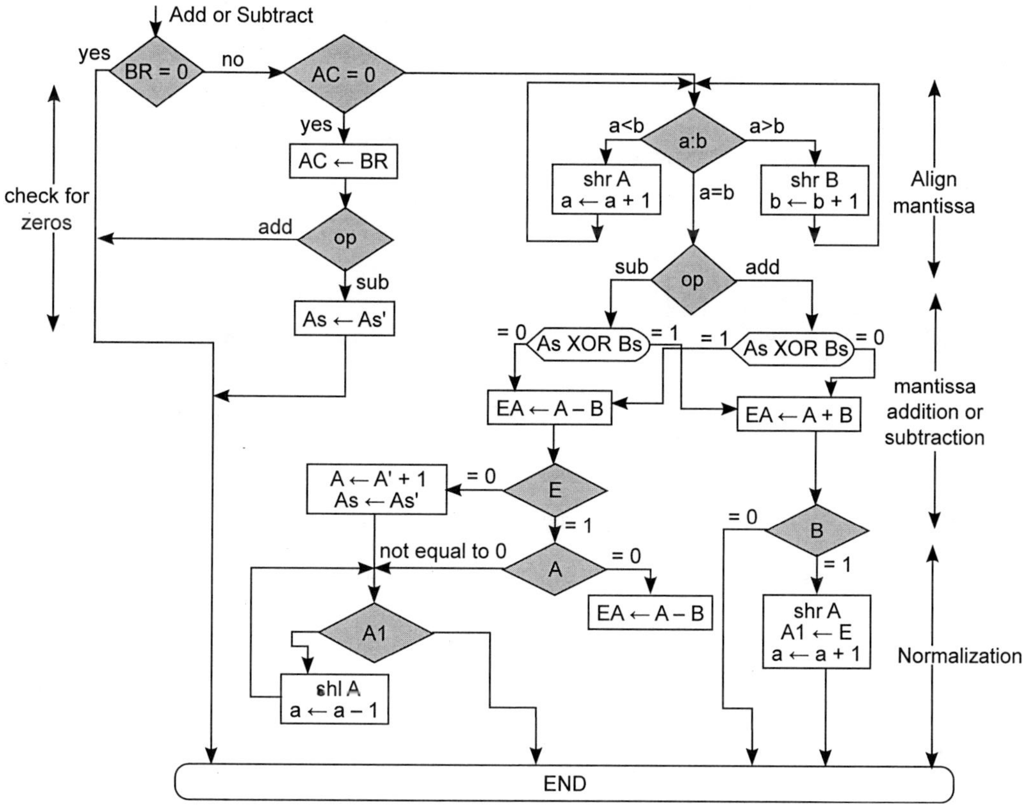

Fig. 2.16: Addition or subtraction of floating point binary numbers

2. **Multiplication:** The following steps can be used to multiply:

   S1: Check for zeros
   S2: Add exponents
   S3: Multiply mantissas
   S4: Result Normalization

   For floating point division example

   Fig. 2.17 depicts these steps in detail. Before multiplying floating point numbers, this is necessary to determine whether it is zero or not. The result is 0 if any number is zero.

   If both numbers are non-zero, the product of the mantissas' multiplication and the exponents' addition is placed in the AC register. If the final result is not in normalised form, it is normalised by moving the result to the left or right, depending on whether the exponent should be increased or decreased.

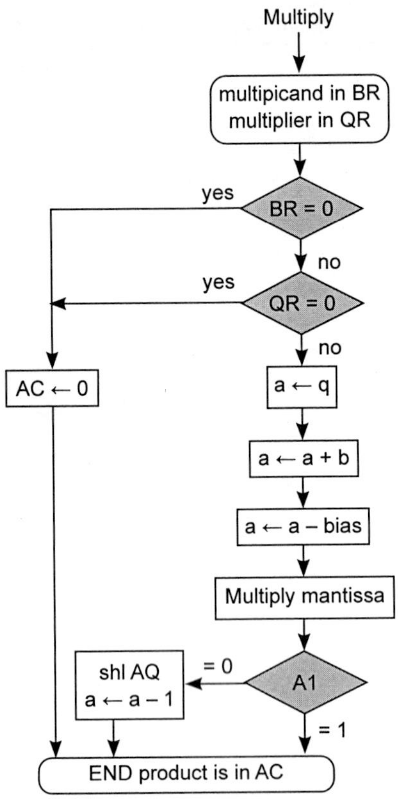

Fig. 2.17: Multiplication of floating point binary numbers

3. **Division:** The division of floating point numbers can be performed using following steps:

   S1: Check for zeros

   S2: Initialize registers and evaluate the sign

   S3: Align the dividend

   S4: Subtract the exponents

   S5: Divide the mantissa

   Fig. 2.19 depicts in detail the procedures required to divide floating point numbers [3]. In division operations, there should be first determine whether or not the divisor is zero. Divide overflow will occur if the divisor is zero. If the divisor is not zero, exponents are subtracted before dividing mantissas, as illustrated in Fig. 2.18.

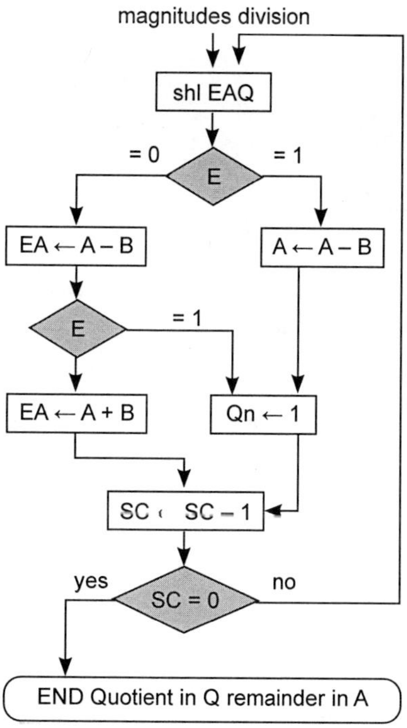

Fig. 2.18: Magnitudes division

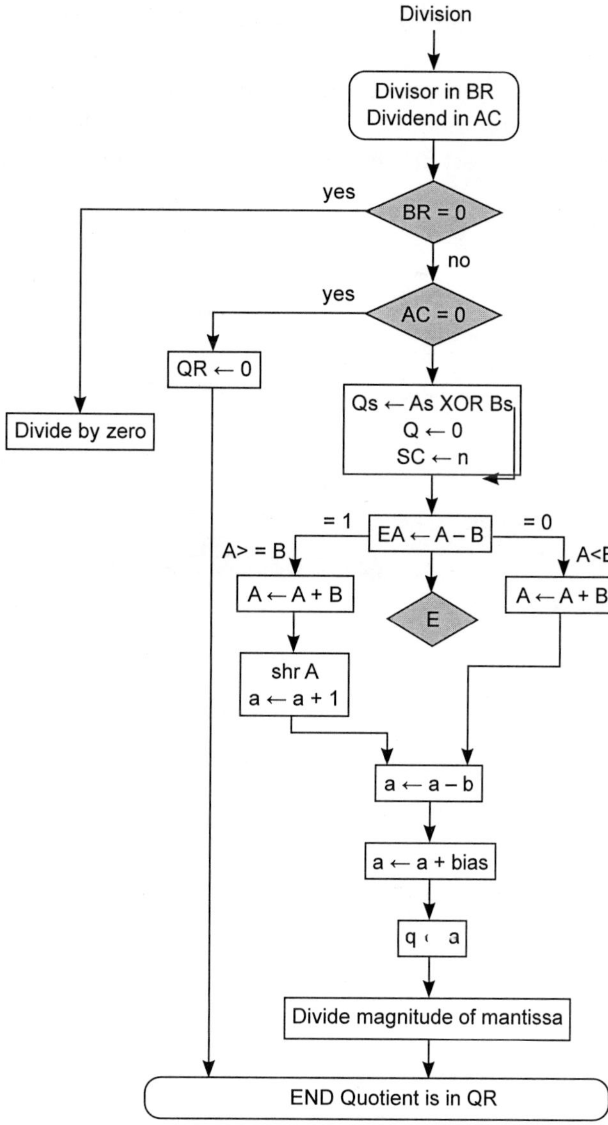

Fig. 2.19: Division of floating point binary numbers

2.6 ARITHMETIC PIPELINE

Pipeline arithmetic units are often seen in supercomputers. They are used to accomplish floating-point operations, fixed-point multiplication, and other calculations found in scientific situations. A pipeline multiplier is just an array multiplier with specific adders that reduce carry propagation time across partial products.

As demonstrated in Fig 2.20, floating-point operations may be easily broken into sub operations. The floating-point adder pipeline gets two normalised floating-point binary values as inputs for a pipeline unit.

$$W = A \times 2^a$$
$$Z = B \times 2^b$$

Mantissas (represented by the letters A and B) and exponents (represented by the letters a and b) make up the expression A and B, respectively. As can be seen in Fig. 2.20, the operations of adding and subtracting with floating-point numbers may be broken down into four segments.

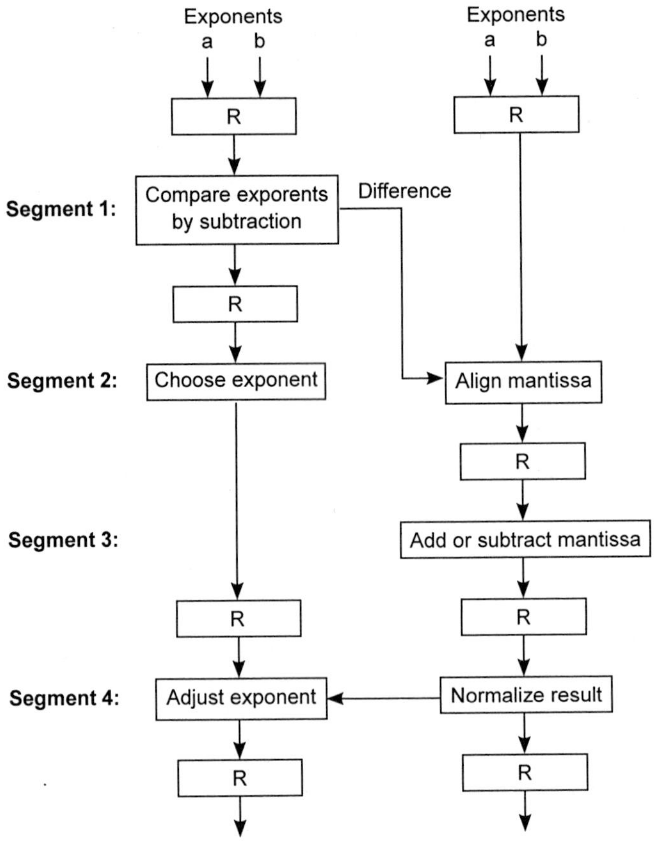

Fig. 2.20: Pipelined execution of floating-point adder

For temporary storage of intermediate data, the segments might be connected with registers denoted by the letter R. The four segments consist of the following sub operations:

S1: Compare the exponents

S2: Align the mantissas

S3: Perform addition/subtraction operation on mantissas

S4: Result normalization

First, subtract the exponents, as illustrated in Fig. 2.20. The exponent difference determines how many times the mantissa of the lower exponent must be moved right or left. This aligns the mantissas. Step three, mantissas are added or subtracted. Normalise the result last. Overflows increase the exponent by one and move the sum or difference mantissa to the right. The amount of leading zeros in the mantissa determines the exponent decrease and how far left the mantissa shifts when there is an underflow.

To understand arithmetic pipeline with example

2.7 INSTRUCTION PIPELINE

Multiple instructions are executed in a single processor clock cycle with instruction pipelining. Non-pipeline architecture, on the other hand, executes instructions sequentially one after the other. Fig. 2.21 depicts three instructions running on a pipelined processor with five stages (fetch (F), decode (D), operand fetch (OF), execute (E), and write back (W)). Each state is completed in a single processor clock cycle. Three instructions in a pipeline require 7 processor clock cycles to execute. Processing three instructions with five stages takes 15 processor clock cycles in the absence of a pipeline.

To know more about instruction pipeline and performance

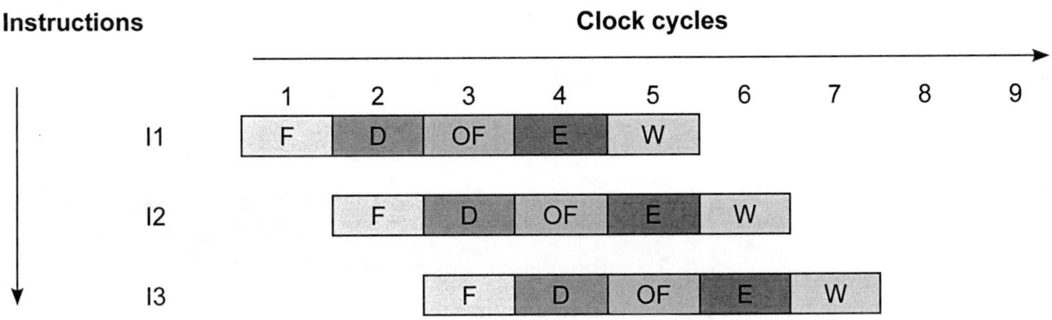

Fig. 2.21: Pipelined execution of instructions

Suppose there are N instructions with K stages and a maximum time delay of T time units between each instruction stage. The time necessary to execute instructions with and without a pipeline can be computed as

- Time required to execute instructions in pipeline = (K + N − 1)T

  Where, K-number of stages, N-total number of instructions, and T-time delay between states
- Time needed to execute N instructions in a non-pipelined processor = NKT
- Speed up factor = NK/(K + N − 1)

There are three types of pipeline hazards that might arise during instruction execution.

2.7.1 Resource or Structural Hazards

Structural hazards may prevent certain instructions from being executed in parallel if there are many instructions in the pipeline. For instance, the main memory only has one port. The processor must use the same port for each read or write operation. Imagine that within a single processor clock cycle, many instructions must access the same primary memory resource. Only one instruction may complete its execution in a single clock cycle due to hardware resource limitations, namely the single main memory. Such resource limitations are considered as structural hazards.

To know structural hazard

In Fig. 2.22, instruction I1 performs a memory writeback in cycle 5, while instruction I5 performs a fetch operation in cycle 5. Similarly Instruction I2 accesses memory to perform write operations, simultaneously Instruction I6 performs fetch operations during the sixth clock cycle. It is not feasible to write and read concurrently to a single port memory, thus between the fifth and sixth clock cycles, the memory is accessed for data writing and instruction reading.

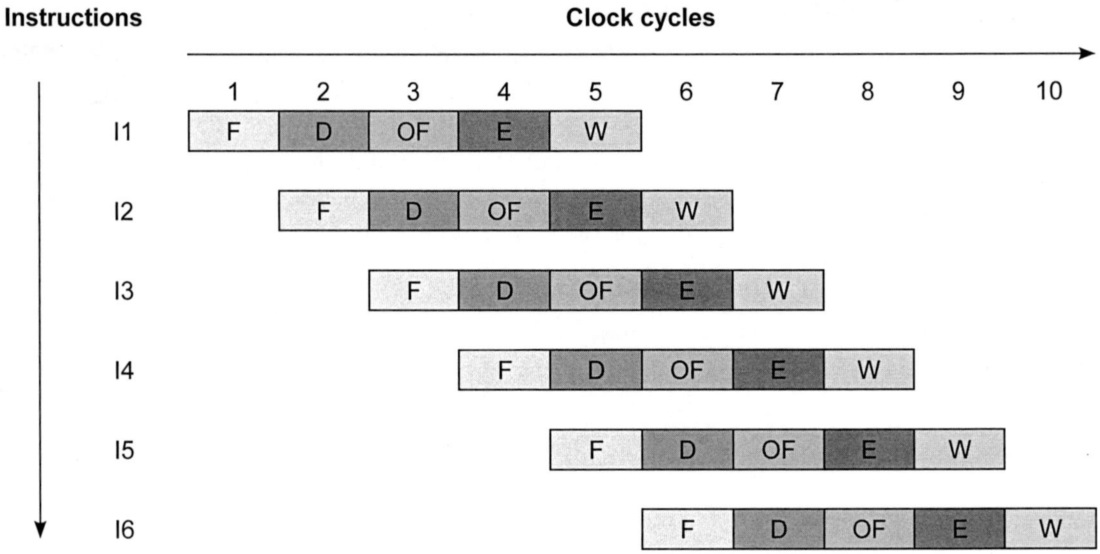

Fig. 2.22: Structural or resource hazard

There is a problem in the pipeline if there are more than two instructions performing different operations on the same resource (memory). This kind of hazard is referred to as structural hazards.

This type of hazard may be reduced by increasing the quantity of accessible resources. In order to avoid structural hazards, modern processors use separate memory for storing instructions and data. Alternatively, the problem may be circumvented by executing a set of instructions, halting the pipeline for a few cycles, executing the set of instructions again, and continuing the process until the program is completed. This solution is shown in Fig. 2.23; after completing the first three steps, the other steps must be executed in sequence.

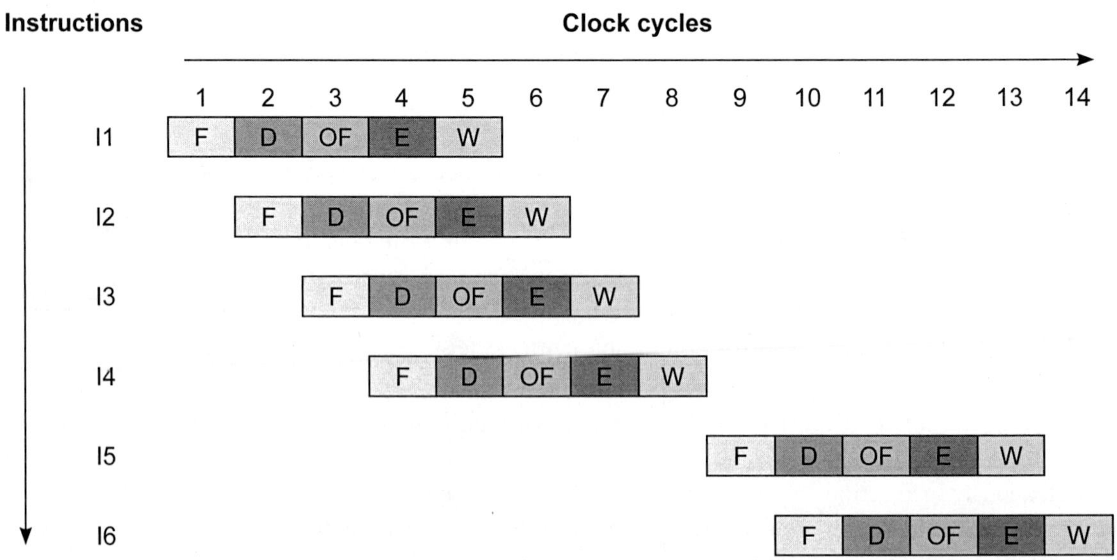

Fig. 2.23: Structural/Resource hazard solution

2.7.2 Data Hazards

When two instructions in the pipeline execute simultaneously, data hazard might arise. If the execution result of the second instruction is dependent on the outcome of the first, data hazard occurs. Data hazards can be classified into RAW hazards, WAR hazards, and WAW hazards.

1. **RAW hazard:** The read after write (RAW) is a true dependency. There is no issue with sequential execution. If the instructions are executed concurrently, they may execute in any sequence, resulting in an incorrect result or output. For example, both the given instructions I1 and I2 use the shared register R3. So the RAW hazard should be checked here.

I1: Add R3, R1, R2

I2: Subtract R5, R4, R3

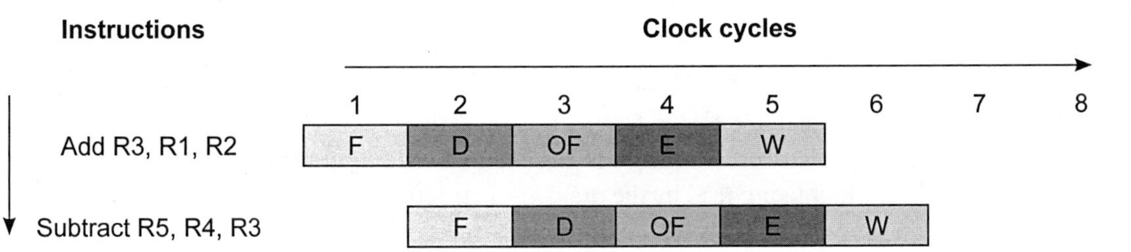

Fig. 2.24: Occurrence of Read after Write (RAW) hazard in pipelined execution of the instructions

As shown in Fig. 2.24, while instruction I1 is in the Decode stage, instruction I2 is in the Fetch stage. The value of operand R3 will be changed after the memory write step. Currently, instruction subtract is executed using the old R3 value. Because the execution of I2 instruction is fully dependent on the completion of I1 instruction. When I2 instruction is executed before I1 instruction write operation completion, the Read after Write (RAW) hazard arises.

To know instruction reordering

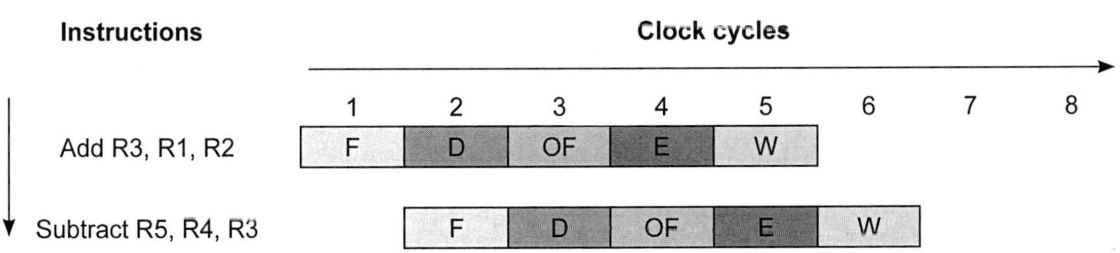

Fig. 2.25: RAW data hazard solution

To eliminate RAW hazard, the instruction I2 operands will be fetched in the 6th clock cycle, following the completion of the instruction I1 write operation as shown in Fig. 2.25.

Because of the NOP (No operation) insertion, the pipeline is slow. RAW hazards may be resolved using two more options. First, rearranging the instructions such that the non-dependent instructions are placed between the dependent instructions. The compiler can perform this reordering of instructions. The second is that the most recent operand computed value may be sent to dependent instructions across pipeline stages.

To know operand forwarding

Example 2.6: How do you execute the Add R3, R7, R1 and Subtract R5, R8, R3 instructions in a pipeline? The operand values are as follows: R1 = 20, R7 = 30, R3 = 10, and R8 = 400.

Solution: For instruction I1, R1 is set to 20, R7 is set to 30, and the result of instruction I1 (Add) is 50, which is kept in register R3 and updated during clock cycle 5. If the I2 instruction needs the R3 operand in the fourth clock cycle and the R3 operand is fetched in the fourth clock cycle, then instruction I2 reads R3 = 10. This is an old value of the operand, resulting in inconsistent data. The final result is R5 = R8 – R3 = 400 – 10 = 390. When both instructions are executed in sequence (one after the other), the result is R3 = R1 + R7 = 20 + 30 = 50; R5 = R8 – R3 = 400 – 50 = 350. For operand R5, the value 350 is correct.

This inconsistency in results is caused by the RAW hazard. To avoid RAW hazards during parallel execution, the operands of instruction I2 should be fetched in the sixth clock cycle while the processor stays idle/stalled/NOP (No operation) in the fourth and fifth clock cycles. As a consequence, the I2 instruction obtains the updated operand (R3 = 50), R8 is 400, and the program produces the correct result (R5 = 350).

2. **WAR hazard:**WAR hazard is also referred to as anti dependency. These hazards arise when instructions are executed concurrently and the destination/output register of one instruction is used immediately after being read by the previous instruction.

$$\text{I1: Mul R6, R7, R8/R6} \leftarrow \text{R7} \times \text{R8/}$$

$$\text{I2: Add R8, R9, R10/R8} \leftarrow \text{R9} + \text{R10/}$$

There is no difficulty, for example, if these instructions I1 and I2 are executed sequentially. However, when I1 and I2 are executed simultaneously, WAR hazard may occur.

Example 2.7: How do you execute the Mul R6, R7, R8 and Add R8, R9, R10 instructions in a pipeline? The operand values are as follows: R7 = 20, R8 = 10, R9 = 30 and R10 = 50.

Solution: A "Write after Read" hazard is less likely in a four- or five-stage pipeline.

$$\text{I1: R6 (200)} \leftarrow \text{R7 (20)} \times \text{R8 (10)}$$

$$\text{I2: R8 (80)} \leftarrow \text{R9 (30)} + \text{R10 (50)}$$

To know more abour register renaming

The register R8 is used by both instructions. If the I2 instruction completes execution before the I1 instruction fetches its operand, then the WAR hazard may occur. However, If I2 is executed after I1, then there will be no problem. But after the I2 instruction write is done, the I1 instruction is executed. There is a WAR hazard because the I1 instruction reads the modified value of register R8.

$$\text{I1: R6 (1600)} \leftarrow \text{R7 (20)} \times \text{R8 (80)}$$

$$\text{I2: R8 (80)} \leftarrow \text{R9 (30)} + \text{R10 (50)}$$

For this reason, the program will give an incorrect value for R6 (1600). However, renaming the register R8 can solve the problem.

to know installation steps of Xillinx ISE design suite

3. **WAW hazard:** A Write After Write (WAW) hazard occurs if the instructions are executed concurrently. If two instructions I1 and I2 are executed concurrently, it is anticipated that Instruction I1 will be delayed while Instruction I2 will be finished. In this situation, the WAW hazard exists. This circumstance occurs as a result of two instructions I1 and I2 writing to the same output register R8.

I1: Add R8, R6, R7/R8 ← R6 + R7/

I2: Add R8, R9, R10 /R8 ← R9 + R10/

Example 2.8: How do you execute the Add R8, R6, R12 and Add R8, R9, R10 instructions in a pipeline? The operand values are as follows: R6 = 50, R12 = 50, R9 = 100 and R10 = 150.

Solution: Here, R6 = 50, R12 = 50, R9 = 100, and R10 = 150. If instructions I1 and I2 are executed in a pipeline, R8 will hold the second instruction execution result after I1 and I2 have completed. In this case, there is no problem.

To understand dynamic branch prediction

I1: R8(100) ← R6(50) + R12(50)

I2: R8(250) ← R9(100) + R10(150)

But, the I1 instruction delayed execution, the I2 instruction completed its execution, and the R8(250) register stores the I2 result. The I1 instruction eventually completed its execution, and the result was written to the R8(100) register. This is referred to as the WAW hazard. This hazard can be solved by renaming the destination register.

2.7.3 Control Hazards

There are control hazards associated with branch instructions. Let's imagine that there are three instructions (I1, I2, and I3) in the pipeline. Assuming that Instruction I2 is a branch instruction, the processor is unaware of this fact until after the decoding phase. The branch address is loaded in a program counter (PC), and the processor then executes the instruction provided by the branch address. Pipeline instructions I1, I2, and I3 are shown in Fig. 2.26. Instruction I2 is decoded during the third clock cycle, and the processor identifies it as a branch instruction. However, instruction I3 is already retrieved from memory during decoding of instruction I2. Therefore, this is the incorrect sequence of pipeline instructions. This is referred to as a control hazard.

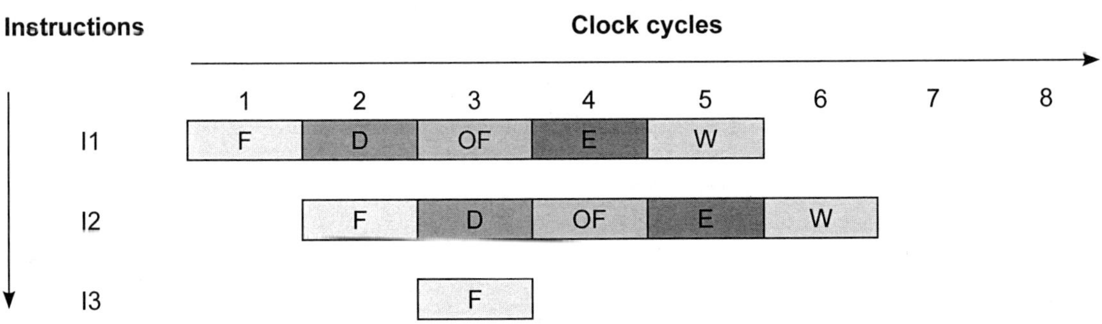

Fig. 2.26: Control hazard situation

If new instruction I3 is inserted in the pipeline during a control hazard, the processor will flush the pipeline. The branch instruction address is loaded into the PC as demonstrated in Fig. 2.27. The unconditional branch instruction jumps to a specific location without performing a conditional check. For example, the Jump 2000 instruction begins instruction execution at the 2000 address location. In contrast, conditional branch instructions examine the condition and execute branch instructions if the condition is true (if, if-else, loops). Other than that, instructions are executed in the order they were received.

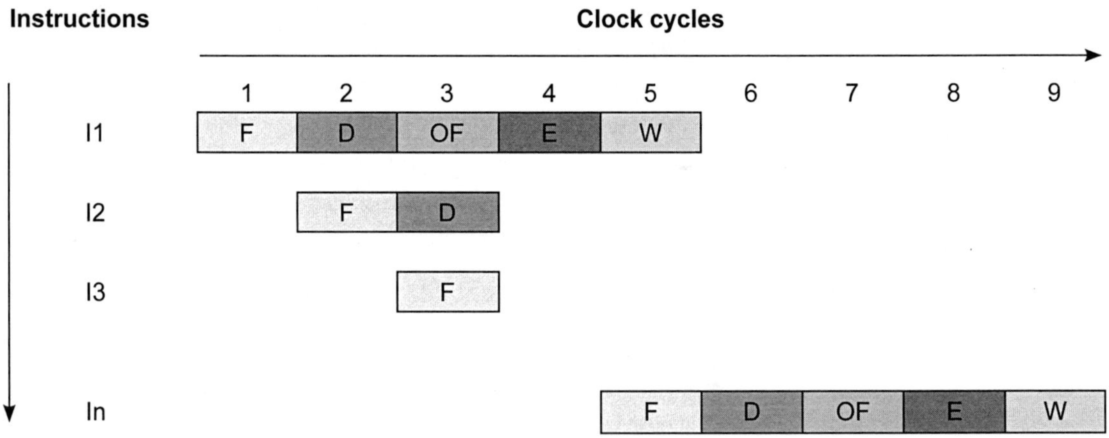

Fig. 2.27: Control hazard solution

Aside from flushing, branch prediction is used to maximize the benefits of the processor's pipelined execution. In the pipeline design, a hardware circuit attempts to predict whether a branch will be taken or not taken. If a branch is identified in the pipeline while it is being executed, the processor waits (stalls or bubbles) for a few clock cycles. Because of this, pipeline performance drops. Predicting for branch instructions before execution speeds up pipelining. There are two approaches for predicting the branch: static and dynamic branch prediction.

1. **Static branch prediction:** Static branch prediction assumes no branch will be taken. It fetches the subsequent instruction in address order. Each inaccurate prediction requires taking the branch. The branch target instruction replaces the previous instruction. Misprediction causes pipeline clock cycle penalties.

   Accelerate the branch instruction's execution if the prediction is accurate. When a conditional branch is met, the same option (assume not taken) is always chosen.

2. **Dynamic branch prediction:** Dynamic branch prediction is a history-based prediction technique. It keeps a branch history table (BHT) with information on the preceding branch. Branches can be dynamically predicted using either one or two bits.

   To understand dynamic branch prediction

   - **1 bit dynamic branch prediction:** The branch history table holds 1 bit of information about the branch that is predicted to be taken (1) or not taken (0) in 1 bit dynamic branch prediction. The processor then retrieves the subsequent instructions from the target branch or sequence based on this.

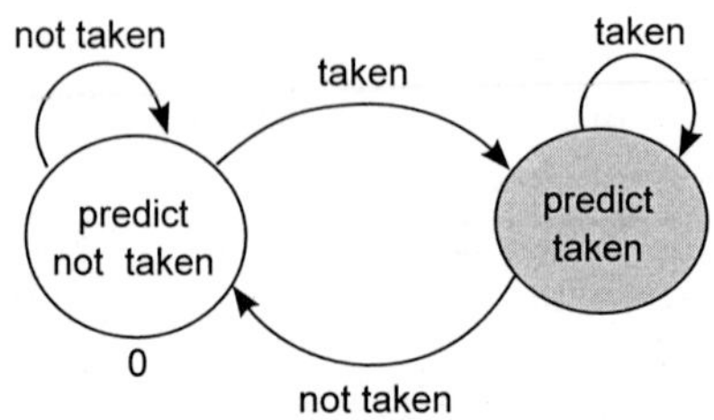

Fig. 2.28: State diagram of 1-bit dynamic branch prediction

Predict taken implies binary value 1, and predict not taken means binary value 0, respectively, in Fig. 2.28. The branch prediction table keeps track of prior branch information. It has been determined that either branch has taken or has not taken based on previous information.

Example 2.9: How many times 1-bit branch predictor correctly predict the branch for the given program? The branch is assumed to have taken in initial state.

```
int a=0;
while(a<5)
{
if(a%2==0){
branch instructions
}
a++;
}
```

Solution: The loop will run as follows. Fig. 2.29 shows the hardware prediction and the actual prediction.

The branch to be taken is the beginning condition. So the branch has taken at a = 0.

Hardware predicts that the branch is taken at a = 1, but that branch must be not taken.

Hardware predicts that the branch is not taken at a = 2, but that branch must be taken.

At a = 3, the hardware assumes that the branch has been taken, but it has not taken.

Hardware assumes that the branch is not taken at a = 4, but it is taken.

	a = 0	a = 1	a = 2	a = 3	a = 4
Actual prediction	T	N	T	N	T

	a = 0	a = 1	a = 2	a = 3	a = 4
Hardware prediction	T	T	N	T	N
	correct	wrong	wrong	wrong	wrong

Fig. 2.29: Actual prediction and hardware prediction

As shown in Fig. 2.29, the branch has taken for at a = 0, a = 2, a = 4 while the branch has not taken for at a = 1, a = 3. However, the branch at a = 0 has been taken because of hardware prediction based on prior branch information. In actual prediction, the branch at a = 1 does not take, but in hardware prediction, the branch at a = 1 take since the preceding history was branch taken. When the actual prediction is compared to the hardware prediction, only one case is accurate at a = 0 and all other cases are incorrect.

- **2 bit dynamic branch prediction:** A 2 bit dynamic branch prediction has an accuracy of 90%, since a prediction must be incorrect twice before the prediction bit is altered. After one incorrect branch prediction in 1-bit branch prediction, the prediction bit is inverted. After two incorrect predictions in 2-bit branch predictions, just the prediction bit is inverted.

2.8 RISC PIPELINE

RISC is an instruction pipeline-efficient reduced instruction set computer. The instruction set's simplicity allows for a pipeline with few sub operations that each take one clock cycle. The fixed-length instruction style allows decoding while the register is determined. All data manipulation instructions use register-to-register techniques. Since all operands are in registers, no effective address or memory retrieval is needed. Thus, the instruction pipeline has two or three steps.

First stage fetches instructions from memory, then executes. A third stage stores the ALU computation in a destination register. RISC data transfer instructions only load and store. These instructions address registers indirectly. Three or four pipeline phases are typical. Most RISC processors contain two buses with two memories-one for instructions and one for data-to minimise memory access conflicts. Instruction(I)-cache and Data(D)-cache can run at the CPU clock.

To understand the working of RISC pipeline

RISC executes one instruction every clock cycle. The CPU is pipelined to execute each instruction in a single clock cycle. RISC has pipeline segments that require only one clock cycle, while CISC has numerous pipeline segments, the largest of which takes two or more clock cycles.

2.9 VECTOR PROCESSING

Standard computers cannot solve certain computing tasks. These problems need a large number of calculations, the completion of which could take a traditional computer several days or even weeks. Vector processing is applicable to a wide variety of scientific and technical problems.

Vector-processing computers are in high demand in specialised applications such as image processing, weather forecasting, mapping the human genome, petroleum explorations, medical diagnosis, seismic data analysis, artificial intelligence and expert systems, aerodynamics and space flight simulations.

For understanding vector operations and matrix multiplication

Many of the essential calculations cannot be accomplished in a reasonable period of time without modern computers. To attain the desired degree of high speed, the fastest and most reliable modern hardware equipped with vector and parallel processing techniques is required.

Many applications require large array arithmetic computation. Floating-point vectors and matrices represent these integers. Vectors are one-dimensional arrays of data objects. The V is a row vector ($V = [V_1, V_2, \ldots, V_n]$) of length n. Column vectors represent data elements in columns. Vector processors' most computationally intensive process is matrix multiplication. The n^2 inner products or n^3 multiply-add operations multiply two n x n matrices. A n x m number matrix is a set of n row vectors or m column vectors.

2.10 ARRAY PROCESSORS

An array processor can process a large array of data. These types of processors are classified into two types: attached array processors and SIMD (single instruction stream multiple data stream) array processors. Both kinds of array processors can manipulate vectors, although they are structured differently.

- **Attached Array Processor:** A general-purpose computer has an attached array processor. Vector processing for complex scientific applications boosts computer speed. The arithmetic unit has pipelined floating point adders and multipliers.

The host computer, a general-purpose commercial computer, is powered by the connected processor. The array processor acts as an external interface to the computer via an input-output controller. A fast bus moves processor data from main memory to local memory. The general-purpose computer offers users conventional data processing while running basic programs. The accompanying array processor operates when complex arithmetic operations are executed. For example, a VAX 11 computer is connected to a Floating-Point Systems FSP-164/MAX to increase the VAX's computational capacity to 100 megaflops.

- **SIMD Array Processor:** In order to process vector data, SIMD array processors make use of several functional units. Parallel processing/functional units are present. These processing units are coordinated to work together by a control unit so that they can accomplish the same goal. Each processing element (PE) contains its own ALUs, floating-point arithmetic unit (FPUs), and registers in addition to its own local memory M. The master control unit is responsible for managing the PEs.

  For circuit design of attached and SIMD array processors

  The programme is stored in the main memory. The master control unit decodes the instructions and determines their execution method. The master control unit directly executes scalar and program control instructions. Vector instructions are concurrently sent to all PEs. Each PE uses local memory to hold operands. Prior to the concurrent execution of an instruction, vector operands are distributed to local memory.

  Consider C = A + B vector addition as an example. The ith components a and b of A and B are first stored in local memory M by the master control unit, where i = 1, 2, 3,...,N. It is possible to perform simultaneous additions since all PEs are given the floating-point add instruction c = a + b. The c components are always stored in the same place in each local memory. The vector sum can be produced with just one cycle of addition. During the execution of vector instructions, masking is used to regulate PE circumstances. When the PE is active, its flags are set, and when it is inactive, they are reset. Only the PEs required for participation are activated during instruction execution.

  The ILLIAC IV computer is a well known SIMD array processor developed at the University of Illinois. This computer is now inoperable. SIMD processors are very specialized for vector or matrix based numerical problems. However, SIMD processors are inefficient with other standard data-processing applications.

UNIT SUMMARY

- A microprogrammed control unit initiates sequences of microoperations in the computer. The functionality can be implemented with either hardwired or microprogramming approach.
- Hardwired approach generates the control signals using hardware. Whereas, microprogramming based control unit stores microprogram that generates a series of microinstructions, and control signals.
- The control memory is kept the collections of microinstructions. Each instruction has its own microprogram stored in the control memory at a specified location.
- The control signals activate various components in the processor like registers, internal bus, ALU and paths between various components.

- Arithmetic operations, i.e., addition, subtraction, multiplication, and division can be done on both unsigned and signed integers.
- Fraction numbers are represented in two forms, fixed point representation and floating point representation. The decimal point does not move in fixed-point notation.
- In floating point representation, the decimal point either goes to the left or to the right. Based on the movement of the decimal point, the exponent is either increased or decreased.
- Arithmetic pipeline units are often used in supercomputers to compute different types of operations in parallel to speed up computation. For example, a supercomputer may use three execution units, i.e., integer numbers arithmetic operations, load/store operations, floating point number arithmetic operations.
- Instruction pipeline can execute multiple instructions in a single processor clock cycle.
- Pipelined instruction execution increases system throughput in the absence of hazards. However, while instructions are being executed, three different types of pipeline hazards, namely structural, data, and control hazards, might occur and significantly impair system performance.
- Structural hazards occur due to hardware resource limitations. This type of hazard may eliminate by replicating hardware resources.
- Data hazard may exist if data dependency exist between the instructions. It can be classified into RAW hazards, WAR hazards, and WAW hazards.
- The control hazards may arise due to branch instructions. The control hazards can mitigate by using branch predictors. There are two approaches for predicting the branch: static and dynamic branch prediction.
- Dynamic branch prediction is a history-based prediction technique.
- RISC is a reduced instruction set computer that can build an instruction pipeline with a minimal number of sub operations, each of which is performed in one clock cycle.
- Vector-processing computers are used for high speed computation of science and engineering problems described in terms of vectors and matrices.
- An array processor can process a large array of data. These types of processors are classified into two types: attached array processors and SIMD (single instruction stream multiple data stream) array processors.

EXERCISES

Multiple Choice Questions

1. The control signals are generated by combinational logic in a __________ controlled unit.
   (a) micro programmed   (b) software
   (c) logic   (d) hardwired
2. A set of microinstructions is called a __________
   (a) program   (b) command
   (c) micro program   (d) micro command

3. Numbers that can be represented in 2's complement notations are
(a) both +ive and –ive numbers
(b) numbers greater than 8 bits
(c) only –ive numbers
(d) only +ive numbers

4. In a four-bit two's complement number representation, the range of negative values is
(a) –1 to –8
(b) –1 to –15
(c) –1 to –7
(d) –1 to –16

5. Which number system is popularly used in modern computers
(a) Sign and magnitude
(b) octal
(c) 1's complement
(d) 2's complement

6. What are the values of difference and borrow for the binary subtraction 0 – 1?
(a) 0, 1
(b) 0, 0
(c) 1, 1
(d) 1, 0

7. What is the outcome of subtracting one binary number from another 0110 – 0010?
(a) 1000
(b) 0100
(c) 0110
(d) 0011

8. How is (–87) 10 represented in 2's complement number system?
(a) 11011011
(b) 10101001
(c) 11010110
(d) 10110011

9. Instruction pipeline does not have __________?
(a) address hazard
(b) control hazard
(c) data hazard
(d) structural hazard

10. If instruction X tries to modify some data before it is written by instruction (X – 1), it can result in a __________ hazard.
(a) RAR
(b) RAW
(c) WAR
(d) WAW

11. There are five instructions, which are given below.

I1: Mul R10, R11, R12
I2: Add R15, R10, R12
I3: Add R13, R10, R14
I4: Mul R12, R11, R13
I5: Sub R15, R16, R17

Consider the following three statements:

1. Instructions I2 and I5 have an anti-dependence
2. Instructions I2 and I4 have an anti-dependence
3. An anti-dependence always creates one or more stalls within instruction pipeline

Which one of the above statements is/are correct?
(a) Statement 1 is true
(b) Statement 2 is true
(c) Statements 1 and 3 are true
(d) Statements 2 and 3 are true

12. Consider the following instructions:

I1 : Add R10, R7, R12; R10 ← R7 + R12

I2 : Sub R12, R7, R10; R12 ← R7 – R10

I3 : Div R12, R9, R12; R12 ← R9/R12

Show the types of data hazards that exist between these instructions.

(a) RAW, WAR, WAW (b) RAW, WAR

(c) RAW, WAW (d) WAR, WAW

13. When 100010010 is divided by 1101, the remainder is

(a) 1 (b) 0 (c) 11 (d) 101

14. There are 2 designs for a pipeline processor. Design-1 has a 5 stage pipeline with execution time of 3 ns, 2 ns, 4 ns, 2 ns and 3 ns. While the Design-2 has 8 pipeline stages each with 2 ns execution time. How much time can be saved using design D2 over design D1 for executing 100 instructions? [**Hint:** Execution time for Pipeline = (K + n − 1) execution time of one stage; where k = no. of stages in pipeline, n = no. of instructions, Execution time of one stage= max (all stages execution time)]

(a) 314 ns (b) 202 ns (c) 96 ns (d) 190 ns

15. In a 7-bit word, a machine stores floating point numbers. The first bit represents the number's sign, the next three represent the biased exponent, and the last three represent the magnitude of the mantissa. In the above word, you must represent 33.35. In this case, the error would be

(a) overflow (b) underflow

(c) error (d) no error

ANSWERS															
1.	(d)	2.	(c)	3.	(a)	4.	(a)	5.	(d)	6.	(c)	7.	(b)	8.	(b)
9.	(a)	10.	(d)	11.	(b)	12.	(a)	13.	(a)	14.	(b)	15.	(a)		

SHORT AND LONG ANSWER TYPE QUESTIONS

Category-I

1. How does the processor control unit function?

2. Define the role of control memory.

3. Describe the features of the horizontal and vertical microprogrammed control unit.

4. What are the primary functions of a microprogrammed control unit?

5. Describe some common microprogramming applications.

6. How do instructions and microoperations relate to one another?

7. Describe the control unit inputs and outputs.

8. Explain the difference between control hazard and data hazard.

9. What are the four main components of a floating-point number?

10. Why is biased representation required for the exponent part of a floating-point number?

11. How to determine negative numbers using sign-and-magnitude and 2's complement representations.

12. How do you perform addition and subtraction for floating-point numbers?
13. What is the difference between vector processing and array processors?
14. Give an example of structural hazard and its solution.
15. What is the difference between static and dynamic branch prediction?

Category-II

16. Explain hardwired and microprogrammed control unit implementations. Is it feasible for a hardwired control unit associated with a control memory?
17. In the control unit, how does address sequencing work? Define the words "microoperation," "microinstruction," and "microprogram" as they are used in the control unit.
18. Consider the following instructions are executed in a computer that has a five-stage pipeline:

    Mul R9, R8, #20

    Add R11, R10, #3   Or   R12, R10, #100

    Subtract R13, R8, R10

    Each pipeline stage requires one clock cycle. Represent instructions' execution via pipeline diagram. Describe the function that each pipeline stage performs.
19. Explain the difference between arithmetic pipeline and instruction pipeline. Discuss the structural hazards, data hazards, and control hazards in a pipeline. Why do these hazards affect the pipeline's performance? Discuss the solutions for dealing with these hazards.
20. Discuss vector processor applications. Create the SIMD array processor's circuit and describe how it works.

Numerical Problems

21. How do you represent the decimal numbers 512 and –29 in sign-and-magnitude and 2's complement number representation using 16 bits?

    [**Ans:** Sign-and-Magnitude: 0000 0010 0000 0000 (512), 1000 0000 0001 1101 (–29); 2's Complement representation: 0000 0010 0000 0000 (512), 1111 1111 1110 0011 (–29)]
22. How do you represent the 2's complement binary values 1101011 and 0101101 in decimal?

    [**Ans:** –21; 45]
23. Assume a 4-segment pipeline system with a clock cycle of 20 ns required in each segment to execute 100 tasks in sequence. What is the speedup ratio? [**Ans:** 3.88]
24. Let's imagine a 2.5 GHz, non-pipelined processor with an average of 4 cycles per instruction. A five-stage pipeline is introduced to the same processor, but the clock speed drops to 2 GHz owing to the pipeline's internal latency. Assume the pipeline is moving forward smoothly with no delays. How much faster is this pipelined processor? [**Ans:** 3.2]
25. Consider a four-stage pipeline processor. The table below shows the number of cycles needed by the four instructions I1, I2, I3, and I4 in stages S1, S2, S3, and S4.

	S1	S2	S3	S4
I1	2	1	1	1
I2	1	3	2	2
I3	2	1	1	3
I4	1	2	2	2

How many cycles are required to complete the following loop?

for (i = 1 to 2) {I1; I2; I3; I4;} **[Ans:** 23]

26. How many mispredictions are there for the given for loop with 1-bit branch predictor?

    for (i = 0; i < 5; i++)

    {

    a + = 5;

    }

    Initially assume to start prediction with a branch taken and you will run this iteration twice. **[Ans:** 3]

27. Perform the A ÷ B using the non restoring division method on the unsigned numbers A = 1000 and B = 0011. What will be the final values of quotient and remainder? **[Ans:** quotient = 0010, remainder = 00010]

28. Given x = 0101 and y = 1010 numbers in 2 's complement notation, use Booth's algorithm to get the product p = x * y. **[Ans:** 1110 0010]

29. How do you write these numbers in IEEE 32-bit floating-point format:

    (a) –5 (b) –1.5 (c) 384 (d) –1/32

    [Ans: (a) 1 10000001 01000000000000000000000

    (b) 1 01111111 10000000000000000000000

    (c) 0 10000111 10000000000000000000000

    (d) 1 01111010 00000000000000000000000]

30. Consider a floating-point format with an 8-bit biased exponent and a mantissa of 23 bits. In this format, show the bit pattern for –720 and 0.645 numbers.

    [Ans: (a) 1 10001000 01101000000000000000000;

    (b) 0 01111010 01001010000111101100000]

PRACTICAL

Aim: Design a hardware circuit that does addition, subtraction, booth's multiplication, and restoring division for 2's complement numbers using the verilog hardware description language.

Tools: Xilinx ISE Design Suite [5].

Verilog tutorial for beginners

Theory: How to construct a basic programme in verilog is previously covered in Chapter 1 (practical). The algorithm of computer arithmetic for 2's complement numbers has previously been discussed in Chapter 1. These algorithms may be implemented in the Xilinx ISE design suite tool using verilog [5]. You may also learn advanced verilog module writing by consulting the verilog tutorial for beginners. You may learn how to create numerous building blocks such as multiplexers, flipflops, and combinational circuits of various functional units.

The number of input and output registers necessary, as well as the combinational circuit has been described in this chapter for executing the following operations using 2's complement numbers.

1. addition
2. subtraction
3. booth's multiplication
4. restoring division

Procedure:

1. First, look into the circuit's number of inputs and outputs.
2. Write the main module

   module signed_arithmetic (list of input and output ports separated by comma)

   (verilog program here)

   endmodule
3. Declare the names of the two input variables that will store two signed numbers.
4. Declare the output port names.
5. Designate a wire as the intermediate output that will become the input of another circuit.
6. A list of the four basic instances for conducting addition, subtraction, booth multiplication, and restoring division.
7. Each instance of a circuit begins with a name, such as addition, subtraction, booth_multiplication, restoring_division followed by the instance output and inputs separated by commas and enclosed in parenthesis.
8. Verify the design by giving input two signed numbers. Create a testbench for circuit verification. Mention all potential input and output combinations in testbench.
9. Run Isim in Xilinx to see the outputs and check the circuit's operation. If outputs are correct with all possible combinations, i.e., two positive numbers, one positive and one negative, both negative numbers then the circuit is correctly designed.

Booth's multiplication program in verilog

Booth's multiplication simulation in xilinx

KNOW MORE

Innovations by Indian: Vinod Dham, the Father of the Pentium Chip, was born in Pune, India in the 1950s. Dham graduated from Delhi College of Engineering with a Bachelor of Engineering in Electrical Engineering in 1971, at the age of 21 [6]. After finishing his engineering degree, he worked for four years at Continental Devices, one of India's few private silicon semiconductor start-ups at the time that partnered with the American Teradyne Semiconductor Company, where he developed an interest in semiconductors. To be successful in this industry, he believed that a better understanding of the physics driving the behaviour of semiconductor devices.

In 1975, he enrolled at the University of Cincinnati in Ohio to pursue a master's degree in physics. After receiving his Master of Science in 1977, he began working as an engineer at NCR Corp in Dayton, Ohio, where he developed advanced non-volatile memory. His pioneering work on non-volatile memories paved the way for NCR's 1985 patent for a mixed dielectric technique and a non-volatile memory device. Later, he became an Intel Corporation engineer. His contribution to the creation of the Pentium Microprocessor has earned him the appellation "Pentium Engineer." In addition, he is one of the original creators of Flash Memory Technology at Intel. He was appointed vice president of Intel's Microprocessor Group.

History of Ayurveda: Ayurveda is a combination of two words: "Ayu", which means life, and "Veda", which means wisdom [7]. The Rig Veda, the Sama Veda, the Yajur Veda, and the Atharva Veda were the foundations for Indian medicine and healthy living. It is well known that Ayurveda is one of the Upavedas that belong to the Atharva Veda.

The Atharva Veda is a collection of magical spells and esoteric disciplines, as well as the medical practise of Ayurveda, which is used to cure illnesses, injuries, infertility, sanity, and overall health. Ayurveda addresses all lifestyles. As a result, patients are given treatment that takes into account all aspects of their health, including yoga, aromatherapy, meditation, gems, amulets, herbs, diet, astrology, colour, and surgical procedures. Marmas are areas of the body known for their sensitivity, and Ayurveda addresses them. Yoga, massages, and other forms of exercise are recommended.

A collection of Sanskrit poems known as the Charaka Samhita was compiled by Charaka in the first century A.D. Both Sushruta and Vagbhata were authors of books as well. The Sushruta Samhita was probably composed some time around the fourth century A.D. Ashtanga Hridaya and Sangraha, the third most important texts, were written by Vaghbata in the fifth century A.D. The medicinal and surgical schools established by Charaka and Sushruta are considered the roots of Ayurveda.

Ayurveda was further developed via the addition of sixteen important supplements known as Nighantus, including Dhanvantari Bhavaprakasha, Raja, and Shaligrama. New drugs have taken the place of older ones that were unsuccessful. It seemed that the applicability was growing, new ailments were being discovered, and other treatments were being found. These dietary supplements included around two thousand different medicinal plants [7, 8].

REFERENCES AND SUGGESTED READINGS

1. M. Morris Mano, Computer system architecture. Prentice-Hall, Inc., Third edition. https://poojavaishnav.files.wordpress.com/2015/05/mano-m-m-computer-system-architecture.pdf (last accessed: Oct 2022)
2. Carl Hamacher, Zvonko Vranesic, Safwat Zaky, and Naraig Manjikian, Computer organization and embedded systems. McGraw-Hill Higher Education, 2011.
3. William Stallings, Computer Organization and Architecture Designing for Performance. 10th edition, 2016.
4. Institute of Electrical and Electronics Engineers, IEEE Standard for Binary Floating-Point Arithmetic, ANSI/IEEE Standard 754-2008, August 2008.
5. Xilinx ISE design suite. https://www.xilinx.com/support/download/index.html/content/xilinx/en/downloadNav/vivado-design-tools/archive-ise.html (last accessed: Oct 2022)
6. Biography of Vinod Dham. http://www.thinklink.in/blog/father-of-the-pentium-chip-vinod-dham (last accessed: Oct 2022)
7. Ayurveda: an overview. https://yehaindia.com/ayurveda-an-overview/ (last accessed: Oct 2022)
8. History of Ayurveda…a heritage of healing. https://poliklinika-harni.hr/images/uploads/434/povijest-ayurvede.pdf (last accessed: Oct 2022)
9. NPTEL Course by Dr. John Jose, Advanced Computer Architecture, IIT Guwahati, 2019. https://archive.nptel.ac.in/courses/106/103/106103206/ (last accessed: Oct 2022)
10. NPTEL Course by Prof. Indranil Sengupta and Prof. Kamalika Datta, Computer Architecture and Organization, IIT Kharagpur, 2017. https://archive.nptel.ac.in/courses/106/ 105/106105163/ (last accessed: Oct 2022)

3 Microprocessor Architecture

UNIT SPECIFICS

The following aspects are discussed in this unit:

- Fundamentals of microprocessor;
- Instruction set architecture;
- Design principles from programmer's perspective;
- Intel 8086 microprocessor case study

The practical applications of the topics are presented for the purpose of fostering greater curiosity and creativity and enhancing problem-solving skills. In addition to a large number of multiple-choice questions, further two categories of questions are designed according to the lower and higher levels of Bloom's taxonomy, i.e., short- and long-answer questions, the unit provides practice assignments in the form of numerical problems, a list of references, and suggested readings. It is also noted that several QR codes have been incorporated into various sections in order to access the required supplementary materials.

The related practical based on the content is followed by a "Know More" section on the topic. This section has been carefully constructed such that the supplementary information it contains is valuable to the book's readers. This section focuses primarily on the contributions of Indian innovators to the development of computer system organization, Indian claypot cooking intact micronutrients found in food, and it plays an important role in preparing nutritional food to stay healthy.

RATIONALE

This chapter discusses standard 8-bit and 16-bit microprocessor architectures. The instruction set architecture of these microprocessors is RISC or CISC. The CISC instruction set has variable length and more sophisticated commands. RISC, on the other hand, uses fixed-length instructions that are less difficult. RISC stores data in registers and has limited memory access via load and store instructions. For the sake of convenience, programmers can use several instruction formats and addressing modes to write the program in an efficient manner. The architecture of the 8086 microprocessor is thoroughly described in this chapter. Microprocessor execution unit is made up of several flags, registers, and special purpose control flags. Whereas the bus interface unit consists of segment registers, an instruction queue, a control unit, and an address calculation processing unit.

PRE-REQUISITE

Computer System Organization (Unit-I)

Assembly Language Programming: Fundamental knowledge of basic instructions (Polytechnic Engineering)

UNIT OUTCOMES

List of outcomes of this unit is as follows:

U3-O1: Describe role of microprocessor in system design

U3-O2: Describe instruction set architecture

U3-O3: Design principles from programmer's perspective

U3-O4: Explain features of Intel 8086 microprocessor

Unit-3 Outcomes	EXPECTED MAPPING WITH COURSE OUTCOMES (1- Weak Correlation; 2- Medium Correlation; 3- Strong Correlation)				
	CO-1	CO-2	CO-3	CO-4	CO-5
U3-O1	3	3	3	3	2
U3-O2	2	2	3	3	2
U3-O3	2	2	3	2	2
U3-O4	3	2	2	1	1

3.1 INTRODUCTION

A microprocessor is a silicon chip with an ALU (Arithmetic Logic Unit), register and control circuitry. A central processing unit (CPU) consists of an arithmetic logic unit for conducting arithmetic logic operations, a register bank for storing intermediate values, from which the CPU often pulls operands, and a control logic that regulates the whole process. Previously, CPU architecture was divided into discrete components such as distinct ALU architecture, separate register circuits, and separate control logic design.

The problem with different modules is that their chips will be distinct. When all of these components are incorporated into a printed circuit board, they are linked through copper wires. The speed of the system is restricted by the speed of the external lines; a very high speed cannot be achieved with this design. Therefore, for a high-speed architecture, it is necessary that all of these CPU components reside on a single chip.

The term microprocessor is a combination of the words "micro" and "processor". A processor is an apparatus for processing data, especially binary integers. This will undergo some processing. The design team for the microprocessor specifies the operations to be performed on the numbers.

Comparing the electronic components of the prior and now, the size, power consumption, and performance are all improving, and one of the primary reasons for this is that the whole system is miniaturised and fits its design into a single chip. In 1970, the microchip was created, and all of the processor's components were put on a single piece of silicon. Thus, the size of the chip shrinks and its speed increases. With the creation of this microchip, the microprocessor was thus born by using the word micro in microprocessor.

A microprocessor is a programmable device that takes in numbers, conducts arithmetic and logical operations according to the programme in memory, and generates results. For example, suppose a circuit is built to scan input bit streams of 1's and detect the pattern four consecutive ones followed by a 0. It will output a 1 unless the output bit is set to 0. A circuit constructed using flip flops and gates can perform this specific operation. The circuit is not programmable because it can only perform specified operations pertinent to a single application. In contrast, microprocessors are programmable devices. Based on the sequence of instructions provided in the given program, they may execute various states of operations on the data they receive. So, microprocessors are led by instructions. Practically every microprocessor features a reset pin to return the device to its initial state. It will begin searching into memory at a specified location and retrieve reset instructions from there. It executes that instruction, then updates its program counter and register type so that it refers to the next instruction, and so on.

for introduction of microprocessor

Modern microprocessors can scan a room's temperature regulation. It first reads the temperature sensor readings, then switches on air conditioners or heaters based on the safe temperature value and the divergence from that. If the same microprocessor is used for anything other than temperature monitoring, such as conveyor belt monitoring. The application is run by the conveyor belt control. In such a situation, the microprocessor will stay unchanged; just the software it was running would change. So now a separate programme in memory will run, and the CPU will perform something else. A programmable component of the microprocessor may modify the program section to perform something else.

A microprocessor is designed to carry out a certain set of instructions or operations. This is referred to as an instruction set. The microprocessor user manual explains which commands this CPU will support. These instructions should only be used to create programs. Programs are written in a high-level language such as C, Java, or C++, and then compiled and translated into the language that the underlying processor understands.

In the case of a computer with an 8085 CPU, a C programme will execute. The 8085-compatible code will be generated by the compiler. If the same program is to be run on an ARM processor, a compiler converts the source code into an instruction set that can be read and understood by the ARM CPU.

The designer of a microprocessor may programme it to understand a set of machine instructions. Users must create their own code in accordance with the stated guidelines. The CPU may connect with other components such as memory and I/O devices.

Memory may therefore be used as an input device if the input values for a program are saved in the memory. For example, if the task is to sort 100 numbers, and the 100 numbers are kept in memory. It will operate on the 100 numbers saved in memory. On the other hand, if a temperature sensor is installed and running, the system should take temperature from that temperature sensor. So, input devices may vary, and the input may originate from the input devices.

These devices carry data from outside world into the system. Therefore, this is the interface with the outside world, and the difficulty is that the outside world is mostly analog. Even though digital circuits are created for microprocessors that operate with digital data, the external environment is analog. So, taking extremely simple types of inputs, such as whether a specific switch is on or off, or whether a particular light is on or off, yields continuous data. So, for instance, a temperature sensor will create a range of voltages based on the temperature it is receiving. Therefore, it is not digital.

There are often data converters, such as analog-to-digital conversion (ADC) for the input and digital-to-analog conversion (DAC) for the output from the input device to the processor. Some processors are equipped with these data converters. So the CPU only processes digital data, but can communicate with the analog environment through these ADC and DAC converters. So, what is occurring is that these devices bring data from the outside world into the system, and devices such as the keyboard, mouse, and switch are all considered input devices.

The next describes how the numbers are modified. What are the possible values it can have? The numbers may be quite large. For instance, integer numbers can have values up to infinity and may be arbitrarily huge, but when it is entered into a computer, it cannot be stored using an endless amount of memory. Therefore, there will be a size limit. A 16-bit signed integer can have a range between –32768 to +32767, while an unsigned number can have a number between 0 to 65,535. Therefore, there is a finite range.

Thus, the microprocessor has a very limited perspective on life, since it only comprehends binary numbers, i.e., zeros and ones, and not octal or hexadecimal integers. Though binary numbers often portray using octal and hexadecimal notations for our own comprehension, the binary number system is always used inside the CPU. And a binary digit, also known as a bit, is used to store numbers because the bit 1 is stored as a high voltage value or as the logic level high, while the bit 0 represents the logic level low.

A microprocessor recognises groups of bits; these groups of bits are known as words. A word may be composed of a specified number of bits, such as 16 or 32. In contrast, when it does elementary operations such as addition, subtraction, multiplication, division, and comparison, it operates at the word level. The designer of the processor thereby determines the processor's word size. Thus, the same holds true for microprocessors.

The number of bits inside a microprocessor word indicates its capabilities. An 8-bit CPU in a microprocessor can process 8-bit values. In integer addition, only 8 bit values are used, with the result consisting of 8 bits plus 1 bit carry for a total of 9 bits. If the basic processor supports 8-bit addition and it is required to do a 16-bit addition. It is possible to construct 16-bit addition in software using 8-bit additions. However, it will take longer than if a processor handles 16-bit words and a 16-bit addition is performed in a single operation. Modern microprocessors have 32-bit and 64-bit word sizes. Therefore, it can manage considerably bigger data sets.

The earliest microprocessors that recognise 8-bit words are the 8085, 8088, Motorola 6800, and 6800. These microprocessors are the only ones that support 8-bit words. Thus, processors such as 8086 and 68000 were developed with 16-bit words. Now, it is important to note that Intel 8086 and 8088 are present. So, why did the 8088 come after the 8086, as the name says, and why is this processor 8 bits while the 8086 is 16 bits? The reason for this is because 8085 came before 8086 and 8088, was highly popular, and was used to construct many systems. It contains 8-bit words, which corresponds to the number of pins on the processor's data lines. Thus, this was 8 bits.

to know more about 8085 microprocessor

When 8086 was launched to the marketplace, it replaced an 8085 chip with an 8086 chip due to the fact that the data size itself has changed from 8 bits to 16 bits. Therefore, the hardware has become incompatible. When this was realised, Intel took one step back and created the 8-bit CPU 8088, whose internal operation is identical to that of the 8086. From the outside, however, it has an 8-bit word interface, therefore all 8085-based systems may be replaced with this 8088 processor while the hardware stays the same. The software must be updated since it is now compatible with the 8088, but the hardware does not need to be modified.

The 8086 microprocessor has words with 16 bits. Modern processors are 32-bit and 64-bit words. There is no standardization or standard entity that corresponds to this 16-bit word. Conventionally, 8 bits make up a byte, but the length of a word depends on the processor. If a word is 16 bits long, the group of 8 bits is known as a half-word or byte, and the group of 4 bits is known as a nibble. So, for a 16-bit word, there are four nibbles. So, 32-bit groups are sometimes referred to as large words. The word size is not standardized because it is determined by the processor's word size.

There are other microprocessors that can manipulate 64, 80, or 128 bits simultaneously. Currently, all processors manipulate at least 32 bits at a time. Thus, it is possible to create superior processors with much increased capacity, allowing to manage bigger data bits with a single instruction.

3.2 INSTRUCTION SET ARCHITECTURE

Computer's instruction set can be classified as either "complex instruction set computer (CISC)" or "reduced instruction set computer (RISC)". Machine language programs are built in accordance with the processor's custom instruction set. Early computers had small and simple sets of instructions because they had to use as little hardware as possible to run them. When integrated circuits came along and made digital hardware cheaper, computer instructions generally tend to get both more and more complicated. There are sometimes even more than 200 instructions in the instruction sets of many computers.

for evolution of instruction set architecture

These computers also use a wide range of data formats and addressing mechanisms. The CISC based computer has a high number of instructions. In the early 1980s, RISC instruction set architecture was designed with fewer instructions. RISC's simple and straightforward architecture allows it to execute faster in the processor, because of its limited memory access.

3.2.1 CISC Characteristics

The following are the key aspects of CISC architecture:

1. A high number of instructions, often between 100 and 250.
2. Some commands that accomplish specific tasks and are often used infrequently
3. A wide range of addressing modes—typically between 5 and 20 distinct modes
4. Instruction formats with variable lengths
5. Instructions can manipulate operands in memory

The design of a computer's instruction set considers both machine language elements and the constraints placed on the usage of high-level programming languages. A compiler is used to translate high-level programming to machine language code. The complex instruction set makes compilation easier and increases total computer speed. Because the statement is automatically carried out by the machine's instructions. One example of CISC architecture is the IBM 370 computer.

CISC uses variable length instruction formats. Instruction operands are only two bytes long, whereas instructions that refer to two memory locations can be up to five bytes long.

A special decoding circuit is required to count the bytes inside the word to fit various types of instructions into a memory word of a fixed length. CISC instructions permit the direct modification of stored operands in memory. More hardware circuitry is needed to implement additional instructions and addressing modes, which can reduce the system's performance.

3.2.2 RISC Characteristics

The following RISC architectural features decrease execution time by reducing the computer's instruction set:

1. There are fewer instructions and addressing modes.
2. Memory is accessed only through "load" and "store" instructions.
3. All operations performed using CPU registers. The processing unit has a large number of registers.
4. Instruction format with a fixed length which can be easily decoded. So the RISC pipeline can be designed efficiently.
5. Execution of instructions take place in a single cycle.
6. Control unit is hardwired rather than microprogrammed.

RISC processors have "load" and "store" instructions only for memory access and rely mostly on register-to-register operations. The operand is loaded into the appropriate CPU register by the "load" instruction. The "store" instruction is used to move results to memory. For storing interim results and speeding up data transfers to other registers, a large number of registers is essential. By putting the most frequently requested operands in registers, register-to-memory transactions may be reduced.

In each clock cycle, a RISC processor may execute one instruction by pipelined execution of instructions. As memory access takes longer than register operations, "load" and "store" instructions need two clock cycles to communicate with memory.

RISC simplifies instruction set architecture by facilitating register manipulation. Because practically all instructions employ basic register addressing. Few addressing modes, such as immediate operands and relative mode, may be provided. The instruction length can be fixed by using a reasonably basic instruction structure. The RISC instruction format is simple to decode. The control logic may be simplified by streamlining instructions and their format. A hardwired control unit is preferred for faster operations.

for comparative study of RISC vs CISC

3.3 DESIGN PRINCIPLES FROM PROGRAMMER PERSPECTIVE

Various features in instruction format and addressing mode are provided to give programmers more freedom and choices when translating high-level programs into machine-readable instructions.

3.3.1 Instruction Format

Each instruction code is interpreted by a specific format within the CPU as listed below.

1. A field for operation code, which represents the type of operation.
2. A field used to specify the address of a memory location or a processor register.
3. A mode field determines operand or effective address computation approach.

In some instances, further special fields may be used, such as specifying the number of shifts in a shift-type instruction. The operation code field describes several processor operations such as add, subtract, complement, and shift. The mode field indicates several options for selecting the operands from the specified address.

Computers may have instructions of variable lengths having a variety of addresses. The number of address fields in a computer's instruction format is dependent on the registers' internal structure. Most computers belong to one of three CPU organization types:

1. **Single accumulator organization:** Every action is executed using an implicit accumulator register (A). This kind of computer's instruction format has a single address field. One of the common example is ADD X instruction, which performs the addition as A ← A + M [X]. Where M [X] is the data stored at location X in memory.
2. **General register organization:** Three register and two address fields are examples of a general register kind of structure. For example, three register fields are represented as ADD R4, R5, R6. This indicates that the ADD operation is performed between registers R5 and R6, and the result is stored in register R4, i.e., R4 ← R5 + R6.

   If the destination and the source registers are identical, the instruction can be represented by two register fields. For example, the instruction ADD R4, R5 represents the operation R4 ← R4 + R5. In this instruction, just the register locations for R4 and R5 must be supplied.

   Transfer instructions, i.e., MOV instruction also uses two address fields. For example, MOV R4, R5 transfers data between registers R4 ← R5 (register R5 transfers data to register R4) or R5 ← R4 (register R4 transfers register data to register R5) depending on the computer. General-purpose computers may use either two or three address fields instructions.
3. **Stack organization:** The stack-organized CPU has PUSH and POP address-field instructions. PUSH X inserts the word on top of the stack and stack pointer is auto-updated. Other operations can be performed directly through instruction, and these instructions do not require the address field to be specified. For instance, the ADD instruction pops the top two values from the stack, adds them, and then pushes the sum to the stack.

3.3.2 Addressing Modes

The operand field of an instruction defines the operation to be performed on data stored in registers or memory [1]. The operand value is determined during program execution by the instruction's addressing mode. The addressing mode specifies how to interpret the instruction's address field before accessing the operand.

Computers can use various addressing modes as follows:

1. The availability of various features provide flexibility in writing code such as data indexing, counters for loop control, memory pointers, and program relocation.
2. It is possible for an assembly language programmer to reduce instruction count and execution time by taking advantage of the many addressing modes available. Thus, lowering the required number of bits in an instruction's address field improves program efficiency.

The control unit of processor performs an operation known as an instruction cycle, which includes reading an instruction from memory, decoding the instruction, and executing the decoded program.

The program counter (PC) is a special computer register that counts how many times each instruction from a programme in memory has been executed. When an instruction is retrieved from memory, its address is stored in the PC, and the PC is incremented by one. In the second stage of decoding, the instruction's operation, addressing mode, and operand locations are determined. After processing the instruction, the computer goes back to step 1 to look for the next instruction in the sequence. It is common practice for certain computers to use a separate binary code for specifying the addressing mode of the instruction, just as they do for specifying the operation code. In other systems, the mode and type of an instruction are both designated by a single binary code. Many different addressing modes may be used to specify an instruction, and often many addressing modes are mixed in a single instruction.

The instruction may or may not include an address field. Any address fields present might be pointed to either a specific memory location or a specific CPU register. The memory address of an operand consists of basically displacement, base address and index value [2]. In addition, the instruction might contain many address fields, each of which could use a different addressing method.

1. **Implied Mode:** There is no operand specified explicitly so this is implied mode addressing. For example– INC

   The INC instruction increments the contents of the accumulator. The stack-based computers generally use this addressing mode.

2. **Immediate Mode:** The operand is given explicitly in the instruction. Immediate-mode instructions may be used to set registers to a constant value. For instance– MOV R4, #300

   In MOV instruction, one operand is the value so this is immediate addressing mode. The MOV instruction places the value 300 in register R4. The number sign (#) in front of the value indicates that this value is to be used as an immediate operand.

3. **Register Mode:** A register contains operands. The register could be either the first or second operand of the instruction. The specific register is chosen from a set of available registers. For example– MOV R1, R4

   Both operands in the MOV instruction are registers so this is register addressing mode. The MOV instruction places the contents of register R4 in register R1.

4. **Absolute(Direct) Mode:** Instruction's address field contains effective address of operands. The operand is stored in memory. The instructions provide a specific address to access the operand. For example– MOV R1, LOC

   The instruction MOV places the value from the memory location LOC into register R2.

5. **Register Indirect Mode:** The memory address or register content specifies the effective address of the operand. For example– MOV R1, (R4)

   The content of register R4 is the memory address where operand value is stored. The register indirect mode may also provide the address in the memory where the address of the operand value is stored. For example– MOV R1, (X)

   The operand value in memory is stored at address Y and this Y address is stored in location X in memory. Here, instead of a register, the memory location X has the address of the operand.

6. **Index Addressing Mode:** The syntax of this addressing mode is X(Ri) or X[Ri], address X + Ri, here X is offset. If the syntax is (Ri) or [Ri] then address Ri where offset(displacement) =

0. The index register is a specialised CPU register used to hold index values. For example– MOV AL, [DI + 2]

The MOV AL, [DI + 2] instruction can also be represented as MOV AL, 2(DI). A displacement (offset) number 2 is added to the register within the [ ], to get the operand value stored in the memory at location [DI + 2]. This is also possible that displacement may be subtracted from the register, for example– MOV AL, [SI – 1].

Example 3.1: Determine the addressing modes of the given instructions.

1. ADD
2. COM
3. ADD R1, R2
4. MOV R1, #100
5. LOAD R2, NUM

Solution:

1. **Implied addressing mode:** In stack-based computers, zero addess instructions are used. As a result, ADD instructions take out (pop) the top two instructions from the stack, add, and then push the result back to the top of the stack.
2. **Implied addressing mode:** Complement the content of the Accumulator.
3. **Register addressing mode:** Because both operands in the instruction are registers. The instruction ADD perform the addition of R1 and R2 registers' content and the result is stored in register R1.
4. **Immediate addressing mode:** The presence of value 100 indicates that this value is to be used as an immediate operand. The MOV instruction places the value 100 in register R1.
5. **Absolute addressing mode:** The instruction LOAD loads the value from the memory location NUM into register R2.

Example 3.2: Determine the addressing modes of the given instructions.

1. LOAD R2, (R4)
2. LOAD R2, (A)

Solution:

1. **Register Indiect addressing mode:** The address of operand is stored in register R4, i.e., LOC

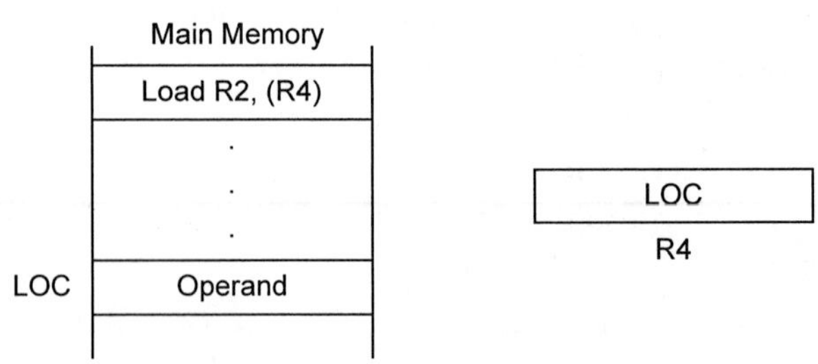

2. **Register Indirect addressing mode:** The address of operand is stored in a memory address A, i.e., LOC

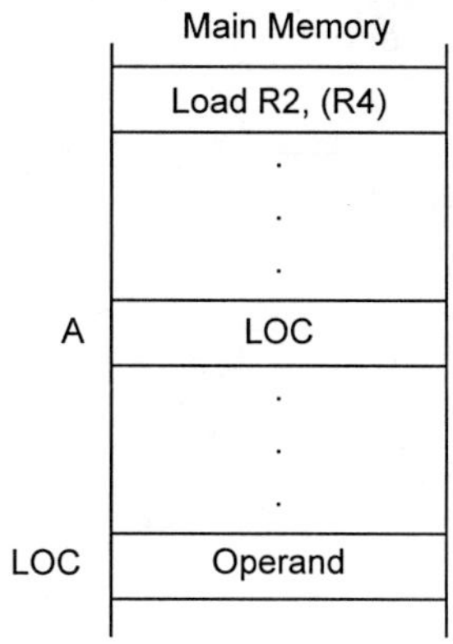

Fig. 3.1: Register indirect addressing mode when operand address stored in a register and when address stored in memory

7. **Base-Index Addressing Mode:** The syntax of base-index addressing is (Ri, Rj) or [Ri, Rj], address Ri + Rj. The sum of base register and displacement register is the effective address of the operand. The base-index addressing mode simplifies program relocation between different memory segments. For example– MOV AL, (BL, DI)

   The interpretation of MOV AL, (BL, DI) instruction is similar to MOV AL, [BL, DI]. A base register BL is added to displacement register DI, i.e., [BL + DI] to compute the address of the operand in memory.
8. **Base-Index Offset:** The syntax of this addressing mode is X(Ri, Rj) or X[Ri, Rj], address X+Ri+Rj. For example– MOV AL, X(BL, DI)

   Here X is an offset(constant) value. This X is added to [BL + DI + X] to get the address of the operand in memory. This flexibility is useful to access multiple components in a record.

Example 3.3: Determine the addressing modes of the given instructions.

1. LOAD R2, 50(R4) when R4 = 2000 2. LOAD R2, (R4, R5)
3. LOAD R2, 10 (R4, R5)

Solution: 1. Index addressing mode

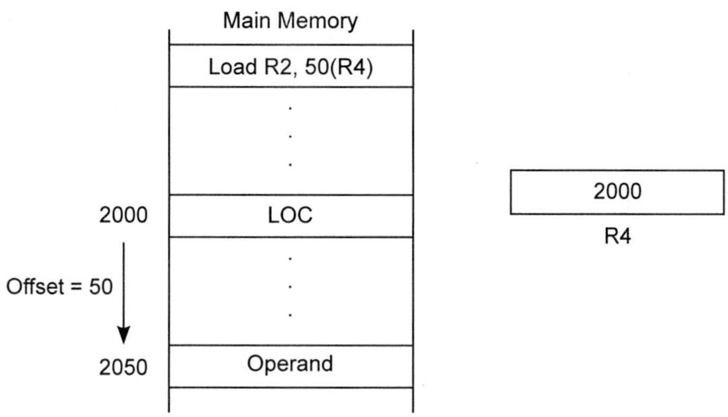

Fig. 3.2: Main memory and register contents in index addressing mode

2. Base-index addressing mode

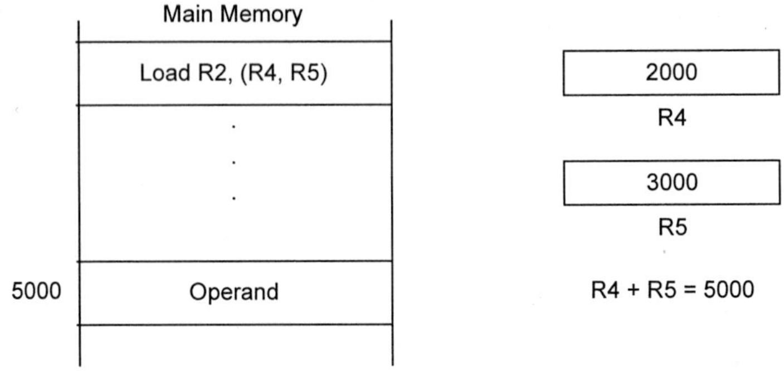

3. Base-index offset addressing mode

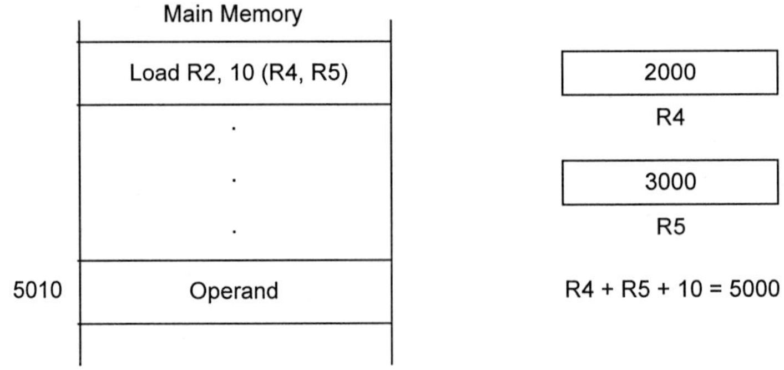

Fig. 3.3: Main memory and register contents in base-index and base-index offset addressing mode

9. **Relative Addressing Mode:** The relative addressing is calculated by using the program counter. When the index value is added to the program counter, the effective address is related to the next instruction's address. The syntax of this addressing mode is X(PC) or X[PC], address PC + X. For example– Branch > 0 LOC

   This address is calculated as an offset from the program counter.

10. **Auto-increment Mode:** This is also known as auto post-increment. It uses a register indirect addressing mode and then increments a register in order to access the next word in memory in a subsequent instruction. The syntax for auto-increment addressing mode is (Ri)+, address Ri + 1xL, where L is the memory word length in bytes. For an example– ST (R1)+, R5

    for 8086 addressing modes

    This instruction saves the contents of register R5 in the memory address contained in register R1, then begins pointing out the next memory location due to auto-increment execution. Thus the address of the next memory location is now stored in register R1. This addressing mode is useful for accessing data items from successive memory locations.

11. **Auto-decrement Mode:** This is also named as auto pre-decrement. The syntax of auto-decrement addressing mode is -(Ri), address Ri-1xL, here L is the length of the memory word in bytes. It uses register indirect addressing mode and then decrements the register to access the previous word in the memory in the current instruction itself. For example– ST – (R1), R5

This instruction first decrements the location stored in register R1. Now R1 has the previous memory location where the content of register R5 is stored. This addressing mode is useful for accessing data items from preceding memory locations.

Example 3.4: Determine the addressing modes of the given instructions. Assume each word length in memory is 4 byte

MOV R2, (R4)+

ADD R3, R4

ADD R6, -(R5)

What are the contents in registers R2, R3, and R6?

Solution: The Mov instruction has auto-increment addressing mode. The first Add instruction has register indirect addressing mode and second Add instruction has auto-decrement addressing mode.

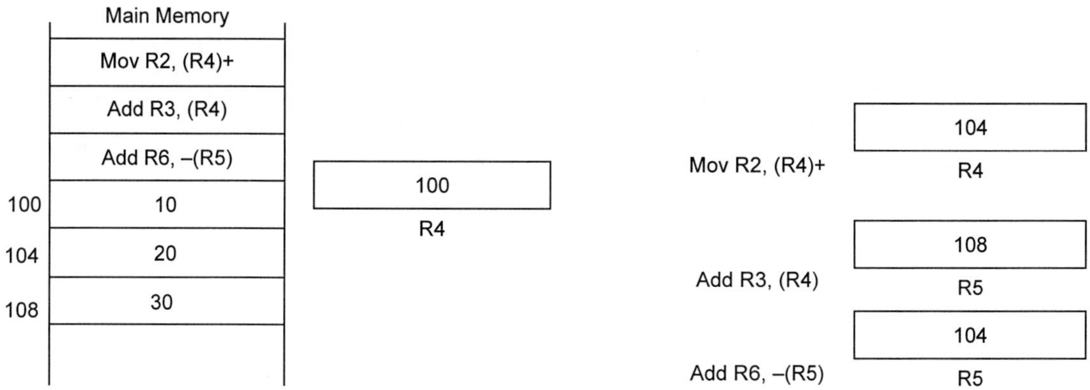

Fig. 3.4: Modification in register address with autoincrement and autodecrement addressing modes

After execution of all three instructions, the register values are R2–10, R3–20, and R6–20 as demonstrated in Fig 3.4.

3.4 ARCHITECTURE OF 8086 MICROPROCESSOR

The 8086 is a 16-bit microprocessor. The microprocessor can read or write 16 bits of data to memory at once via using a 20-bit address bus. The maximum 1MB RAM can be used by this microprocessor.

for functional parts of 8086 microprocessor

3.4.1 8086 microprocessor functional units

The execution unit (EU) and bus interface unit (BIU) are the major functional units of the 8086 microprocessor architecture as shown in Fig 3.5.

- **Execution Unit (EU):** The execution unit instructs the BIU where to obtain the data, and the BIU is then responsible for decoding and executing those instructions. Its job is to manage data operations using the ALU and instruction decoder. The system buses are not directly connected to the execution unit.

- **FLAG Registers:** It is a 16-bit register. It consists of two types of flags-conditional flags and control flags. The flags' state varies based on the value stored in the accumulator register.
  - **Conditional or Status flags:** The following conditional flags represent the outcome of previously executed arithmetic or logical operation:

    1. **Carry flag (C):** When adding two n-bit binary numbers, if the outcome exceeds n-bit, the carry flag sets as C = 1, otherwise, C = 0.
    2. **Auxiliary flag (AF):** For BCD numbers, the auxiliary flag is the same as the CF. When adding two numbers and carry is generated from lower nibble to higher nibble, then AF = 1. Otherwise, AF = 0.
    3. **Overflow flag (O):** The C flag and the overflow flag are similar. If the outcome of any arithmetic or logical operation on a signed integer exceeds the register's specified capacity, it is set to 1. If not, the O flag is set to 0.
    4. **Parity flag (P):** The parity flag is even parity. If the number of 1's in the binary value is even, then set P = 1, otherwise P = 0.
    5. **Zero flag (Z):** If the result of an arithmetic or logical operation in the Accumulator register is zero, then set Z = 1, otherwise Z = 0.

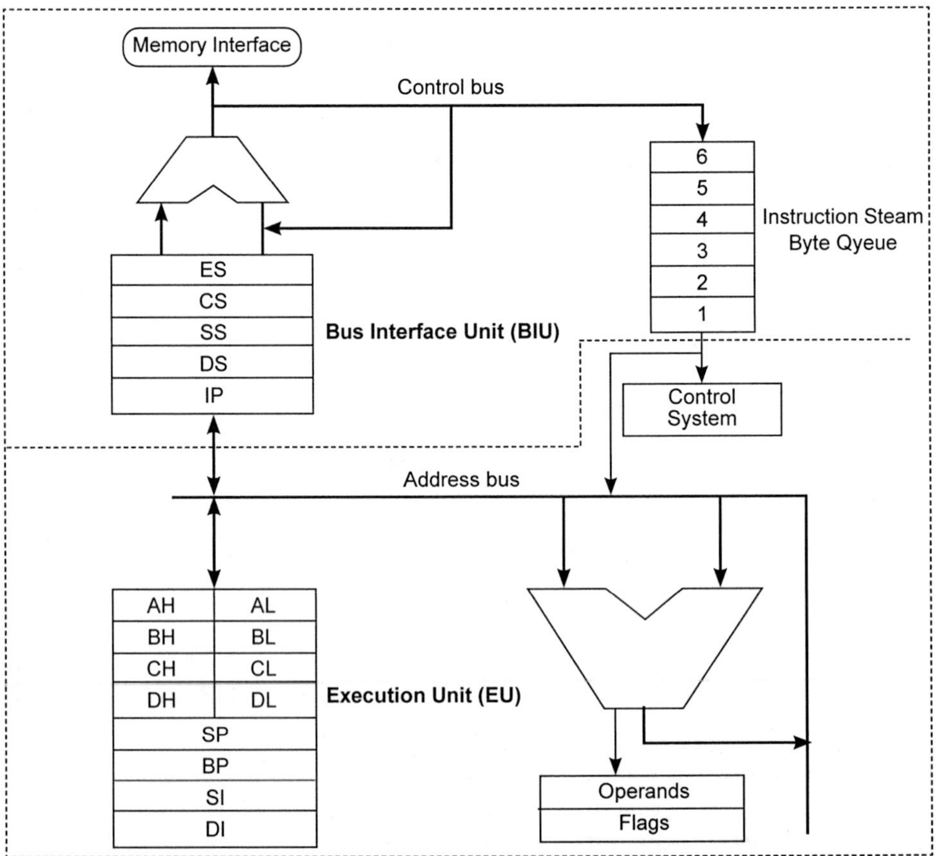

Fig. 3.5: 8086 Microprocessor architecture

6. **Sign flag (S):** After an arithmetic or logical operation, if the result sign is positive, then set S = 1, otherwise S = 0.

- **Control flags:** The interrupt flag, direction flag, and trap flag are the control flags.
    1. **Interrupt flag (I):** When peripheral devices send the interrupt control signal to the microprocessor, I = 1; otherwise, I = 0.
    2. **Directional flag (D):** The directional flag is set to 1 when a string is accessed from a higher byte to lower byte in memory. It is set to 0 when a string is accessed from a lower byte to higher byte in memory.
    3. **Trap flag (T):** On-chip debugging is performed using the trap flag. When T = 1, the function operates in single-step mode. An internal interrupt is triggered on execution of each instruction. This enables sequential execution of instructions.

- **General-purpose registers:** There are four 16-bit general-purpose registers; those are "AX", "BX", "CX", and "DX" in the 8086 microprocessor and eight 8-bit general-purpose registers; those are ("AH", "AL"), ("BH", "BL"), ("CH", "CL"), and ("DH", "DL"). These registers are used to store data during arithmetic or logical operations.

1. **Accumulator register (AX):** The "AX" register has a capacity of 16 bits. It is split into two 8-bit registers. These are the "AH" and "AL" registers, respectively. It stores data before arithmetic or logical operations. The result is available in "AX" register.
2. **Base register (BX):** The base register is a 16-bit register. It is used to store the offset address of a value (operand). It has two 8-bit registers (BH and BL). In the following example, 300H is the offset address of a value and is stored in the BL register.

   mov bl, [300] (bl ← 300H)

3. **Count register (CX):** The count register is a 16-bit register. It is divided into two 8-bit registers called CH and CL. It is used for loop instructions. In the following example, the loop is repeated until cx reaches 0.

   ```
   mov cx, 08
   loop
   ```

4. **Data register (DX):** The data register is a 16-bit register. It is also divided into two 8-bit registers; those are DH and DL. This register is used for division and multiplication operations. The remainder is stored in the DX register and the quotient is stored in the AX register.
5. **Stack pointer (SP):** It is a 16-bit register that is used to point the topmost stack element of the stack segment.
6. **Base Pointer (BP):** The base pointer register is also a pointer to the stack segment. This 16-bit register is used to access elements passed by the stack.
7. **Source index (SI):** Source index register is a 16-bit register. It uses pointer addressing of data. It points to the data segment.
8. **Destination index (DI):** The destination index register is a 16-bit register. "DI" register is used in the pointer addressing of data.
9. **Arithmetic and logic unit (ALU):** All arithmetic and logical operations are performed in the ALU circuit.

- **Bus interface unit (BIU):** The bus interface unit has segment registers, an instruction queue, a control unit, and a processing unit for address calculation. The BIU is connected to the memory interface through the system bus.
  - **Instruction queue:** Bus interface unit has 6-byte instruction queue. The bus interface unit retrieves and stores memory's next instructions in the instruction queue. The execution unit executes faster with the instruction queue.
  - **Segment registers:** The bus interface unit has four segment registers–"CS", "DS", "SS", and "ES" which store memory addresses for data and instructions that the processor uses to access memory addresses.
  - **Code segment (CS):** The executable program is stored in a 16-bit code segment register. This register contains the address of the memory's code segment.
  - **Data segment (DS):** Data segment register of 16-bit addresses 64 KB program data. The general registers ("AX", "BX", "CX", "DX") and index registers ("SI", "DI") reference data in the data segment. The POP and LDS instructions can modify the data segment directly.
  - **Extra segment (ES):** The extra segment is a 16-bit register with the 64KB segment address. The string stores extra destination information in ES.
  - **Stack segment (SS):** During execution, memory is managed using a 16-bit stack segment register to store data and addresses.
  - **Instruction pointer (IP):** A 16-bit instruction pointer register comprises the address of the next instruction.
- **Effective address calculation:** The microprocessor cannot access data with a 16-bit address because the memory has a 1 MB storage capacity. Each memory has a 20-bit address, so before accessing data or instructions from memory, the effective or physical address is calculated.

  $$\text{physical address} = \text{segment register} * 10\text{H} + \text{offset}$$

  Here segment register is CS and offset is instruction operand address.
- **Control unit (CU):** The control unit coordinates data transfer between CPU registers and ALU. The control unit controls every part of the computer, coordinating all parts, traffic, etc.

3.4.2 Instruction Types in 8086

Data transfer instruction, logical instruction, arithmetic instruction, string manipulation instruction, process control instruction, and control transfer instruction are among the eight kinds of instructions supported by the 8086 instruction set. Some of them are familiar to us, such as data transfer, arithmetic, and logic, among others. In contrast, string manipulation instructions are quite new. In addition, certain control transfer instructions will include various forms of branch calls, etc., making them processor-specific.

- **Data transfer instructions** transfers data from source to destination.
  1. MOV transfers data from source to destination. For example, mov ax, bx transfer data from bx register to ax register.
  2. PUSH places word on the top of the stack.
  3. POP removes word from the top of the stack.
  4. XCHG exchanges data between two registers.

- **Input/Output port transfer instructions** are as follows.
  1. IN reads word/byte from the provided port to the accumulator register.
  2. OUT writes word/byte from the accumulator register to the provided port.
  3. LEA loads operand address to the provided register.
  4. LDS load data segment register and other register from the memory.
  5. LES loads extra segment register and other register from the memory.
- **Arithmetic instructions** can be defined as
  - **Addition**
    1. ADD – it used to add a byte/word to another byte/word.
    2. ADC – perform addition with carry
    3. INC – byte/word incremented by 1. It is addition operation only.
  - **Subtraction**
    1. SUB – it used to subtract a word/byte from another word/byte.
    2. SBB – subtraction with borrow.
    3. DEC – either word or byte subtracted by 1.
    4. CMP – two registers operand subtracted and result compared with zero.
  - **Multiplication**
    1. MUL – multiplication of two unsigned numbers.
    2. IMUL – for two signed numbers multiplications.
  - **Division**
    1. DIV – for two unsigned numbers division.
    2. IDIV – for two signed numbers division.
- **Bit manipulation instructions:** These are logical operations like NOT, OR, AND, XOR, etc.
- **Shift instructions:**
  - Shift left instruction – each bit shifted to the left and in rightmost bit position zero is added. For example– shl al, 1

    Where, all bits of AL is shifted one position to the left and in the rightmost position zero is added.
  - Shift right instruction – All bits are shifted to the right and in the leftmost bit position zero is added. For example– shr al, 2

    Where, all bits of AL are shifted towards right and in the leftmost position zero is added.
  - Arithmetic right shift – The leftmost bit remains same in the position and all bits are shifted towards right one position. For example– ashr al, 1

    Where, bits of AL are shifted towards right and in the leftmost bit value is added in the last bit position.
- **Branch Instructions:** The following branch instructions are used in 8086:
  1. JA compares unsigned numbers. After a CMP or SUB instruction, the JA instruction transfers control to the label immediately if the first operand is greater than or equal to the second.

2. JE jumps to the label if equal.
3. JC jumps if the carry flag = 1.
4. JZ jumps if zero flag = 1.

- Loop instruction: The loop instruction is repeated until cx reaches 0.

UNIT SUMMARY

- A microprocessor is a silicon chip with an ALU (Arithmetic Logic Unit), register and control circuitry. A central processing unit (CPU) consists of an arithmetic logic unit for conducting arithmetic logic operations, a register bank for storing intermediate values, from which the CPU often pulls operands, and a control logic that regulates the whole process.
- The 8085 and 8086 microprocessors are the standard 8-bit and 16-bit microprocessor architectures.
- A microprocessor is a programmable device that takes in numbers, conducts arithmetic and logical operations according to the programme in memory, and generates results.
- Computers use two kinds of instruction sets: "complex instruction set computer (CISC)" and "reduced instruction set computer (RISC)".
- CISC instructions are variable length and complex instruction formats. These types of instructions permit the direct modification of stored operands in memory.
- RISC processors have "load" and "store" instructions for memory access and rely mostly on register-to-register operations. The load instruction loads operand into the appropriate CPU register. The "store" instruction is used to save results to memory.
- Most computers belong to one of three CPU organization types: single accumulator organization, general register organization, and stack organization.
- The addressing mode specifies how to interpret the instruction's address field before accessing the operand.
- The operand field of an instruction defines the operation to be performed on data stored in registers or memory.
- The 8086 is a 16-bit microprocessor. The microprocessor can read or write 16 bits of data to memory at once via using a 20-bit address bus.
- The major functional units of the 8086 microprocessor architecture are the execution unit (EU) and bus interface unit (BIU).
- Execution unit is made up of several flags, registers, and special purpose control flags. Whereas the bus interface unit consists of segment registers, an instruction queue, a control unit, and an address calculation processing unit.
- The execution unit instructs the BIU where to obtain the data, and the BIU is then responsible for decoding and executing those instructions.
- Instruction set of 8086 comprises data transfer instruction, logical instruction, arithmetic instruction, string manipulation instruction, process control instruction, and control transfer instruction.

EXERCISES

Multiple Choice Questions

1. The smallest unit of binary data
   (a) Bit (b) Byte (c) Nibble (d) Word
2. A 64 bit word consists of
   (a) 4 bits (b) 8 bits (c) 4 bytes (d) 8 bytes
3. Single Flip-Flop can store __________ bits of information.
   (a) 2 (b) 32 (c) 64 (d) 1
4. How many pins does the 8086 microprocessor have?
   (a) 20 (b) 60 (c) 40 (d) 30
5. 1 MB memory equivalent to
   (a) 1024 bits (b) 1024 KB (c) 1024 bytes (d) 1024 GB
6. Which of the following is correct
   (a) A microprocessor contains ALU, flash memory and control units
   (b) A microprocessor contains ALU, registers and control units
   (c) A microcontroller contains ALU and control units only
   (d) A microprocessor contains ALU only
7. In an 8086 microprocessor, an address bus
   (a) counts 16 bits at once (b) may get two 8-bit values at once
   (c) has 20 address lines (d) none of the above
8. The register that stores information about the nature of the outcomes of arithmetic and logic operations is known as the
   (a) Flag Register (b) Accumulator (c) Program Counter (d) Process status register
9. A program that uses mnemonics is called
   (a) Object program (b) Fetch cycle
   (c) Assembly language (d) Micro instruction
10. Identify addressing mode of following 8086 instruction.
    ADD R1, R2
    (a) Direct (b) Immediate (c) Implied (d) Register
11. In an 8086 microprocessor, the Program Status Word register pair is implemented as which of the following register pairs?
    (a) Program Counter and Stack Pointer (b) Program Counter and Accumulator
    (c) Program Counter and Flag Register (d) Status Flags and Control Flags

12. Which of the following about an 8086 microprocessor's stack is NOT TRUE?
    (a) Stack is a last-in-first-out structure
    (b) When you push on the stack, information is saved there.
    (c) The register for the stack is made up of 8 bits.
    (d) Information is retrieved on the stack by popping it off.
13. In an 8086 microprocessor, a conditional branch statement does not change any of the following flags.
    (a) Zero flag (b) Carry flag
    (c) Sign flag (d) None of the given options
14. The __________ addressing mode adds the offset and index register to get the effective address of the operand.
    (a) index (b) base-indexed (c) register indirect (d) relative

ANSWERS													
1.	(a)	2.	(d)	3.	(d)	4.	(c)	5.	(b)	6.	(b)	7.	(c)
8.	(a)	9.	(c)	10.	(d)	11.	(d)	12.	(c)	13.	(d)	14.	(a)

Short and Long Answer Type Questions

Category-I

1. What is the purpose of input and output ports?
2. Distinguish between a microprocessor, a microcontroller, and a microcomputer.
3. What is the significance of the AD7-0 pins?
4. What do you mean by a programmer's perspective on a processor?
5. What is a register, and what are its advantages and disadvantages over other General Purpose Registers?
6. What distinguishes A register from the other General Purpose Registers?
7. Describe how the "AX", "BX", "CX", and "DX" registers may be used.
8. What distinguishes the HL pair from the other register pairs?
9. Why do users often specify addresses and data in hexadecimal notation?
10. Describe the development of microprocessors in brief.
11. Explain the push and pop instructions in 8086.
12. Why is the 8088 microprocessor an 8-bit microprocessor instead of 16-bit?

Category-II

13. How is a microprocessor different from a microprogram? Can a microprocessor be made without the use of a microprogram? Is it true that all microprogrammed computers also function as microprocessors?

14. What is instruction set architecture? Explain the difference between RISC and CISC instruction set architecture. Give the name of the microprocessor or processors which are using RISC or CISC.

15. Explain the various instruction formats. How to decide which instruction format is suitable for a specific microprocessor?

16. What is the need of addressing modes in microprocessors? Explain different addressing modes and their applications in detail.

17. Explain in detail the functional parts of the 8086 microprocessor.

Numerical Problems

18. Registers R3 and R4 contain values 300 and 1200 respectively in decimal, and the word length of the processors 32 bits. The effective address of the instruction "STORE R5, 90 (R3, R4)" in decimal will be __________. [**Ans:** 1590]

19. A two-word instruction is placed at address "A" and "B" represents the instruction's address field, which is located at "A+1". The operand utilised during instruction execution is stored at the address "C". In an index register, the value X is stored. Explain how "C" is computed from the other addresses if the addressing mode of the instruction is

(i) indirect, (ii) direct, (iii) indexed, and (iv) relative.

[**Ans:** (i) C = M[B] (ii) C = B (iii) C = B + X (iv) C = B + A + 2]

20. There is a branch instruction at memory address 600. The address of the branch is specified to 300 decimal places.

(i) Determine the relative address in decimal and binary numbers.

(ii) Find the binary representation of "300" in PC after the fetch phase. Then, show that 300 in binary is equal to the sum of the program counter (PC) and the relative address found in (i).

[**Ans:** (i) Relative address – 300 – 601 = – 301; 301 = 000100101101; – 301 – 111011010011

(ii) PC = 601 = 001001011001, 300 = 000100101100; PC = 001001011001(601), RA = 111011010011(– 301), EA = 300 = 000100101100]

21. If the instruction is (i) computational and requires an operand from memory, or (ii) a branch, determine the number of memory accesses performed by the control unit in order to fetch and execute the instruction in indirect addressing mode. [**Ans:** (i) 3 (ii) 2]

22. In indexed addressing mode, what value should be entered into the address field of an instruction for it to be considered equivalent to a register indirect mode instruction? [**Ans:** zero]

23. An instruction is stored at memory address 500 with its address field at 501 memory location. The value of the address field is 400. The R1 register of the processor contains the number 200. Evaluate the effective address if the instruction addressing mode is

(i) immediate (ii) direct (iii) register indirect (iv) relative or

(v) index with R1 index register.

[Ans: (i) 501, (ii) 400, (iii) 200, (iv) 502 + 400 = 902, (v) 200 + 400 = 600]

24. The value of 16 bits is 10011010110010101. What operation is required to:
   (i) clear the first four bits, i.e., b0 to b3, to 0?
   (ii) set the last four bits, i.e., b12 to b15, to 1?
   (iii) complement the middle four bits, b6 to b9?

[**Ans:** (i) AND with 1111111111110000 or AND with 1111111111111010 (ii) OR with 1111000000000000 or OR with 0110000000000000 (iii) XOR with 0000001111000000]

25. Create a binary representation of each of the signed integers that are presented below.
   (i) First, carry out the binary addition of the numbers (+68) and (–83), and then evaluate the outcome of this operation.
   (ii) Carry out the subtraction of the binary numbers (–68) – (+83), and determine the occurrence of overflow.
   (iii) Shift the value of binary –68 to the right by one position, and show the result in decimal form. [**Hint:** Perform arithmetic shift right because this is signed number]
   (iv) Move binary –83 one position to the left, and then determine the occurrence of overflow.

[**Ans:** + 83 = 01010011, + 68 = 01000100, – 83 = 10101101, – 68 = 10111100
(i) – 83 (10101101) + 68 (01000100) = – 15 (11110001) (in 2's complement)
(ii) – 68 (10111100) – 83 (10101101) = –151 (01101001), overflow
(iii) – 34 = 11011110, (iv) –166 ≠ 01011010, overflow]

26. Determine status bit values C, S, Z, and O according to the below instructions. In each example, register R begins with the number 72 (hexadecimal) and it is an 8-bit register.
   (i) ADD C6, R (ii) ADD 1E, R (iii) SUB 9A, R (iv) AND 8D, R
   (v) XOR R, R

[**Ans:** (i) 138 (00111000); C = 1, S = 0, Z = 0, O = 0 (ii) 90 (10010000); C=0, S = 1, Z = 0, O = 1 (iii) D8 (11011000); C = 0, S = 1, Z = 0, O = 1 (iv) 00 (00000000); C = 0, S = 0, Z = 1, O = 0 (v) 00(00000000); C = 0, S = 0, Z = 1, O = 0]

27. Consider the 8-bit values of registers A = 01010101 and B = 10101010.
   (i) Perform the addition of binary values stored in registers A and B under the assumptions that they are signed numbers.
   (ii) Provide the decimal equivalent under the assumptions that the result obtained in (a) is (i) unsigned and (ii) signed.
   (iii) Determine status bit values C, S, Z, and O after performing addition.

[**Ans:** (i) A + B = 11111111 (ii) unsigned = 255, signed = –1 (iii) C = 0, S = 1, Z = 0, O = 0]

28. Two unsigned numbers, A=01000001 and B=10000101 are compared by a computer program. Determine binary result of subtraction (A-B) and values of status bits C and Z.

[**Ans:** A – B = 10111100, C = 1; Z = 0]

29. Two unsigned numbers, A = 01000001 and B = 10000100 are compared by a computer program. Determine binary result of subtraction (A-B) and values of status bits S, Z and O.

[**Ans:** A – B = + 65 (01000001) – –124 (10000100) = 189 (10111101)
= 010111101 (9 bits); S = 1, Z = 0, O = 1 (overflow)]

30. The stack pointer has the value 3560, while the top of the memory stack has the value 5320. A two-word call subroutine instruction is located in 1120 followed by the address field of 6720 at location 1121. What are the content of PC, SP, and the top of the stack:

(i) Prior to fetching call instruction from memory?

(ii) After execution of the call instruction?

(iii) After the subroutine's return?

[**Ans:** (i) PC: 1120 (initial), 6720 (after call), 1122 (after return)
(ii) SP: 3560 (initial), 3559 (after call), 3560 (after return) (iii) Top of Stack:
5320 (initial), 1122 (after call), 5320 (after return)]

PRACTICAL

Aim: Perform addition and subtraction using 16-bit numbers. Assume initially both the numbers are residing in memory. You have to load these numbers into CPU registers, perform the addition and subtraction of these numbers and store the result back to memory.

Tools: 8086 Microprocessor kit [3], Power Supply

Theory: The ADD instruction performs addition, while the SUB instruction performs subtraction. The ADD instruction can add immediate data or the contents of a memory location or source register specified in the instruction to the contents of a destination register or memory location.

To understand the working of 8086 microprocessor kit

The outcome is stored in the destination operand. The source and destination operands, however, cannot both be memory operands. Because it is not feasible to add memory to memory. All condition code flags are affected by the outcome. In addition, the status of the carry flag must be checked, and the result and carry flag are both saved to a memory location. Similarly, execute the subtraction operation and check the overflow condition to ensure that the result is correct.

The microprocessor can operate with the help of certain commands as follows.

Reset

Enter

Starting Address

Fill program instruction by instruction

Execute

Result Store in Memory

For performing subtraction on 8086 microprocessor kit

Procedure for 16-bit addition:

1. First you have to write an assembly language program, one program for performing addition and second program for performing subtraction.
2. You have to prepare a table comprising the column's name as memory address, machine opcode, mnemonics, operands.
3. Start the program.

4. Load first data in AX register and the second data in BX register.
5. Clear CL register for carry.
6. Perform Add operation between AX and BX registers and get the result in AX register.
7. Store the result in memory locations.
8. If carry = 1 then go to next step. Otherwise, go to step 11.
9. Increment the carry in memory.
10. Store the carry in memory.
11. Stop the program.

For performing addition on 8086 microprocessor kit

KNOW MORE

Innovations by Indian: SHAKTI is India's first open-source industrial-grade processor [4]. It is developed by the "Reconfigurable Intelligent Systems Engineering" group at IIT Madras under supervision of Professor V. Kamakoti. The objective of the team is to develop SoCs that are competitive with commercial products in terms of space, power consumption, and performance. All SHAKTI source code is open-source. The Shakti processors are intended for embedded applications, robotic controllers, and Internet of Things boards [7].

The health benefits of using rejuvenated traditional Indian clay cookware: Indian proverb "we reach the other people's heart through stomach" [5]. Food affects us mentally too. Cooking requires mixing,

heating, and combining components. The cooking utensils and heating agent (charcoal, clay stove, kerosene stove, gas stove, microwave) make up the heating ingredients. Ancestors cooked using cast, copper, brass, iron, and clay utensils.

These utensils keep food's nutritional worth intact [6]. Modern utensils, such as the modern pressure cooker, aluminium, steel, plastic, and nonstick, are unable to maintain the majority of the micronutrients found in the food. Infact, plastic, aluminium, and nonstick utensils actually add some toxins to the food. For instance, cast iron utensils play a significant role in boosting the iron content of food, especially in the case of acidic foods. Copper has a special ability to strengthen the collagen booster in meals. Brass is excellent in preserving water, which boosts the human immune system. Similarly, silver has a calming impact on the mood illness, but it is prohibitively expensive and difficult to acquire. Importantly, clay utensils have a significant impact on immunity. Whenever we think about clay utensils, we can consider our nearly extinct clay potters. In place of clay cups, tea vendors now use either plastic cups containing Bisphenol A (BPA) or paper cups (containing styrene), both of which are extremely harmful to human health.

Clay utensils concern us for these reasons. Food that has been cooked in clay retains more nutrients and tastes better. Clay pottery creates jobs. In order to foster a lifestyle that is simultaneously healthier and more tasty, it is important to promote cooking in earthen pots and the amazing food of India. Earthen pots use less water for cooking and take up no waste space. Indians are deeply rooted with soil, now it's time to use this soil for maintaining some livelihood to distribute taste and health throughout and outside the country.

REFERENCES AND SUGGESTED READINGS

1. M. Morris Mano, Computer system architecture. Prentice-Hall, Inc., Third edition. https://poojavaishnav.files.wordpress.com/2015/05/mano-m-m-computer-system-architecture.pdf (last accessed: May 2023)
2. Carl Hamacher, Zvonko Vranesic, Safwat Zaky, and Naraig Manjikian, Computer organization and embedded systems. McGraw-Hill Higher Education, 2011.
3. Microprocessor and Interfacing Lab Manual. https://webstor.srmist.edu.in/web_assets/srm_mainsite/files/2017/cse-lab-manual-microprocessor.pdf (last accessed: May 2023)
4. Shakti Processor. https://shakti.org.in/ (last accessed: May 2023)
5. Debdip Khan, Sudatta Banerjee, Revitalizing ancient Indian clay utensils and its impact on health. International Journal of All Research Education and Scientific Methods (IJARESM), ISSN: 2455-6211, Volume 8, Issue 7, July 2020.
6. Vedic cooking for long life. https://vedichindustan.org/vedic-cooking-long-life/ (last accessed: May 2023)
7. NPTEL Course by Santanu Chattopadhyay, Microprocessors and Microcontrollers, IIT Kharagpur, 2023. https://nptel.ac.in/courses/108105102. (last accessed: May 2023)

For 8085 pin diagram

For 8086 pin diagram

4 Assembly Language Programming

UNIT SPECIFICS

The following aspects are discussed in this unit:

- Assembly language generic structures;
- Assembler directives, procedures and macros;
- Assembly language programs involving arithmetic, logical, branch and call instructions;
- Programs for evaluation of arithmetic expressions, string manipulation, and sorting.

The practical applications of the topics are presented for the purpose of fostering greater curiosity and creativity and enhancing problem-solving skills. In addition to a large number of multiple-choice questions and short- and long-answer questions marked in two categories according to the lower and higher levels of Bloom's taxonomy, the unit provides practice assignments in the form of numerical problems, a list of references, and suggested readings. It is crucial to note that several QR codes, which may be scanned for further information on various topics of interest, have been included in different parts and can be used to obtain necessary supporting data.

The related practical based on the content is followed by a "Know More" section on the topic. This section has been carefully constructed such that the supplementary information it contains is valuable to the book's readers. This section focuses primarily on the contributions of Indian innovators to the development of computer system organization and history of instruction set architecture. Indian practices of yoga and pranayam are also discussed for mind-body healing to achieve good health.

RATIONALE

This chapter examines the fundamental ideas behind assembly language, as well as its structure, generic concepts, and terminology, using the open-source NASM assembly programming language. The necessity of assembly language from the standpoint of hardware developers is discussed. The examination of the generic semantics of assembly languages lays the foundation for writing simple to complicated programmes in assembly language. This chapter explains the use of various types of instructions for writing the assembly language programs. From the basic program to advanced programs such as the assembly program involving arithmetic, logical, branch and call instructions, evaluating arithmetic expressions, string manipulation, and sorting are discussed in this chapter. This chapter serves as an introduction and lays the foundation for a more in-depth study of instruction sets and assembly languages.

PRE-REQUISITE

Microprocessor Architecture (Unit-III)

Digital Electronics: Number systems binary, octal, and hexadecimal (Polytechnic Engineering)

Operating System: Basics of system call, kernel etc. in Linux operating system

UNIT OUTCOMES

List of outcomes of this unit is as follows:

U4-O1: Describe role of assembly language programming in processor design

U4-O2: Describe the key features of writing simple assembly programs

U4-O3: Explain assembler directives

U4-O4: Explain the importance of procedures and macros

U4-O5: Design principles of writing complex assembly programs

Unit-4 Outcomes	EXPECTED MAPPING WITH COURSE OUTCOMES (1- Weak Correlation; 2- Medium Correlation; 3- Strong Correlation)				
	CO-1	CO-2	CO-3	CO-4	CO-5
U4-O1	3	3	3	1	2
U4-O2	3	1	2	1	2
U4-O3	2	2	3	1	2
U4-O4	3	3	3	3	2
U4-O5	3	3	3	2	3

4.1 INTRODUCTION

The assembly language simplifies program development. The programmer can write a program for hardware of computer systems. Assembly language is instruction set architecture (ISA) and assembler-specific low-level programming. Assembly language programmes comprise of assembly statements. Each computer instruction is a textual identifier like "ADD", "SUB", "LOAD", etc. Assembly language programming uses all symbolic names and their rules. Each instruction also includes a list of operands with their values or locations. The values of the operands are either numeric or are stored in registers or memory.

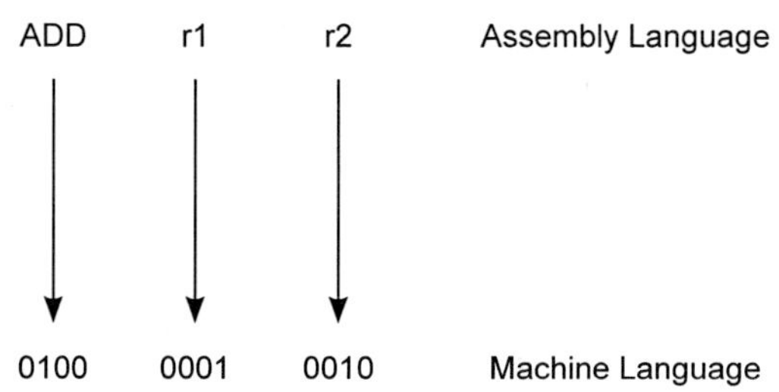

Fig. 4.1: Assembly language ADD instruction representation in machine language

Assembly language programmes are converted into machine instructions by assemblers. Utility programmes, such as the assembler programmes, are included in computer system software. Assemblers, like other software, are stored as machine instructions in computer memory. Machine instructions are made up of binary patterns. It is challenging to programme using such structures. Therefore, the symbolic names reflect binary code patterns in assembly language.

The programmer runs the assembler after composing the assembly language program to convert it into a computer-executable machine language programme. Fig 4.1 shows an example of assembly language instruction, i.e., ADD r1, r2 and the machine language instruction that might be generated from it. This ADD instruction performs addition of values stored in registers r1 and r2 and stores result in register r1.

Compare NASM with MASM and GAS Assembly Languages

The Assembly language instructions are in human readable form and elegant written representation of the machine code. It makes writing programmes much easier, neatly used. However, programming is tedious because of the small amount of work done by each instruction and the instructions available to the programmer differ from machine to machine.

If a programmer wants to run a program on a different type of computer, the program had to be completely rewritten in the new computer's assembly language.

In practice, standalone assembly programmes can be written and converted to executables using an assembler. Both C and C++ have the ability to include pieces of assembly code. The second option is the more common choice. The combined programming is then converted by the compiler into machine code. Assembly languages offer a number of benefits. Assembly code is expressive in the same way that machine code is, and the reason for this is because each line represents one machine instruction.

Keyboard input stores user programmes in memory or on a hard disc. The user programme is now lines of alphanumeric characters. The assembler programme analyses the user programme and builds a machine-language programme with patterns of 0s and 1s that the computer will execute. Source programmes are user programmes in alphanumeric text format, while object programmes are machine-language programmes. Computer assembly language may or may not discriminate between capital and lower-case letters.

The assembler stores object programmes on the hard drive. Loading the object programme into main memory is required for execution. This necessitates the presence of a loader utility programme in memory. When the loader is run, it transports the machine-language programme from the hard drive to memory. The programme length and memory address must be known to the loader. The assembler puts this information in a header before the object code. After loading the object code, the loader branches to the first instruction, such as START. The address is placed in the object code header by the assembler for the loader to use at runtime.

Online compiler for Assembly Language Programs

In this chapter, assembly program instructions are based on Intel 32 processors. There are various machine encodings for the same instruction. The following assemblers are widely used for assembly programming:

- Microsoft Assembler (MASM)
- Borland Turbo Assembler (TASM)
- GNU assembler (GAS)
- NASM assembler

In this chapter, all the assembly language programs are discussed using NASM assembler. NASM is free to download on both Linux and Windows operating systems. NASM is an Intel x86 architecture assembler and disassembler. It is a popular option for low-level programming and is commonly used in the design of operating systems, device drivers, and other system-level programming activities. In this chapter, basic syntax and instruction formats of NASM are demonstrated that are used for the discussed programs. NASM is well documented. The advanced programs can be designed by following the QR codes and references discussed in this chapter.

4.2 ASSEMBLY LANGUAGE PROGRAMS

Ubuntu operating system is free to download and its continuous support is available. So the NASM assembler is installed on the Ubuntu operating system. The following steps can be followed to start writing assembly programs with NASM assembler.

Learn NASM Assembly Language

1. Install 64 bit ubuntu on desktop or laptop systems (if your system is 64-bit)
2. Then type the command in the terminal of ubuntu to install NASM

sudo apt-get -y install nasm

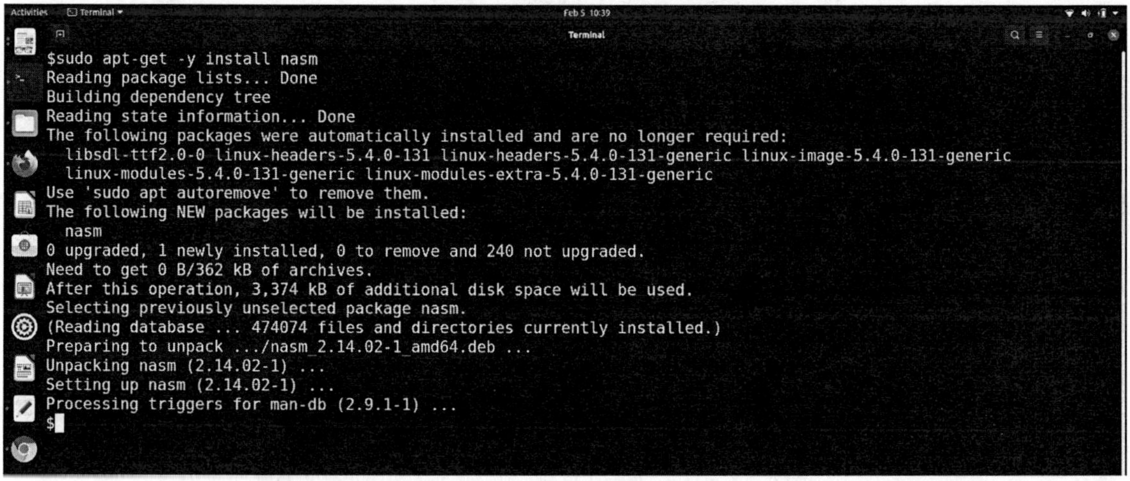

3. After installation, the NASM installation location can be checked by the following command

whereis nasm

4. You can check the version of installed nasm by using the command

nasm –version

5. If you want clear the terminal screen, use the command

clear

```
Terminal
$nasm --version
NASM version 2.14.02
$clear
```

6. The present working directory of the terminal can be checked as

pwd

```
Terminal
$pwd
/home/user
$
```

7. Now you can start to write assembly language program in geditor. Type the following command to check whether gedit is installed or not

sudo apt-get install gedit

```
Terminal
$sudo apt-get install gedit
[sudo] password for user:
Reading package lists... Done
Building dependency tree
Reading state information... Done
gedit is already the newest version (3.36.2-0ubuntu1).
The following package was automatically installed and is no longer required:
  libsdl-ttf2.0-0
Use 'sudo apt autoremove' to remove it.
0 upgraded, 0 newly installed, 0 to remove and 247 not upgraded.
$
```

Enter the system password to start the installation. If it is already installed, then you get the message that gedit is already installed as shown in the screenshot. The next section covers writing the first assembly programme, its syntax, and how to run it.

4.2.1 First Assembly Program with NASM

Step 1: Open the terminal and type the command

gedit print_name.asm

```
Terminal
$gedit print_name.asm
```

Here print_name is the name of the program and .asm extension is used for the assembly program.

This command open the gedit window with program name print_name.asm

Step 2: Comments in assembly language begin with a semicolon (;). They are used to elaborate the details of program and syntax to enhance the readability and understanding of the program.

Write the details of the program what to perform and command to execute the program in the header by using the comments with syntax ;

To learn NASM installation through GUI

However, this is an optional step. In this chapter, all the program's details are mentioned in the beginning using comments.

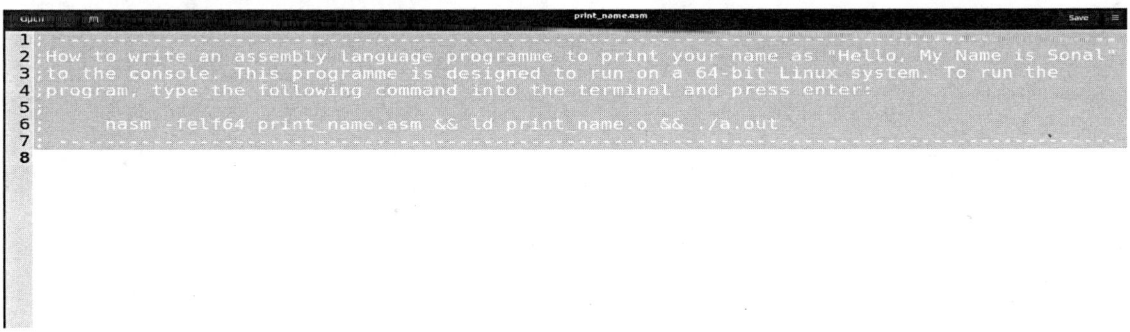

Step 3: Write the complete assembly language program. A generic assembly statement has three fields: a label, also known as an identifier of the instruction, a key, also known as an assembly instruction or a directive to the assembler, and a comment. These fields make up the general structure of an assembly statement. These three fields are completely optional. Nevertheless, at least one of these fields is required for every assembly statement to be valid. These are explained in detail in subsequent steps.

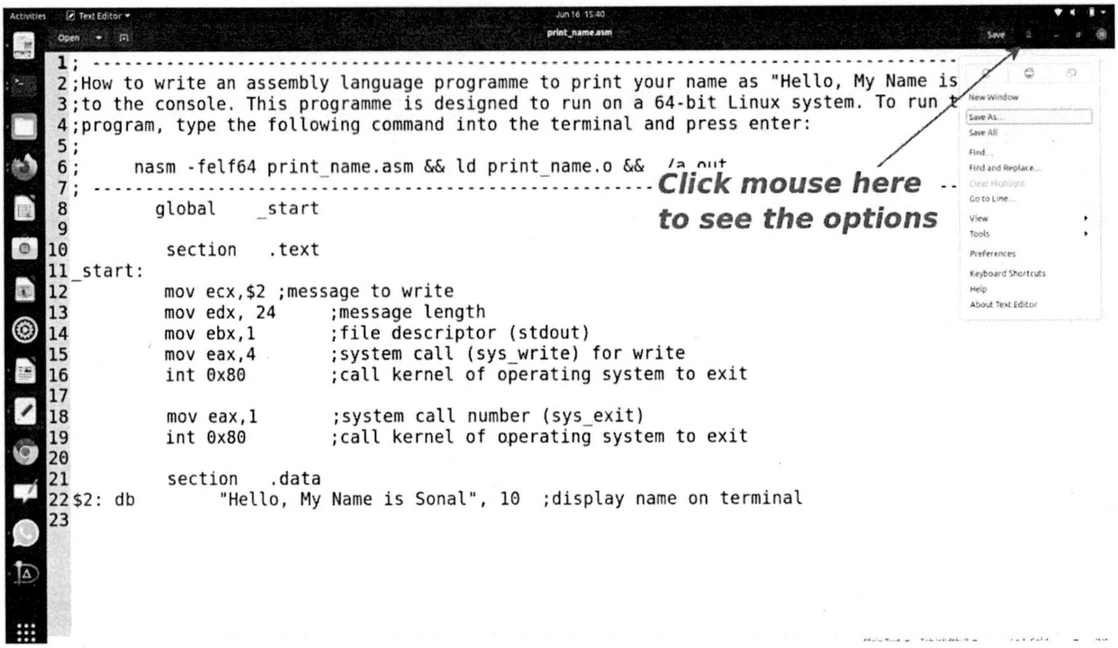

Step 4: You can save the program with keys ctrl+s or can save the program with a different name by using the keys ctrl+shift+s keys together as available in the keyboard. Alternatively, you can click on the three lines as displayed in right side of above screenshot by using the mouse cursor and you will see the options to apply different options. For save as, you will get the following options:

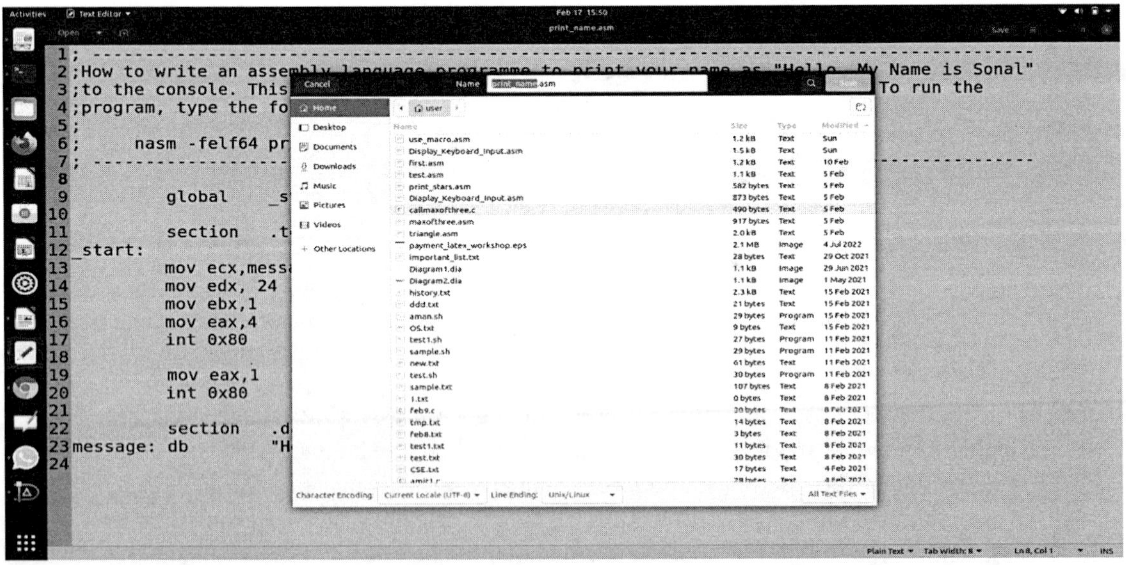

Step 5: On clicking save as, you will get the option to rename the program and display the location where it will be saved. Here, you have the option to change the save location as well.

Step 6: A label is a textual identifier of an assembly statement. Labels are used to specify the branch jump location while implementing branch instructions. For example, a label can be shown as follows.

label: add r1, r2

After the label and colon, an assembly instruction "add" is written and given a list of operands, i.e., r1, r2. A label can consist of valid alpha-numeric characters [a – z][A – Z][0 – 9]. However, a label cannot start with a digit. In the following screenshot of print_name.asm program labels are highlighted in line number 12 and 23.

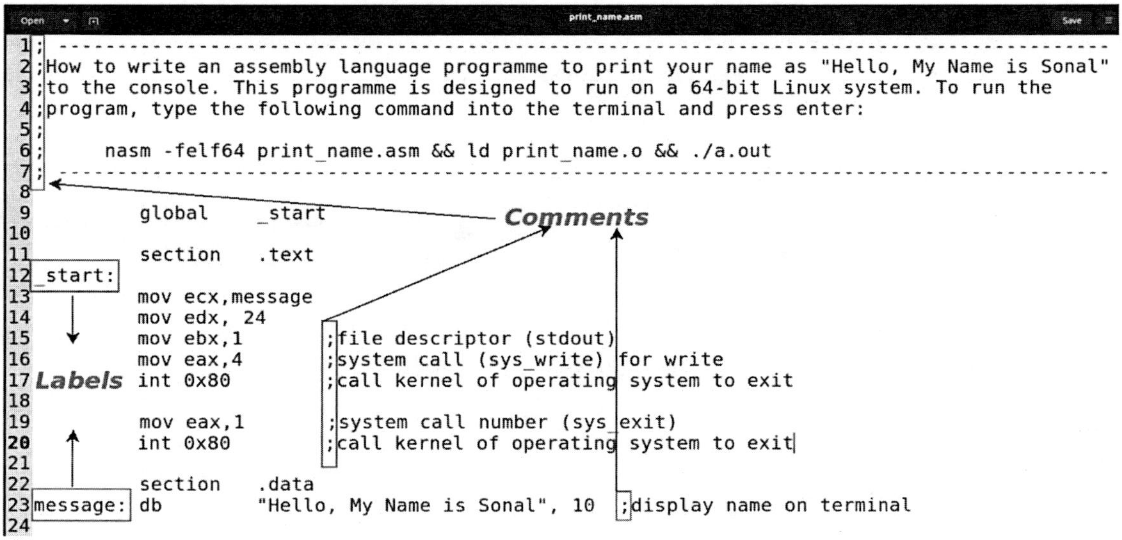

Step 7: The linker searches for the statement global _start. Basically, _start tells linker the entry point of the program.

Step 8: The assembler directive starts with a period (.), It is used to start a new section or declare a constant. The directive accepts a list of parameters. Regular assembly instructions start with letters.

Sections: The following three different sections are used in assembly program:

- **data section:** The data and constants are declared/initialized in the data section. This data does not change at runtime. This section is declared as

  section .data

- **bss section:** The variables are declared in bss section. This section is declared as

  section .bss

- **text section:** This section begins with declaration of global _start to tell the kernel that program execution begins here. The actual code is written after a label _start as shown below:

```
section .text
global _start
_start:
```

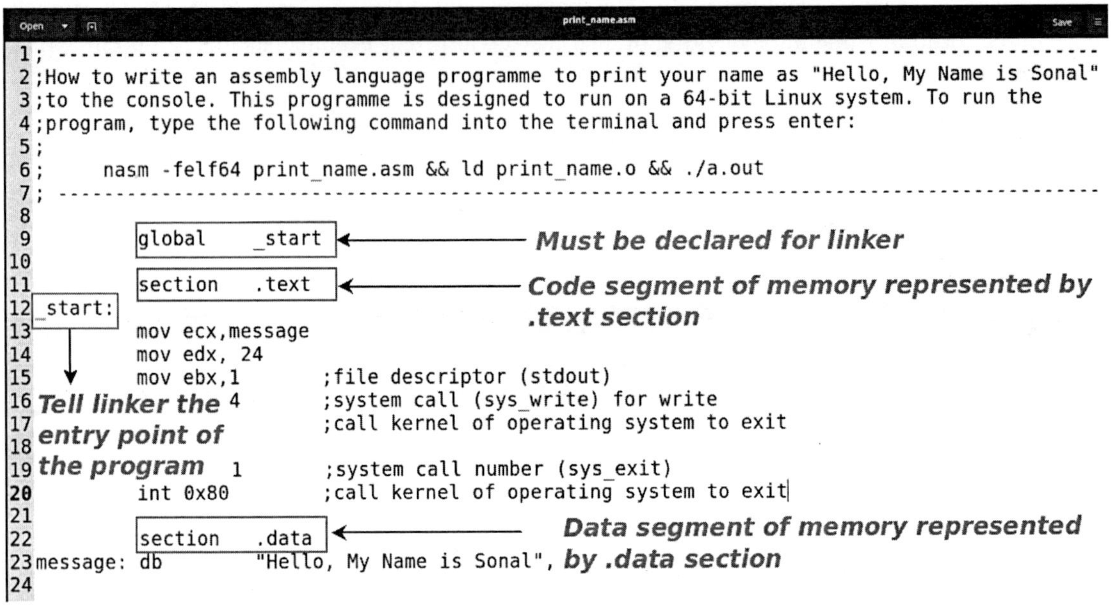

Step 9: The specialised instructions are used for system calls to transfer control from a user level program to the system call such as int 0x80 to call operating system kernel to exit.

Step 10: Four 32-bit data registers called "EAX", "EBX", "ECX", and "EDX" are utilised for various operations like arithmetic, logic, and others. The "AX", "BX", "CX", and "DX" are 16-bit data registers. "AH", "AL", "BH", "BL", "CH", "CL", "DH", and "DL" may be used as eight 8-bit data registers. These registers hold system call arguments.

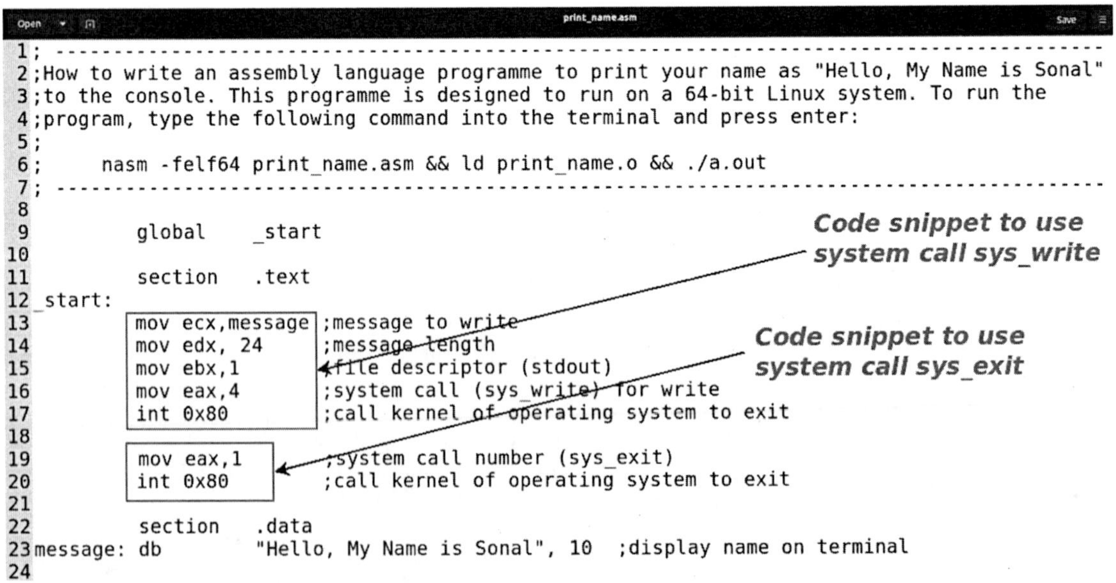

The characteristics of these registers are as follows:

- "AX" is used as an accumulator.

- "BX" is used as a base register for indexed addressing.
- "CX" is used as a count register for count in iterative operations.
- "DX" is used as a data register.

Each syscall and its corresponding number (the one to save in EAX before calling int 0x80) can be found in the file /usr/include/asm-generic/unistd.h.

Step 10: NASM uses define assembler directive to reserve/initialize bytes in storage space such as DB (Define Byte) allocates 1 byte.

Step 11: The following command is used to run the program. Only the name of the program (in the given example print_name.asm is program name) will be changed, the rest of the command will be the same.

nasm -felf64 print_name.asm && ld print_name.o && ./a.out

Step 12: Display output of the program print_name.asm on the terminal

```
$nasm -felf64 print_name.asm && ld print_name.o && ./a.out
Hello, My Name is Sonal
$
```

4.3 ASSEMBLER DIRECTIVES

Assembler directives are used to supply data to the source program. For example, the EQU directive is used for defining constants.

CONSTANT_NAME EQU expression

Suppose that the name YEAR is used to represent the value 2023.

YEAR EQU 2023

During the translation of a source programme into an object programme, the assembler replaces the name YEAR with the value 2023 wherever it occurs in the programme. Such statements are called assembler directives. The following statements illustrates the use of YEAR in the program:

mov ecx, YEAR
cmp eax, YEAR

Program 4.1: use_directive.asm

Write an assembly language program to illustrate the use of the EQU directive and print messages on the terminal.

```
; ---------------------------------------------------------------------------------
;How to write an assembly language programme to print the message
;"Hello, programmers!
;Start playing with Assembly. It is a language like all other languages!
;Practice makes you perfect..."
;using assembler directives to the console. This programme is designed to run on a 64-bit
;Linux system. To run the program, type the following command into the terminal and
;press enter:
;
;     nasm -felf64 use_directive.asm && ld use_directive.o && ./a.out
: ---------------------------------------------------------------------------------
```

```

; Define assembler directives
SYS_EXIT equ 1
SYS_WRITE equ 4
STDIN equ 0
STDOUT equ 1

; program code begins here
        section .text
        global _start

_start:
        mov eax, SYS_WRITE
        mov ebx, STDOUT
        mov ecx, str1
        mov edx, len1
        int 0x80

        mov eax, SYS_WRITE
        mov ebx, STDOUT
        mov ecx, str2
        mov edx, len2
        int 0x80

        mov eax, SYS_WRITE
        mov ebx, STDOUT
        mov ecx, str3
        mov edx, len3
        int 0x80

        mov eax, SYS_EXIT
        int 0x80 ;call kernel

        section .data
str1:   db 'Hello, programmers!',0xA,0xD
len1:   equ $- str1
str2:   db 'Start playing with Assembly. It is a language like all other languages!', 0xA,0xD
len2:   equ $- str2
str3:   db 'Practice makes you perfect...', 0xA,0xD
len3:   equ $- str3
```

Output:

```
Terminal
$nasm -felf64 use_directive.asm && ld use_directive.o && ./a.out
Hello, programmers!
Start playing with Assembly. It is a language like all other languages!
Practice makes you perfect...
$
```

4.4 PROCEDURES AND MACROS

When a programme repeats a set of instructions. There are two methods to avoid repetition. One is to develop a procedure with a specific set of instructions and call upon it whenever needed. The stack stores the return address of the procedure. This procedure's invocation and return cause overhead time. Nonetheless, this is minimal for large group of instruction. Procedures are not recommended for small groups of instructions since overhead and execution time are equivalent in this case. Macros are preferred for simple instructions. When a macro is invoked, the assembler generates machine codes for instruction. The process of calling and returning macro is instant. Each macro call generates inline code, which consumes extra memory.

4.4.1 Procedures

When a particular sequence of instructions are repeated in different points in a program. These sequences of instructions in the program can be written as a "subprogram" called a procedure. The "call" instruction, together with the beginning address of the procedure in memory, may be used to carry out the execution of this series of instructions at each and every time. At the end of the procedure, there is a "ret" instruction, which causes the execution to proceed to the next instruction in the main program.

The procedures can be "nested" such that one procedure invokes another as part of its instruction sequence. The benefits and drawbacks of the procedure are:

Advantage:

1. The machine codes for the group of instructions within the procedure only need to be loaded once into memory.

Disadvantage:

1. The stack is required for procedure storage.
2. There is some timing overhead. The time it takes to invoke the procedure and then return to the programme that invoked it.

Program 4.2: procedure.asm

Write an assembly language program using procedure sub to subtract the numbers stored in ECX and EDX registers. The output is stored in EAX register.

```
; ------------------------------------------------------------------------------
;How to write an assembly language programme to perform the subtraction of numbers
;8 and 3 by calling a procedure sub. Display the result on the terminal.
;This programme is designed to run on a 64-bit Linux system. To run the
;program, type the following command into the terminal and press enter:
;
;     nasm -felf64 procedure.asm && ld procedure.o && ./a.out
; ------------------------------------------------------------------------------

        section .text
        global _start
_start:
        mov ecx, 8
        sub ecx, 0
        mov edx, 3
        sub edx, 0
        call sub            ;call sub procedure

        mov [res], eax
        mov ecx, msg
        mov edx, len
        mov ebx,1           ;file descriptor (stdout)
        mov eax,4           ;system call number (sys_write)
        int 0x80            ;call kernel
```

```
        mov ecx, res
        mov edx, 1
        mov ebx, 1          ;file descriptor (stdout)
        mov eax, 4          ;system call number (sys_write)
        int 0x80            ;call kernel

        mov ecx,newline     ;message to write
        mov edx,nlen        ;message length
        mov ebx,1           ;file descriptor (stdout)
        mov eax,4           ;system call number (sys_write)
        int 0x80            ;call kernel


        mov eax,1           ;system call number (sys_exit)
        int 0x80            ;call kernel

sub:
        mov eax, ecx
        sub eax, edx
        add eax, '0'
        ret

        section .data
msg: db "Subtraction using procedure, the output of 8-3 =", 0xA,0xD
len: equ $- msg
newline:  db  " ", 0xa      ; for the newline by the end of the program
nlen:     equ $ - newline   ; length of message

        segment .bss
        res resb 1

```

Output:

```
$nasm -felf64 procedure.asm && ld procedure.o && ./a.out
Subtraction using procedure, the output of 8-3 =
5
$
```

4.4.2 Macros

When the repeating set of instructions is too short, a "macro" is used instead of a procedure. A macro is a set of instructions that is named at the start of the program. The assembler inserts the specified block of instructions in lieu of "call" every time the "macro" is invoked. In other words, the macro call is a shorthand statement that informs the assembler, every time a macro name appears in the programme, it is replaced by the group of instructions defined as that macro at the start of the programme.

Assemblers generate machine codes for each macro call. Instructions replace macros in expansion. Since the generated machine codes are in line with the programme, the assembler does not need to go away and return. Thus, using a macro eliminates procedure call and return overhead.

The drawback of producing in-line code each time a macro is invoked is that the programme will consume more memory than if a procedure is used. Table 4.1 shows a comparison between procedures and macros.

Table 4.1: Difference between procedure and macro

S. No.	Procedure	Macro
1	Accessed during program execution through "call" and "ret" instructions.	Accessible during assembly program with the name of defined macro.
2	Machine code for instructions is stored in memory only once.	When a macro is called, machine code is generated for the instructions.
3	Procedures require less memory.	More memory is required when using macros.
4	Parameters can be passed in registers, memory locations, or stack.	Parameters provided as part of the macro statement.

Macro sequences execute more quickly than procedures since there are not any CALL and RET instructions to execute. The macro instructions are inserted into the code by the assembler when it is executed. This process is known as macro expansion. The macro prototype is written as follows.

```
%macro macro_name number_of_params
<macro body>
%endmacro
```

Where macro_name specifies the macro's name, number_of_params specifies the number of parameters.

Program 4.3: use_macro.asm

```
;---------------------------------------------------------------------------------------
;How to write an assembly language programme to print the message
;"Hello, programmers!
;Start playing with Assembly. It is a language like all other languages!
;Practice makes you perfect..."
;to the console. This programme is designed to run on a 64-bit Linux system. To run the
;program, type the following command into the terminal and press enter:
;
;     nasm -felf64 use_macro.asm && ld use_macro.o && ./a.out
;---------------------------------------------------------------------------------------

; A macro with two parameters, implements the write system call
%macro display_message 2
        mov eax, 4
        mov ebx, 1
        mov ecx, %1
        mov edx, %2
        int 80h
%endmacro

        section .text
        global _start

_start:
        display_message str1, len1
        display_message str2, len2
        display_message str3, len3

```

```
        mov eax,1 ;system call (sys_exit)
        int 0x80  ;call kernel

        section .data
str1:   db 'Hello, programmers!',0xA,0xD
len1:   equ $- str1
str2:   db 'Start playing with Assembly. It is a language like all other languages!', 0xA,0xD
len2:   equ $- str2
str3:   db 'Practice makes you perfect...', 0xA,0xD
len3:   equ $- str3
```

Output:

```
$nasm -felf64 use_macro.asm && ld use_macro.o && ./a.out
Hello, programmers!
Start playing with Assembly. It is a language like all other languages!
Practice makes you perfect...
$
```

4.5 ASSEMBLY PROGRAMS

Following subsections explain simple to complicated programs to demonstrate various types of instructions and their structure used in NASM.

For simple programs in NASM

4.5.1 Simple Programs

The simple programs use arithmetic operations such as add, subtract, multiply, etc. The syntax of the arithmetic instructions and data transfer are as follows:

Program 4.4: display_keyboard_input.asm

```
; ------------------------------------------------------------------------------------------
;How to write an assembly language programme to read a number from the keyboard and display it
;on the console screen. This programme is designed to run on a 64-bit Linux system. To run the
;program, type the following command into the terminal and press enter:
;
;     nasm -felf64 display_keyboard_input.asm && ld display_keyboard_input.o && ./a.out
; ------------------------------------------------------------------------------------------

; Define assembler directives
SYS_EXIT equ 1
SYS_WRITE equ 4
STDOUT equ 1


%macro keyboard_input 2
        mov eax, SYS_WRITE
        mov ebx, STDOUT
        mov ecx, %1
        mov edx, %2
        int 80h
%endmacro

        ;Code segment
        section .text
        global _start

_start:

```

```
        keyboard_input userMsg, lenUserMsg

        ;Read and store the user input
        mov eax, 3
        mov ebx, 2
        mov ecx, num
        mov edx, 8 ; up to 8 bytes of data can store
        int 80h

        ;Output the message 'The entered number is: '
        keyboard_input dispMsg, lenDispMsg

        ;Output the number entered
        keyboard_input num, 8

        mov eax, SYS_EXIT                  ; Exit
        mov ebx, 0
        int 80h

        ;Data segment
        section .data
userMsg: db 'Please enter a number: '      ;Ask the user to enter a number
lenUserMsg: equ $-userMsg                  ;The length of the message
dispMsg: db 'You have entered: '
lenDispMsg: equ $-dispMsg

        section .bss                       ;Uninitialized data
        num resb 8
```

Output:

```
Terminal
$nasm -felf64 display_keyboard_input.asm && ld display_keyboard_input.o && ./a.out
Please enter a number: 1234567
You have entered: 1234567
$
```

4.5.2 Arithmetic Programs

Arithmetic instructions perform addition, subtraction, multiplication, and division operations. The syntax of arithmetic instructions and data transfer are as follows.

For multiplication and division programs

Table 4.2: List of arithmetic operations

Operation	Operands	Comments
ADD/SUB	destination, source	Perform addition/subtraction of numbers stored in destination and source registers. Result stores in the destination register.
MUL/IMUL	multiplier	multiply unsigned/signed data
DIV/IDIV	Divisor	division on unsigned/signed data
INC/DEC	destination	incrementing/decrementing an operand by one

Program 4.5: add_sub.asm

```
; ----------------------------------------------------------------------------------------
;How to write an assembly language programme to add and sub the values 5 and 3.
;What is the value in AL register after performing addition and subtraction operation.
;This programme is designed to run on a 64-bit Linux system. To run the
;program, type the following command into the terminal and press enter:
;
;     nasm -felf64 add_sub.asm && ld add_sub.o && ./a.out
; ----------------------------------------------------------------------------------------

        section .text
        global _start
_start:                     ;tell linker entry point

        mov ecx,message ;message to write
        mov edx,len     ;message length
        mov ebx,1       ;file descriptor (stdout)
        mov eax,4       ;system call number (sys_write)
        int 0x80        ;call kernel

        mov al, 5       ;store 5 in the al
        mov bl, 3       ;store 3 in the bl
        add al, bl      ;add al and bl registers, the output is stored in al register
        add al, byte '0';converting decimal to ascii
        mov [result], al

        mov eax, 4
        mov ebx, 1
        mov ecx, result
        int 0x80        ;call kernel

        mov ecx,newline ;message to write
        mov edx,nlen    ;message length
        mov ebx,1       ;file descriptor (stdout)
        mov eax,4       ;system call number (sys_write)
        int 0x80        ;call kernel

        mov ecx,message1 ;message to write
        mov edx,len1    ;message length
        mov ebx,1       ;file descriptor (stdout)
        mov eax,4       ;system call number (sys_write)
        int 0x80        ;call kernel

        mov al, 5       ;store 5 in the al
        mov bl, 3       ;store 3 in the bl
        sub al, bl      ;sub al and bl registers, the output is stored in al register
        add al, byte '0';converting decimal to ascii
        mov [result], al

        mov eax, 4
        mov ebx, 1
        mov ecx, result
        int 0x80        ;call kernel


        mov ecx,newline ;message to write
        mov edx,nlen    ;message length
        mov ebx,1       ;file descriptor (stdout)
        mov eax,4       ;system call number (sys_write)
        int 0x80        ;call kernel


        mov eax,1       ;system call number (sys_exit)
```

```
        int 0x80        ;call kernel

        section .data
message:  db  "Addition of (5+3):", 0xa       ; display the message on the terminal
len:      equ $ - message                      ; length of message

message1:  db  "Subtraction of (5-3):", 0xa      ; display the message on the terminal
len1:      equ $ - message1                    ; length of message

newline:  db  " ", 0xa      ; for the newline by the end of the program
nlen:     equ $ - newline   ; length of message

        section .bss
result: resb 1
```

Output:

```
$nasm -felf64 add_sub.asm && ld add_sub.o && ./a.out
Addition of (5+3):
8
Subtraction of (5-3):
2
$
```

4.5.3 Logical Instructions

Logical instructions are used for data processing such as compute bitwise or, and, exclusive or, and not instructions.

Table 4.3: List of logical operations

Operation	Operands	Comments
AND/OR/XOR	operand 1, operand 2	Perform logical AND/OR/XOR operation between operand 1 and operand 2. Result is stored in operand 1
NOT	operand 1	Perform logical NOT operation and result store in operand 1

Program 4.6: logical_xor_operation.asm

```
;------------------------------------------------------------------------------------
;How to write an assembly language programme to store the value 5 and 3 in the AL and the BL
;register respectively. What is the value in AL register after performing XOR AL, BL operation.
;This programme is designed to run on a 64-bit Linux system. To run the
;program, type the following command into the terminal and press enter:
;
;     nasm -felf64 logical_xor_operation.asm && ld logical_xor_operation.o && ./a.out
;------------------------------------------------------------------------------------

        section .text
        global _start    ;must be declared for using gcc
_start:                  ;tell linker entry point

        mov eax,4        ;system call number (sys_write)
        mov ebx,1        ;file descriptor (stdout)
        mov ecx,message  ;message to write
        mov edx,len      ;message length
        int 0x80         ;call kernel

        mov al, 5        ;store 5 in the al
```

```
        mov bl, 3        ;store 3 in the bl
        xor al, bl       ;xor al and bl registers, the output is stored in al register
        add al, byte '0';converting decimal to ascii
        mov [result], al

        mov eax, 4
        mov ebx, 1
        mov ecx, result
        int 0x80         ;call kernel


        mov eax,4        ;system call number (sys_write)
        mov ebx,1        ;file descriptor (stdout)
        mov ecx,newline  ;message to write
        mov edx,nlen     ;message length
        int 0x80         ;call kernel


        mov eax,1        ;system call number (sys_exit)
        int 0x80         ;call kernel

        section .data
message:  db  "Output of (5 XOR 3):", 0xa      ; display the message on the terminal
len:      equ $ - message                      ; length of message

newline:  db  " ", 0xa      ; for the newline by the end of the program
nlen:     equ $ - newline   ; length of message

        section .bss
result: resb 1
```

Output:

```
Terminal
$nasm -felf64 logical_xor_operation.asm && ld logical_xor_operation.o && ./a.out
Output of (5 XOR 3):
6
$
```

4.5.4 Branch Instructions

Branch instructions jump the program execution control to different parts of the program. The "for" loops and "if-then-else" statements are the examples of the branch instructions. Branch instructions can be unconditional or conditional jump.

For more programs of branch instructions

1. In unconditional jump, the "JMP" instruction transfers programme execution control to a different point of an instruction, bypassing the present execution of the instruction.
2. In conditional jump, a "CMP" instruction checks the condition and uses an appropriate jump instruction from the available range of jump instructions in the program based on the condition. The conditional jump interrupts the sequential execution flow and transfers control to a new location.

The "CMP" instruction is used in conjunction with the conditional jump instruction. It subtracts one operand from the other to determine if the operands are equal.

CMP destination, sourceC

The destination operand may be either a register or memory, while the source operand can be either constant (instant) data, a register, or memory. As an example,

```
CMP DX, 00      ; Compare the DX value with zero
JE L7           ; If yes, then jump to label L7
.
.
L7: ...
```

Program 4.7: array_sum.asm

```
;------------------------------------------------------------------------------------
;Write an assembly language program to store four values in array x: 1, 4, 3, and 1.
;Perform the addition of the array elements and display the sum.
;This programme is designed to run on a 64-bit Linux system. To run the
;program, type the following command into the terminal and press enter:
;
;     nasm -felf64 array_sum.asm && ld array_sum.o && ./a.out
; ----------------------------------------------------------------------------------

; Define assembler directives
SYS_EXIT equ 1
SYS_WRITE equ 4
STDOUT equ 1


%macro display_message 2
        mov eax, SYS_WRITE
        mov ebx, STDOUT
        mov ecx, %1
        mov edx, %2
        int 80h
%endmacro


        section .text
        global _start      ;must be declared for linker (ld)
_start:

        mov eax,4       ;number bytes to be summed
        mov ebx,0       ;EBX will store the sum
        mov ecx, x      ;ECX will point to the current element to be summed

top:    add ebx, [ecx]
        add ecx,1        ;move pointer to next element
        dec eax          ;decrement counter
        jnz top          ;if counter not 0, then loop again

done:
        add ebx, '0'
        mov [sum], ebx ;done, store result in "sum"

        display_message msg, len

        display_message sum, 1

        display_message newline, nlen

```

```
        mov eax, STDOUT ;system call number (sys_exit)
        int 0x80 ;call kernel

        section .data
msg db "The sum of array elements is: ", 0xA,0xD
len equ $- msg

newline:  db  " ", 0xa      ; for the newline by the end of the program
nlen:      equ $ - newline   ; length of message

        global x
x:
db 1
db 4
db 3
db 1
sum:
db 0

```

Output:

```
$nasm -felf64 array_sum.asm && ld array_sum.o && ./a.out
The sum of array elements is:
9
$
```

4.5.5 Evaluation of Arithmetic Expressions

Infix notation is used to describe expressions, in which arithmetic operators like as addition, subtraction, multiplication, division, and so on are written between two operands, i.e., "A + B". To distinguish "(A + B)*C" from "A + (B * C)", this notation needs parentheses or operator precedence.

Program 4.8: evaluate_expression.asm

```
; ------------------------------------------------------------------------------------------
;How to write an assembly language programme to evaluate the expression 8/4+2x2-1
;What is the value in AL register after evaluating given expression.
;This programme is designed to run on a 64-bit Linux system. To run the
;program, type the following command into the terminal and press enter:
;
;     nasm -felf64 evaluate_expression.asm && ld evaluate_expression.o && ./a.out
; ------------------------------------------------------------------------------------------

        section .text
        global _start
_start:                     ;tell linker entry point

        mov ecx,message ;message to write
        mov edx,len     ;message length
        mov ebx,1       ;file descriptor (stdout)
        mov eax,4       ;system call number (sys_write)
        int 0x80        ;call kernel

        mov al, 8       ;store 8 in the al
        mov bl, 4       ;store 4 in the bl
```

```
        div bl          ;divide dividend stored in al by divisor stored in bl register
        add al, 2       ;add intermediate result stored in al with value 2
        mov cl, 2
        mul cl          ;divide multiplicand stored in al by multiplier stored in bl register
        sub al, 1       ;subtract intermediate result stored in al with value 1
        add al, byte '0';converting decimal to ascii
        mov [result], al

        mov eax, 4
        mov ebx, 1
        mov ecx, result
        int 0x80        ;call kernel

        mov ecx,newline ;message to write
        mov edx,nlen    ;message length
        mov ebx,1       ;file descriptor (stdout)
        mov eax,4       ;system call number (sys_write)
        int 0x80        ;call kernel


        mov eax,1       ;system call number (sys_exit)
        int 0x80        ;call kernel

        section .data
message:  db  "The output of arithmetic expression (8/4+2x2-1) is :", 0xa ;display message
len:      equ $ - message                       ; length of message

newline:  db  " ", 0xa      ; for the newline by the end of the program
nlen:     equ $ - newline   ; length of message

        section .bss
result: resb 1              ;reserve 1 byte
```

Output:

```
Terminal
$nasm -felf64 evaluate_expression.asm && ld evaluate_expression.o && ./a.out
The output of arithmetic expression (8/4+2x2-1) is :
7
$
```

4.5.6 String Manipulation

String manipulation actions include copying the string, reversing the string, counting the characters, and so on [1]. String instructions for 32-bit information employ ESI and EDI registers to refer to the source and destination operands, respectively. However, for 16-bit data, the SI and DI registers are utilised to indicate the source and destination, respectively. String processing consists of five fundamental instructions.

- MOVS instruction transfers 1 Byte, Word, or Doubleword of data between memory locations.
- LOAD instruction retrieves memory-based data. AL register is loaded with a single byte operand, AX register is loaded with a single word operand, and EAX register is loaded with a doubleword operand.
- STOS instruction writes data from registers (AL, AX, or EAX) to memory.
- CMPS instruction compares two elements of memory-based data. Sizes of data include byte, word, and doubleword.

- SCAS instruction evaluates the contents of a register (AL, AX, or EAX) against those of a memory location.

Program 4.9: encrypt.asm

```
; ------------------------------------------------------------------------------------
;In cryptography, a caesar cipher encrypts a data by simply replacing each alphabet in it
;with a shift of two alphabets, so a will be substituted by c, b with d and so on.
;Write an assembly language program to encrypt the string 'assembler'.
;This programme is designed to run on a 64-bit Linux system. To run the
;program, type the following command into the terminal and press enter:
;
;     nasm -felf64 encrypt.asm && ld encrypt.o && ./a.out
; ------------------------------------------------------------------------------------


section .text
   global _start                ;must be declared for using gcc

_start:                         ;tell linker entry point
   mov  ecx, len
   mov  esi, s1
   mov  edi, s2

loop_continue:
   lodsb                        ; loads byte into the al register from memory
   add al, 02
   stosb                        ; stores byte from register to memory
   loop         loop_continue
   cld                          ; clear direction flag (DF)
   rep          movsb           ; moves 1 byte

   mov edx,20   ;message length
   mov ecx,s2   ;message to write
   mov ebx,1    ;file descriptor (stdout)
   mov eax,4    ;system call number (sys_write)
   int 0x80     ;call kernel

   mov ecx,newline ;message to write
   mov edx,nlen ;message length
   mov ebx,1    ;file descriptor (stdout)
   mov eax,4    ;system call number (sys_write)
   int 0x80     ;call kernel

   mov eax,1            ;system call number (sys_exit)
   int 0x80             ;call kernel

   section .data
s1 db 'assembler', 0    ;source
len equ $-s1

newline:  db  " ", 0xa      ; for the newline by the end of the program
nlen:     equ $ - newline   ; length of message

   section .bss
s2 resb 10              ;reserve 10 bytes for destination
```

Output:

```
Terminal
$nasm -felf64 encrypt.asm && ld encrypt.o && ./a.out
cuugodngt
$
```

4.5.7 Sorting

Sorting is an important and often used procedure in computer science. Sorting in NASM assembler may be accomplished by the use of numerous algorithms, including bubble sort, insertion sort, selection sort, and quicksort. The procedure of bubble sort is demonstrated in program 4.10.

Bubble sort compares adjacent components and swaps them if they are out of order. The list is traversed again and again until it is sorted.

Program 4.10: sorting_integers.asm

```
; -----------------------------------------------------------------------------
;Write an assembly language programme to sort unsorted items 9 8 7 6 5 4 3 2 1 0.
;The sorted elements list 0 1 2 3 4 5 6 7 8 9 should be displayed on the terminal.
;This programme is designed to run on a 64-bit Linux system. To run the program,
;type the following command into the terminal and press enter:
;
;     nasm -felf64 sorting_integers.asm && ld sorting_integers.o && ./a.out
; -----------------------------------------------------------------------------

section .text

startnew:

        mov ecx,newline
        mov edx,1
        mov eax,4
        mov ebx,1
        int 0x80
        ret

convert:
        mov ecx,[inp]
        mov bl,10
        mov al,cl
        sub al,30h

        cmp ch,10
        je converted
        mul bl
        sub ch,30h
        add al,ch

converted:
        mov byte[inp],al
        ret

```

```
takeinput:
        mov ecx,msg_element
        mov edx,length_msg_element
        mov eax,4
        mov ebx,1
        int 0x80

terminal_input:

        mov ecx,inp
        mov edx,3
        mov eax,3
        mov ebx,0
        int 0x80

        call convert

        ret

global _start
_start:

        mov ecx,num_elements
        mov edx,length_num_elements
        mov eax,4
        mov ebx,1
        int 0x80

        call terminal_input

        mov al,byte[inp]
        mov byte[n],al

        mov ebx,0
        mov bl,[n]
        mov edx,0
taking:
        push dx
        call takeinput
        mov al,byte[inp]
        mov edx,0
        pop dx
        mov byte[input+edx],al
        add dx,1
        mov bl,[n]
        cmp dl,bl
        jne taking

        mov edx,0
sort:
        mov bl,byte[input+eax]
        mov cl,byte[input+eax+1]
        cmp bl,cl
        jl no_swap
        mov byte[input+eax+1],bl
        mov byte[input+eax],cl
no_swap:
        add eax,1
        mov bl,byte[n]
        sub bl,1
```

```
        cmp al,bl
        jne sort
        mov eax,0
        add edx,1
        mov bl,byte[n]
        add bl,1
        cmp dl,bl
        jne sort

        call startnew

        mov ecx,sorted_list_msg
        mov edx,length_sorted_list_msg
        mov eax,4
        mov ebx,1
        int 0x80

        mov edx,0
        mov esi,0

output:

        push 29h
        mov ebx,0
        mov bl,byte[input+esi]
        mov ax,bx
        mov ebx,0
        mov bl,10
break:
        mov edx,0
        div bx
        add dl,30h
        push dx
        cmp al,0
        jne break

        mov edx,0
        pop dx

prints:

        mov byte[printdata],dl

        mov ecx,printdata
        mov edx,1
        mov eax,4
        mov ebx,1
        int 0x80

        mov edx,0
        pop dx
        cmp dl,29h
        jne prints

        mov ecx,space
        mov edx,1
        mov eax,4
        mov ebx,1
        int 0x80


        add esi,1
        mov ebx,0
        mov bl,byte[n]
        cmp esi,ebx
        jne output
```

```
        call startnew
        call startnew

        mov eax,1
        mov ebx,0
        int 0x80

section .bss
        input resb 100

section .data
        inp dd 30h
        temp db 30h
        space db 32
        newline db 10
        n db 30h
        printdata db 30h
        num_elements db "Enter the number of elements: ",32
        length_num_elements equ $-num_elements
        msg_element db "Enter the data: ",32
        length_msg_element equ $-msg_element
        sorted_list_msg db "Sorted elements list",10
        length_sorted_list_msg equ $-sorted_list_msg
```

Output:

```
$nasm -felf64 sorting_integers.asm && ld sorting_integers.o && ./a.out
Enter the number of elements:  10
Enter the data:  9
Enter the data:  8
Enter the data:  7
Enter the data:  6
Enter the data:  5
Enter the data:  4
Enter the data:  3
Enter the data:  2
Enter the data:  1
Enter the data:  0

Sorted elements list
0 1 2 3 4 5 6 7 8 9

$
```

UNIT SUMMARY

- Machine instructions can be coded in Assembler. In general, one statement in an assembly language programming equals to one machine instruction.
- An assembler converts programmes written in assembly language into machine code.
- Assembly languages are ISA and assembler-specific.
- Assembly language is used to design programs for the kernel and device drivers that support an operating system.
- Assembly languages help hardware designers comprehend ISA semantics. It provides direction for the design.
- NASM assembler is free to download on both Linux and Windows operating systems.

- NASM runs the program using the command "nasm -felf64 filename.asm && ld filename.o && ./a.out".
- An assembly program's data section initialises data, the bss section defines variables, and the text section contains the actual code.
- Assembler directives allow the programmer to specify other information needed to translate the source program into the object program. The EQU directive is used for defining constants.
- Procedure is defined in assembly language when a group of instructions repeated in the program and the size of these instructions are too long.
- When the repeated group of instructions is too short or not appropriate to be written as procedure, a "macro" is used.
- The group of instructions defined as macro in the beginning of the program. For each macro name in the program, replace it with machine codes for the group of instructions.
- The simple assembly programs perform simple arithmetic operations such as addition, subtraction, division, multiplication.
- Any arithmetic expression comprises more than one arithmetic operation. So these are complex assembly programs.
- Branch instructions jump the program execution control to different parts of the program. The "for" loops and "if-then-else" statements are the examples of the branch instructions.
- Assembly language programs are written for string manipulation. Such as copy string, reverse the string, count the characters, etc.

EXERCISES

Multiple Choice Questions

1. Assembler converts the programs written in __________ into machine instructions.
   (a) C language (b) C++ language
   (c) Assembly language (d) Python language
2. The __________ instruction performs the addition of two numbers.
   (a) MOV (b) ADD (c) SUB (d) DIV
3. The assembler directive Sum EQU 200 does __________
   (a) assigns value 200 to first occurrence of Sum
   (b) assigns value 200 to every occurrence of Sum
   (c) add 200 to its original address
   (d) assigns 200 bytes of memory starting the location of Sum
4. Assembly language is a __________ programming language specific to each instruction set architecture (ISA) and assembler.
   (a) high-level (b) middle-level (c) low-level (d) object-oriented

5. How do you use the comments in the NASM assembly language
   (a) semicolon (;)
   (b) percent sign (%)
   (c) forward slash (/)
   (d) comma (,)
6. Assembler automatically translates an assembly language program into a sequence of ________
   (a) byte code
   (b) binary numbers
   (c) special characters
   (d) machine instructions
7. Which of the following is the name of the assembler?
   (i) MASM (ii) TASM (iii) GAS (iv) NASM
   (a) (i), (iii), and (iv)
   (b) (i), (ii), and (iii)
   (c) only (i) and (ii)
   (d) all
8. When a particular sequence of instructions are repeated in different points in a program. These sequences of instructions in the program can be written as a "subprogram" called a ________.
   (a) directive (b) program (c) procedure (d) macro
9. Assembler stores the object program on the ________.
   (a) cache memory
   (b) primary memory
   (c) secondary memory
   (d) ROM memory
10. In procedure, ________ instruction executes sequence of instructions and ________ instruction returns execution to the next instruction in the program.
    (a) call, ret (b) begin, end (c) start, return (d) do, while
11. Which system call is used in NASM program for system exit
    (a) int 0×80 (b) mov eax, 4 (c) mov eax, 1 (d) mov ebx, 2
12. The ________ brings the object code into memory for execution.
    (a) linker (b) extractor (c) fetcher (d) loader
13. Which section does not use in NASM assembler
    (a) data (b) text (c) bss (d) code

ANSWERS													
1.	(c)	2.	(b)	3.	(b)	4.	(c)	5.	(a)	6.	(d)	7.	(d)
8.	(c)	9.	(c)	10.	(a)	11.	(c)	12.	(d)	13.	(d)		

Short and Long Answer Type Questions

Category-I

1. What is assembler?
2. List four popular assemblers.
3. What is assembly language programming?
4. What are machine instructions?

5. Define the assembler, loader, and linker.
6. List the number of logical operations used in NASM.
7. List the arithmetic operations can be performed in NASM.
8. Which addressing mode is preferable for accessing the elements of an array stored in consecutive memory locations?
9. What is the difference between the unconditional and conditional branches?
10. Give the example of two string manipulations operations.
11. What command do you use to run assembly language program in linux 64-bit computer?
12. What is the difference between high-level and low-level languages?
13. What is the meaning of system calls 1 and 4?
14. How do you use labels and comments in NASM?
15. Explain the utility of define byte (DB) in NASM?

Category-II

16. Explain the installation steps of NASM.
17. How are procedures and macros defined in NASM assembly language programmes? What is the difference between macros and procedures?
18. What is a nested procedure? List the benefits and drawbacks of procedure and macros.
19. What is an assembler directive? Explain with examples.
20. List the system calls available in the NASM directory.
21. Explain the CALL and RET instructions in procedures.

Numerical Problems

22. Display your name and parents name on the terminal using an assembly language program (ALP).
23. Write an ALP to subtract 12 from the number 40. Then, on the result, execute the NOT operation and show the result on the screen.
24. Write an ALP for the AND and OR logical operations on the integers 3 and 2 using macros.
25. Write an ALP for AND operation between the integers 5 and 2. Then, multiply the value by 4 to get the final result. What does the terminal show as the end result?
26. Write an ALP to divide the number 16 by the number 2. Show the result on the terminal.
27. Write an ALP using the branch instruction. If the number is greater than 5, perform a logical OR of 1 and 2; otherwise, perform a logical AND on the same numbers. Display the result on the terminal.
28. Write an ALP that will store the input element in an array and display it on the terminal. System calls should be written as procedures to facilitate their frequent use in the program.

PRACTICAL

Aim: Write an assembly language program to design an arithmetic calculator that can perform addition, subtraction, multiplication, and division operation. Compute the expressions (a + b) * 3 – c/d using NASM assembler. Where a = 8, b = 2, c = 4, and d = 1

Tools: NASM assembler [1]

Theory: Details of NASM assembler is already discussed in the chapter.

Procedure: Detailed instructions for installing Linux 64-bit on a computer are already covered in this chapter.

To learn NASM assembler programming

KNOW MORE

Innovations by Indian: As the leader of the Think Tank Team and a computer scientist and inventor, Pranav Mistry is best known for his contributions to SixthSense.

SixthSense is an innovative augmented reality (AR) technology that enables users to project a screen onto a wall by moving their fingers and controlling it with their fingertips in the air.

To know more about Pranav Mistry inventions

History of Instruction Set Architecture: The ARM and the x86 are popular instruction set architectures. ARM is an acronym for "Advanced RISC Machines." It is a well-known business located in Cambridge, United Kingdom. In 2012, approximately 90% of mobile devices were powered by ARM-based processors. Intel and AMD use x86 processors, which dominates over ninety percent of the desktop and laptop market. The instruction set of ARM is RISC, whereas the instruction set of x86 is CISC.

To know more about ARM and x86

Indian Yoga and Pranayam: Pranayama is the practice of controlling the breath. "Prana" is a person's breath or vital energy. The "ayama" technique allows the practitioner to manage prana, or the pranic energy that gives life [2].

Pranayama is the practise of controlling the respiration to connect the body and mind. Patanjali describes pranayama as a method for attaining higher states of consciousness. It is an essential component of yoga, a physical and mental health-promoting practice. "Prana" means life energy in Sanskrit, and "yama" means control [3].

Pranayama involves various breathing exercises and patterns. You intentionally inhale, exhale, and retain your breath in a particular order. Pranayama is used in conjunction with other yoga practices such as physical postures (asanas) and meditation (dhyana). Collectively, these practices account for many of the benefits of yoga. Pranayama is the ancient practice of regulating the timing, duration, and frequency of each breath and hold. It provides oxygen to the body while eliminating toxins. It balances the actions of the numerous pranas, resulting in a healthy body and mind.

The benefits of pranayama have been studied scientifically in the context of contemporary lifestyle. Thousands of years ago, India was the birthplace of yoga. With the expansion of yoga's scientific study, its therapeutic aspects are also being investigated. Yoga and pranayama may benefit health in a variety of ways, such as reducing tension, enhancing sleep quality, enhancing mindfulness, lowering high blood pressure, enhancing lung and brain function, the digestive system, boosting the immune system, and strengthening the respiratory system.

REFERENCES AND SUGGESTED READINGS

1. Muhammed Yazar Y, Introduction to NASM. https://usermanual.wiki/Document/NASM20 Manual.116 4426225/view (last accessed: May 15, 2023)
2. What is pranayama and its types & techniques? https://www.artofliving.org/in-en/yoga/what-ispranayama-and-its-types-techniques (last accessed May 14, 2023)
3. Health Impacts of Yoga and Pranayama: A State-of-the-Art Review. https://www.ncbi.nlm.nih.gov/pmc/articles/PMC3415184/ (last accessed: May 14, 2023)
4. NPTEL Course by Prof. Janakiraman Viraraghavan, C Programming and Assembly Language, IIT Madras, 2019. https://nptel.ac.in/ courses/108105102 (last accessed: May, 2023)

To learn the use of C library with assembly programs

5 Memory and Digital Interfacing

UNIT SPECIFICS

The following aspects are discussed in this unit:

- Memory addressing and address decoding;
- Interfacing RAM, ROM, EPROM;
- Programmable peripheral interface and modes of operation;
- Various techniques of interfacing to processor;
- Interfacing with keyboard, and display

The practical applications of the topics are presented for the purpose of fostering greater curiosity and creativity and enhancing problem-solving skills. In addition to a large number of multiple-choice questions and short- and long-answer questions marked in two categories according to the lower and higher levels of Bloom's taxonomy, the unit provides practice assignments in the form of numerical problems, a list of references, and suggested readings. It is crucial to note that several QR codes, which may be scanned for further information on various topics of interest, have been included in different parts and can be used to obtain necessary supporting data.

The related practical based on the content is followed by a "Know More" section on the topic. This section has been carefully constructed such that the supplementary information it contains is valuable to the book's readers. This section focuses primarily on the contributions of Indian innovators to the development of computer system organization and Indian meditation practices to stay energised, focused, and stress-free in daily life.

RATIONALE

This chapter discusses several memory technologies and how they have evolved to satisfy storage capacity and data transfer speed demands. Semiconductor technology advancements have resulted in considerable improvements in the speed and capacity of memory, as well as significant fall in the cost per bit. The classification of different memory technologies helps in understanding the requirements of distinct technologies for diverse applications. Memory-to-cache data mapping techniques are also covered. Furthermore, discussing secondary memory allows you to compare the speed, capacity, and technology with primary memory. This chapter also covers memory and I/O interfaces. The numerous interfacing techniques for peripheral devices, processors, keyboards, displays, and so on are thoroughly described.

PRE-REQUISITE

Computer System Organization (Unit-I)

Digital Electronics: Number systems- binary, octal, and hexadecimal (Polytechnic Engineering)

UNIT OUTCOMES

Outcomes of this unit are as follows:

U5-O1: Describe role of various memory interfacing for processors

U5-O2: Describe role of the memory technology RAM, ROM, EPROM in memory design

U5-O3: Explain programmable peripheral interface and various modes of operations

U5-O4: Explain various techniques of interfacing to processor

U5-O5: Explain the interfacing with keyboard and displays

Unit-5 Outcomes	EXPECTED MAPPING WITH COURSE OUTCOMES (1- Weak Correlation; 2- Medium Correlation; 3- Strong Correlation)				
	CO-1	CO-2	CO-3	CO-4	CO-5
U5-O1	3	3	3	2	2
U5-O2	3	3	2	1	2
U5-O3	2	1	3	1	2
U5-O4	3	3	2	1	1
U5-O5	3	3	3	1	3

5.1 INTRODUCTION

Interface is the communication path between two components. Interfacing is of two types, memory interfacing and I/O (input/output) interfacing as shown in Fig 5.1. In memory interfacing, during instruction execution, processors communicate with memory for read and write operations. Processor reads data from memory or writes data into memory. Before read/write operation, the microprocessor sends read/write control signals to the memory. In I/O interfacing, processors communicate with I/O devices

For memory interfacing and addressing

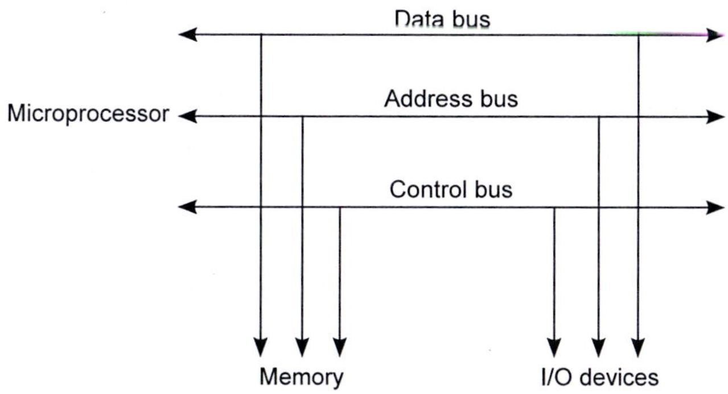

Fig. 5.1: Memory and I/O interfacing

through I/O modules which contain logic for performing communication between peripheral devices and system bus [1].

Fig 5.2 demonstrates that I/O module is required as an important interface between peripherals and the system bus because

- Many different types of peripherals exist, each with its own unique way of functioning. Not all devices can be controlled by a single central processing unit (CPU), as it would be impracticable to contain the necessary functionality within the processor.
- Peripherals data transfer rate is slower than the main memory/CPU. For this reason, it is not possible to communicate with a peripheral device over the high-speed system bus.

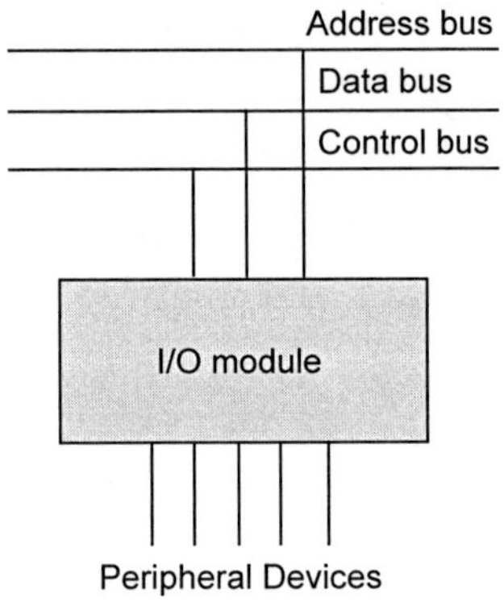

Fig. 5.2: Peripheral devices

- Many peripherals store and transfer information in different formats and with a different word length that are incompatible with the host computer.

The block diagram of the I/O module is demonstrated in Fig 5.3. The left hand side interface connected with the system bus and right hand side interface connected to external devices like keyboard, mouse, external memories etc.

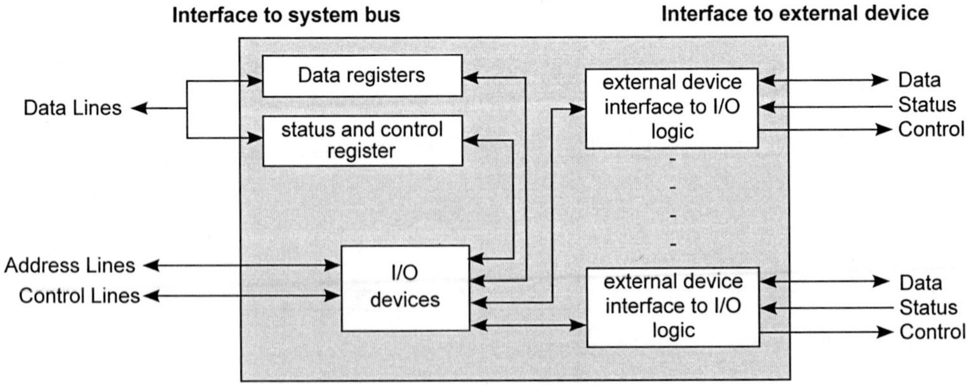

Fig. 5.3: Block diagram of I/O module

The control signals are required to coordinate the timing of flow of information between internal resources and external devices. The processor interrogates the I/O module to know the device status.

The data is transferred to the processor through the I/O module if the device is ready. The I/O module obtains data from the external device.

5.2 MEMORY TYPES AND CHARACTERISTICS

This section covers various types of memory that a computer system can use. Each memory characteristic and working principle is thoroughly discussed.

5.2.1 Types of Memory

Memory is classified into several types based on the circuit design technique used, the volume of temporary or permanent storage capacity, the size, cost, and location within the system.

1. **Registers:** Registers are part of the CPU such as general purpose registers, segment registers, pointer registers, and index registers. The storage capacity of the register is defined in bytes. Registers are the fastest access memory elements.
2. **Semiconductor Memories:** The semiconductor memories are classified into random access memory and read only memory.

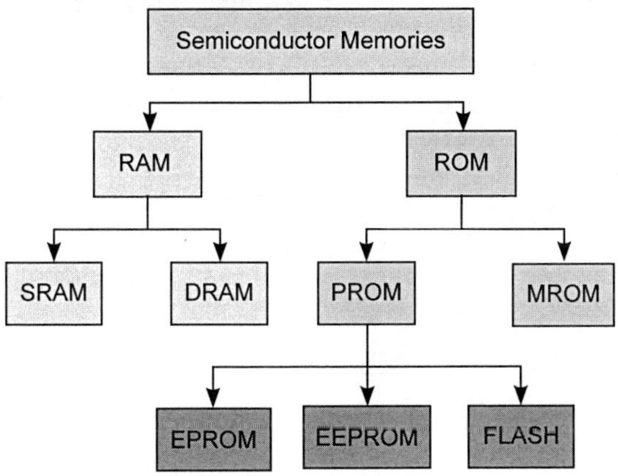

Fig. 5.4: Classification of semiconductor memories

5.2.2 Random access memory (RAM)

For SRAM and DRAM circuit design

Random-access memory (RAM) is used to store data and programmes temporarily before they are used. Data can be read/written from/to specific locations in physical memory. RAM has multiplexing and demultiplexing circuits to connect the data lines to the address lines, allowing for the reading and writing of individual data elements [2]. RAM's memory cells are essentially electronic circuits that can store data for a computer. The set and reset logic is used to store the data in memory cells, "set" means "1" (greater than 0.5 volts) and "reset" means "logic 0" (below 0.5 volts). It is a volatile memory. The RAM memory is classified into dynamic RAM (DRAM) and static RAM (SRAM). Both types of memory are volatile memory. If power fails then data is lost in memory.

A DRAM is also known as primary or main memory and its storage capacity is MB to GB. Each DRAM memory cell is made up of only one transistor and a capacitor. Data is stored in capacitors, and each capacitor's charge level determines whether a bit is a logical 1 or 0. Because information may be lost if the capacitor discharges, the memory cell stores either 0 or 1 while the capacitor is charged. These memory cells are automatically refreshed at regular intervals. Because DRAM is implemented using MOS capacitors. Therefore, a lot of power is required to store data.

Whereas, SRAM is used to design the cache memory. Each SRAM cell circuit requires six transistors, four to store the bit and two to control access to the cell. In SRAM, the data does not need to be refreshed periodically [3]. SRAM memory cells are typically MOSFET-based flip-flop circuits. Cache memory has KB to MB of storage space, which is more than register storage space. Data used recently is stored in cache memory. In comparison to register access time, cache memory access time is longer.

Table 5.1: Difference between SRAM and DRAM

SRAM	DRAM
It has lower access time, so SRAM is faster than DRAM.	It has a longer access time, so DRAM is slower than SRAM.
It is costlier than DRAM.	It is less expensive than SRAM.
It needs to be powered on all the time, so SRAM uses more power.	DRAM uses less power because it stores information in a capacitor.

The features of SRAM and DRAM memory are compared in Table 5.1. The data stored in static RAM is lost if the power is off. SRAM is significantly faster than DRAM. It is more expensive than DRAM because each cell requires six transistors.

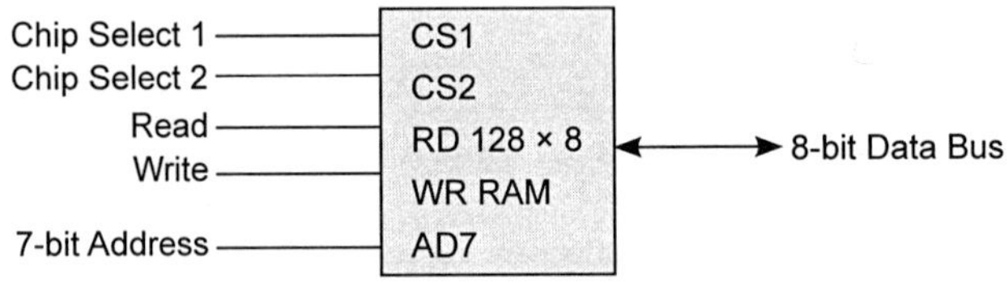

Fig. 5.5: A typical RAM chip with 7 address lines and 8 bidirectional data lines

A $2^n \times d$ RAM chip has n address lines and d bidirectional data lines. Figure 5.5 shows the structure of a RAM chip, which includes two selection lines (CS1 and CS2), seven address lines (AD7), and bidirectional eight-bit data lines. The read/write operation is activated based on the bit value selected. The RAM chip has 128 (2^7) memory locations that can be represented with a 7-bit address and the capacity of each memory location is 8 bits. The processor can access 8 bit data from the RAM chip or write 8 bit data into the RAM chip at a time. The RAM memory is a type of temporary memory.

5.2.3 Cache Memory Mapping Techniques

The computer perceives that the main memory operates at a faster speed because of the cache memory. Loops, nested loops, and functions are examples of instructions that call each other repeatedly in a programme. Many instructions in specific areas of the programme are executed repeatedly over time. This is known as the "locality of reference". This is classified into two types: spatial locality and temporal locality. The use of data elements within relatively close storage locations, such as arrays, is referred to as spatial locality. Temporal locality believes that a recently executed instruction has a high possibility of being executed again.

Caches are classified into two types: "write-through" caches and "writeback" caches. The "write-through" cache simultaneously modifies the cache and main memory locations. In writeback cache, only the cache location is updated and the associated flag bit is marked as updated; this bit is commonly known as the dirty or modified bit. When this block is removed, it is stored in memory. Caches that use this method are called "writeback" or "copying back" caches. This process occurs when a cache block is removed from the cache to make space for new cache blocks.

Blocks of main memory can be mapped to cache memory in three different ways: direct mapping, fully associative mapping, and set-associative mapping. These mapping schemes have a significant impact on the cache hit ratio and, as a result, system performance. Each strategy has benefits and drawbacks. These mapping methodologies are discussed in detail further below.

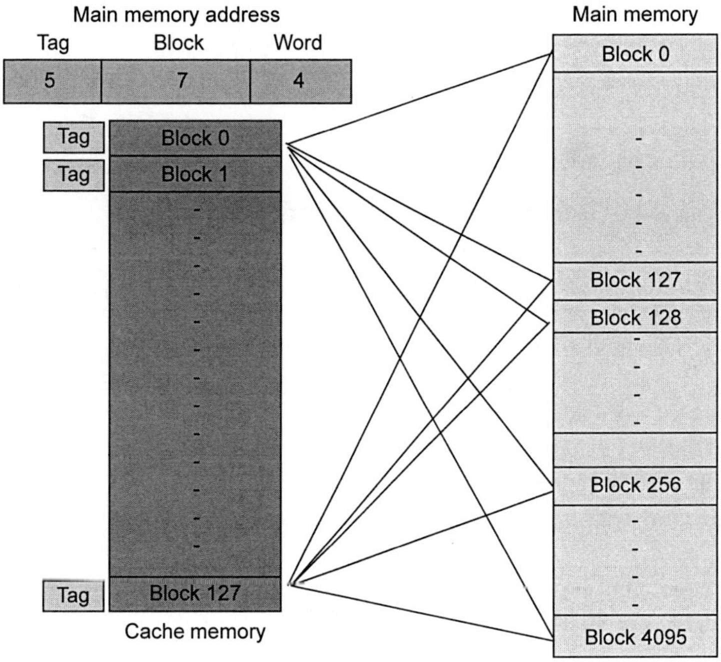

Fig 5.6: Direct cache block mapping of typically 4096 main memory blocks to 128 cache blocks

1. **Direct mapping:** The capacity of cache memory is lesser than that of main memory. The cache address uses C bits, which is less than N bits in main memory. Assume the main memory has a capacity of 2^N bytes, which is partitioned into B blocks (0 to B – 1 integer value). Each block stores D bytes of data. If cache miss occurs, the required block is mapped into 2^C cache memory. Block j of main memory (where $0 \leq j < B$) is therefore mapped to the cache block number computed as

$$\text{Cache block number} = \text{block j modulo } 2^C$$

Figure 5.6 depicts the direct mapping technique in which the cache consists of 128 blocks and the size of each cache block is 16 (2^4) words. The main memory address is 12 + 4 = 16 bits, where the least significant four bits of the memory address represent the word address. The required number of bits for cache block address is 128 (2^7). The total number of bits needed for the tag address is determined as follows:

Total number of bits required for the tag address = Number of bits in the main memory address – Number of bits for block address – Number of bits for word address

Therefore, total number of bits required for the tag address = 16 – 7 – 4 = 5 bits.

The cache block 0 loads main memory blocks 0, 128, 256, ..., and cache block 1 stores blocks 1, 129, 257, ... It is also feasible to predict where a main memory block will be mapped in cache. For example, main memory block 856 will be mapped to cache block 856 modulo 128 = 88.

Example 5.1: Consider that your computer's byte-addressable main memory is 2^{32} bytes in size and is divided into blocks. A block of data can contain 32 bytes. This computer has a 512-block direct mapped cache. How many bits are used by the cache memory's tag field?

Solution: Given that it is a byte addressable memory, and the main memory is 2^{32} bytes in size. So the main memory's physical address is 32 bits long.

Each block is $32 = 2^5$ bytes in size. The first 5 bits of the 32-bit main memory address represent the word address.

There are $512 = 2^9$ cache blocks for cache memory, and because it is a direct mapped cache, the 9 bits are used for cache block addresses.

Main memory physical address 32-bits

Tag (18-bit)	Block (9-bit)	Word (5-bit)

There number of bits of main memory physical address for a directed mapped cache is equal to the sum of the number of bits used in cache tag address + number of bits for block address + number of bits for word address.

Thus, the number of bits used in the cache's tag address + 9 + 5 = 32.

Number of bits used in cache tag address = 32 – 14 = 18.

The direct mapping technique has following advantage and disadvantage:

Advantage:

1. The direct mapping approach is **simple and easy** to implement.
2. Word searches are **faster** as only the tag field has to match.
3. The **tag** field is **short**.
4. Direct mapping is **less expensive** than associative and set-associative cache mapping.

Disadvantage: Direct mapping **performs worse** due to conflict misses. Although empty cache blocks are available, filled blocks are frequently replaced because the new block can be mapped to a fixed position in the cache. Conflict miss occurs when filled cache blocks are replaced despite the presence of empty cache blocks.

2. **Associative mapping:** Associative mapping is the most efficient and flexible mapping approach. It identifies a block using tag address and word address. Because of associative mapping, each position in cache can store any word from main memory.

LRU replacement algorithm

Figure 5.7 depicts the typical associative mapping technique. Assume the main memory has a capacity of 4096 (2^{12}) blocks. Each block is 16 (2^4) bytes in size. The physical address in the main memory has 12 + 4 = 16 bits. Because the cache memory may hold 128 blocks and the needed number of bits for word addresses is 4. So, the number of bits necessary to represent the cache tag address is 16 – 4 = 12 bits.

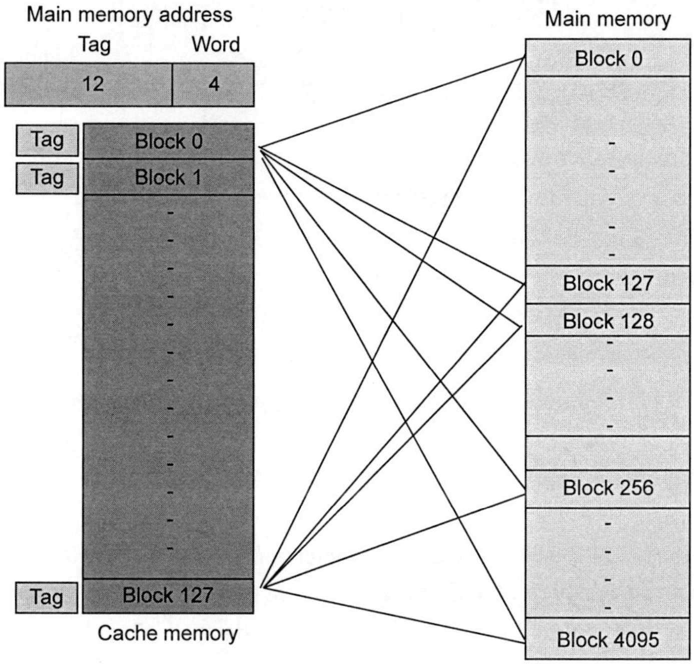

Fig 5.7: Associative mapping

When the cache is full, the existing block is replaced to bring a new block in cache. In this case, an algorithm is used to select the block to be replaced. Many replacement algorithms are possible, but least recently used (LRU) is popularly used for associative caches.

Example 5.2: Consider a 16 KB associative mapped cache with a 256-byte block size. The main memory is 128 KB in size. How many bits are used for the address of the tag?

Solution: Given that

Cache memory size = 16 KB

Block size = 256 bytes

Main memory size = 128 KB

The memory is considered as byte addressable.

Since main memory capacity = 128 KB

$= 2^7 \times 2^{10} = 2^{17}$ bits

Thus, number of bits in main memory physical address = 17 bits.

Main memory physical address 17-bits

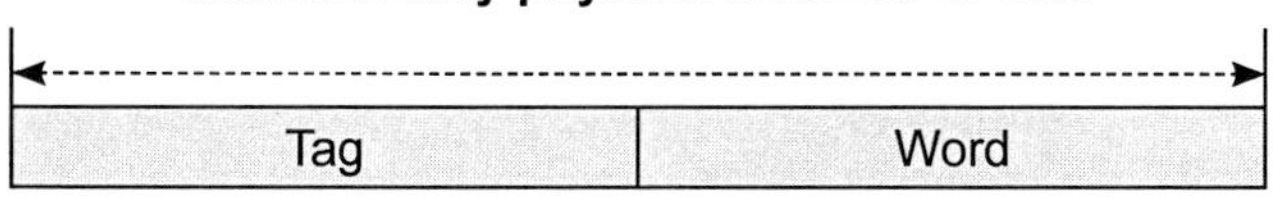

Since the block size of cache memory = 256 bytes = 2^8 bits

The number of bits for word address = 8 bits

Thus, the first 8 bits of the main memory address are used for word addresses.

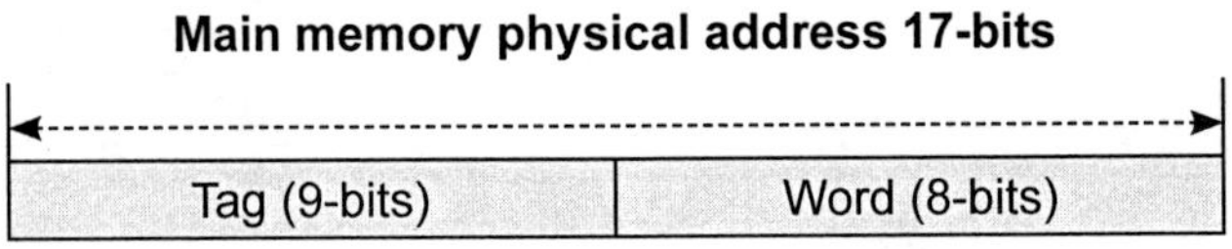

Therefore, number of bits for tag address

= Number of bits in physical address – Number of bits for word address

= 17 bits – 8 bits = 9 bits

Thus, Number of bits for tag address = 9 bits

The associative mapping has following advantage and disadvantage–

Advantage:

1. The associative mapping is the most flexible approach when a new block is read into the cache.
2. The hit rate is better than the other two cache mapping techniques.

Disadvantage:

1. All tag patterns need to be searched to determine the desired cache block. So associative caches are more **complex** than direct-mapped caches.
2. Tags are searched in parallel to avoid a long search delay. But this kind of **search is expensive** to implement.
3. The tag field is long.

3. **Set-Associative mapping:** Set-associative mapping combines the features of both direct and associative mapping. A main memory block can be inserted into any block in a set. This mapping provides more flexibility than direct mapping, however it is not as flexible as associative mapping.

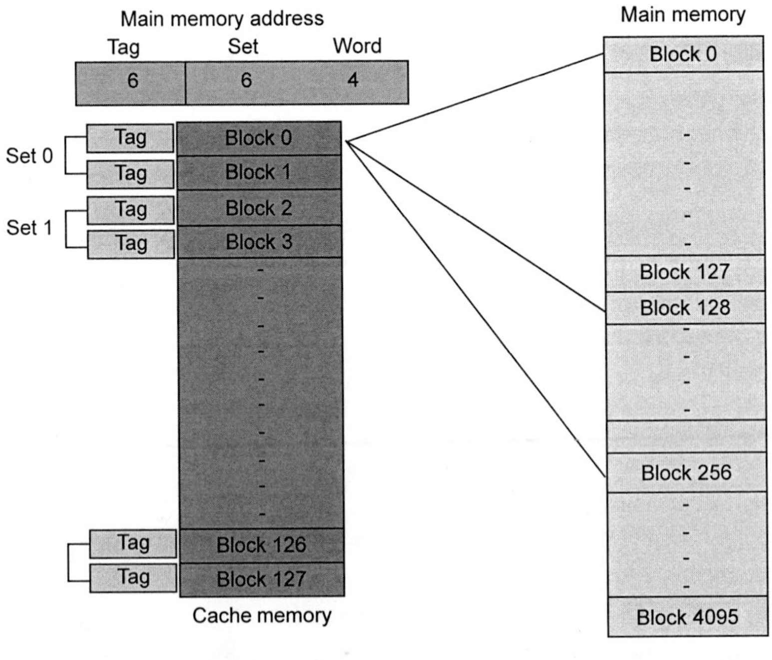

Fig 5.8: Set-associative mapping

Fig 5.8 depicts set-associative cache memory with 128 cache blocks organised into 64 sets, each set containing two cache blocks. Given that the total number of sets is 64 (2^6), a specific set can be identified using an address consisting of 6 bits. If each of the six bits is 0, it indicates the first set. Each block contains 16 bits; therefore, identifying a specific word within a block requires a 4-bit binary value. If the four least significant bits are 0000, the first word block is identified. The four bits are 0011, which indicates that this is the fourth word in the block. Because there are 4096 blocks and 16 bits in each block, the main memory's physical address is 16 bits long, and the memory's total capacity is $2^{12+4} = 2^{16}$.

Example 5.3: Consider a 2-way set associative mapped cache of sixe 16 KB with block size 256 bytes. The size of the main memory is 128 KB. Compute the number of bits required for tag, set and word address.

Solution: Given that

Set size = 2

Cache memory size = 16 KB

Block size = 256 bytes

Main memory size = 128 KB

The memory is considered as byte addressable.

Size of main memory = 128 KB = 2^{17} bytes

Thus, Number of bits in physical address = 17 bits

Total number of blocks in cache = Cache size/block size

= 16 KB/256 bytes = 214 bytes/2^8 bytes = 2^6 blocks

Thus, Number of blocks in cache = 64 blocks

Total number of sets in cache = Total number of blocks in cache/Set size

= 64/2 – 32 sets = 2^5 sets

Thus, Number of bits in set number = 5 bits

Main memory physical address 17-bits

Tag (4-bit)	Set (5-bit)	Word (8-bit)

Number of bits in tag = Number of bits in physical address – (Number of bits in set number + Number of bits in word address)

= 17 bits – (5 bits + 8 bits) = 17 bits – 13 bits = 4 bits

Thus, Number of bits in tag = 4 bits

Cache set 0 maps memory blocks 0, 64, 128, ..., 4032 to its two block places. To determine if the required block is present, the address tag field must be compared associatively with the tags of the two blocks in the set. This two-way associative search implementation is simple. The number of blocks in each set can be modified according to the system requirements.

Set-associative mapping has the following advantages and disadvantages.

Advantage:

1. Having multiple block positioning options reduces the direct mapping's contention issue.
2. By decreasing the number of associative searches, hardware costs can be reduced.

Disadvantage:

1. Set-Associative cache memory is too expensive. The cost increases with the size of the set.
2. Overall, associative mapping outperforms all others, but its implementation is expensive. Therefore, set-associative mapping is preferred in common practices [4].

Memory management unit (MMU)

The run-time mapping between the processor-generated logical address and the main memory's physical address is carried out by a hardware component known as the memory management unit (MMU). The logical address is a virtual address generated by the CPU when a programme is running. When processes move between the disk and main memory, the operating system manages how they move in and out. Both memory availability and utilisation are monitored by the operating system.

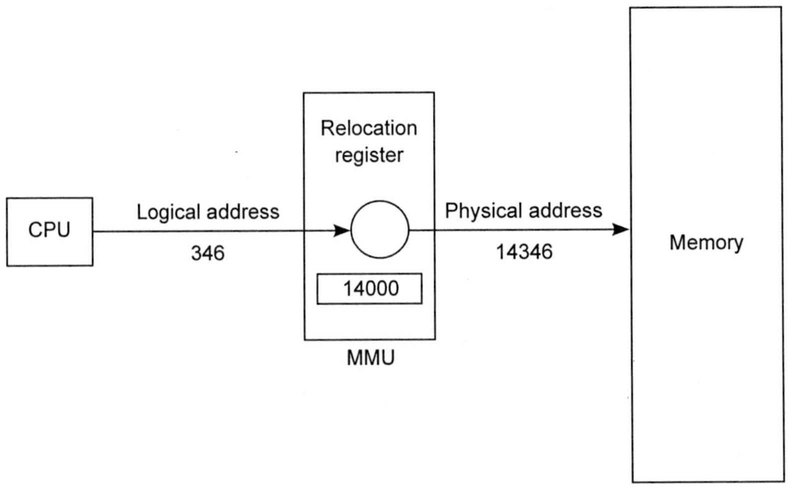

Fig 5.9: Logical address to physical address mapping using memory management unit

The address generated by the CPU is a logical address. The memory management unit (MMU) generates the actual main memory address (physical address) by adding the logical address L to the value B of the relocation register (base register). The processor can access data or instructions for programme execution from this location. Figure 5.9 shows how the CPU's logical address 346 is added to the relocation register value 14000 to produce the physical address 14346 of the main memory where this instruction/data will be stored.

Example 5.4: The CPU generated address is 500 and relocation register values is 10000. Then what is the physical address of memory to access the data?

Solution: Given that the logical address 500 is added with relocation register (base register) value 10000 and result 10500 is generated from MMU to memory. This result 10500 will be the actual memory address (physical address), from this location processor access either data or instruction for program execution.

5.2.4 Read Only Memory (ROM)

Read only memory (ROM) is a type of primary memory but this memory holds system programs. It is referred to as system memory, and the processor can read data from the ROM chip only. It is a non-volatile memory and data is stored permanently, even when the power is removed [5].

RAM vs ROM Memory

The architecture of the ROM chip, consists of n-bit address and d-bit unidirectional data bus. This ROM's storage capacity can be expressed as $2^n \times d$. A ROM chip with 9-bit address lines and 8-bit data lines is shown in Fig 5.10. With a 9 bit address, there are $2^9 = 512$ memory locations, and each memory location can store 8 bits. Over time, various ROM versions have evolved for use in various applications.

- **ROM** is a nonvolatile memory in which data is written once and never changed. A firmware program called the basic input/output system (BIOS) is stored in ROM.

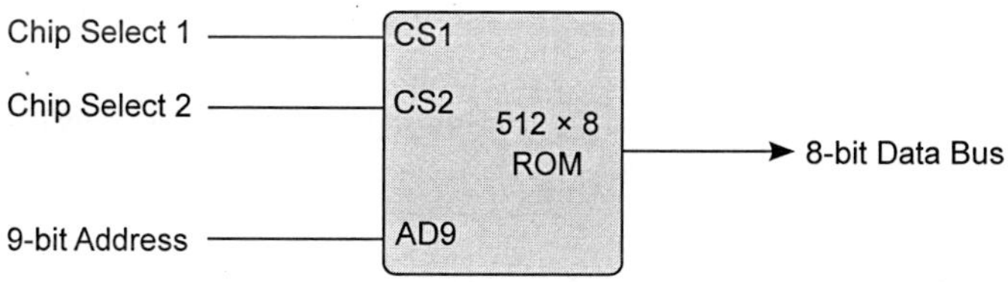

Fig. 5.10: A typical ROM chip with 9 address lines and 8 unidirectional data lines

- **PROM** is an abbreviation for "programmable read-only memory". This type of memory can only be programmed once and requires a special tool known as a "PROM programmer" to program it.
- **EPROM** stands for "electrically programmable read-only memory". After the memory has been programmed, ultraviolet light can be used to erase it.
- **EEPROM** stands for "electrically erasable programmable read-only memory". With an electric voltage, you can write data to it and erase it.
- **Flash memory** allows you to write and erase data. The data can be rewritten. The digital cameras and cell phones both use flash memory cards.

Example 5.5: For a 2048*16 RAM and ROM chips, how many address lines add data lines are there?

Solution: The chip capacity is 2048*16. Since 2048 – 2^{11}, the RAM chip has 11 address line and 16 bidirectional data lines and ROM chip has 11 address lines and 16 unidirectional data lines.

5.3 SECONDARY MEMORY

The secondary memory is based on serial access memory technology. The data can be allocated in contiguous memory blocks and data can be deleted from contiguous memory blocks. It is non-volatile memory, data can be stored permanently. The example of permanent storage devices are magnetic disk, magnetic tape, CD-Drive, etc. These devices have more storage capacity compared to all other memories. The storage capacity ranges from GB to TB. The CPU access time is more compared to all other memories.

To know types of secondary memory

In a hard disk, data is organized in a concentric set of rings called track. A read/write head is used for reading/writing a portion of the platter. Each track is further divided into sectors. Universal size of each sector is 512 bytes. Data density is more in the innermost track because the inner sector has less memory space. The outermost track has a lower data density because its sector memory capacity is larger. Memory space is wasted in the outer tracks. Zones are used instead of sectors to prevent memory waste. There are equal-length zones on each track where a fixed amount of data is kept. In comparison to the outer track, which has more zones, the inner track has fewer zones. The disk capacity can be computed as

$$\text{Disk capacity} = \text{surfaces} \times \text{tracks} \times \text{sectors} \times \text{bytes}$$

Disk capacity is the product of #surfaces, #tracks per surface, #sectors per track and #bytes per sector. Here # symbol indicates the number of the given units.

Disk performance: The performance of a disk is dependent on seek time, rotation latency, and data transfer rate.

- **Seek time (Ts):** The amount of time required for the read/write head to locate the correct track.
- **Rotational latency (T_R):** The disk controller waits until the desired sector spins to line up with the head of the selected track that is called rotational latency (T_R). The default rotational latency is

$$T_R = (½) \times \text{rotation time}$$

- **Disk access time (T):** The sum of seek time and rotational latency is disk access time.

$$T = T_S + T_R$$

- **Transfer time (T_T):** The disk rotational speed (r) decides the transfer time as follows

$$T_T = (b/r) \times N$$

The number of bytes to be transmitted (*b*) is divided by the rotational speed (*r*) in revolutions per second, which is then multiplied by the number of bytes (*N*) on a track.

Average access time of disk (T_{avg}) = $T_S + T_R + T_T$

$T_{avg} = T_S + (½) \times r + (b/r) \times N$

Example 5.6: A disk has

- 8 data recording surfaces
- each surface has 4096 tracks
- each track has 256 sectors
- each sector contains 512 bytes

What is the total capacity of the disk?

Solution: Disk capacity = #surplus × #tracks × #sectors × #bytes

Total disk capacity = 8 × 4096 × 256 × 512 = 4294967296 bytes

5.4 PROGRAMMABLE PERIPHERAL INTERFACE

The 8255 IC features 24 input/output pins to increase the capacity of the microprocessor's input/output interface. All I/O pins are categorized into A, B, and C ports. Both A and B ports operate as 8-bit input/output ports. Port C may be configured in a number of different ways, such as an 8-bit I/O port, two 4-bit I/O ports, or as a handshake port for ports A and B. These ports are divided into two groups

- Group A: port A and the port C upper part
- Group B: port B and the port C lower part

According to the values of address lines A1 and A0, each port or a control register accesses a data register as summarized in Table 5.2.

Table 5.2: Address lines bit values for port selection

A_1	A_0	Selected port
0	0	Port A
0	1	Port B
1	0	Port C
1	1	Control register

5.4.1 Operational modes of 8255

The 8-bit control register, as shown in Table 5.2, not only controls the modes of operation but also identifies the ports for the input/output. Bit set/reset mode and input/output mode are the two operational modes. These modes are determined by the control register's most significant bit (MSB) D7.

Table 5.3: Control register format for BSR mode

D7	D6	D5	D4	D3	D2	D1	D0
0	X	X	X	B2	B1	B0	S/R

Always 0 for BSR mode | Don't care | Part C selection bits | Set/Reset

- **Bit Set/Reset (BSR) mode:** If the D7 bit is set to 0, the 8255 operates in BSR mode, which is only available on port C. By altering the control register value, each line of port C from PC0 to PC7 may be set/reset. Although the BSR and I/O modes exist independently, none affects the other's operation.

  The remaining bits D6, D5, and D4 are Don't care (X). The bits D3, D2, and D1 are used to choose the port C pin. Bit D0 is used to set/reset port C pin.

Table 5.4: Pin selection of port C

D_1	D_2	D_1	Port C Pin Selection
0	0	0	PC0
0	0	1	PC1
0	1	0	PC2
0	1	1	PC3
1	0	0	PC4
1	0	1	PC5
1	1	0	PC6
1	1	1	PC7

- **Input/Output mode (I/O mode):** This I/O mode is chosen when the D7 bit of the control register is set to 1. It has three different I/O modes: mode 0, mode 1, and mode 2.
  1. **Mode 0:** In mode 0, ports A and B can perform basic I/O operations without handshaking. Port C might be a single 8-bit port or two 4-bit ports. Port C's two halves may be set as input and output ports since they are separate.
  2. **Mode 1:** It is possible to set up port A and B to function in different modes when using mode 1. For example, port A may run in mode 0 while port B operates in mode 1. In addition, handshake input or output can be sent over either port A or port B. You can use either port. Handshake lines are implemented on a portion of port C's pins.
  3. **Mode 2:** In mode 2, only port A can be initialized for bidirectional handshake data transfer (the same eight lines can be used for input or output) through PA0 to PA7 pins. Port A's handshake lines are PC3 through PC7. Port C pins PC0-PC2 may be utilised as input/output lines if group B is initialised in mode 0. Group B may utilise the remaining pins for port B handshaking in mode 1.

5.4.2 Interfacing to Processor

The following tasks are performed for interfacing of processor with peripheral devices:

For memory mapped I/O vs I/O mapped I/O

1. The I/O module sends a signal on the control bus according to commands received from the processor/CPU.
2. The CPU and I/O module exchange data.
3. The I/O module communicates its status to the CPU through status signals like BUSY and READY.
4. The I/O module recognizes each peripheral device with a unique address.
5. The I/O module receives status signals from the peripheral devices. The device's state is sent to the CPU through the I/O module.
6. Data is sent and received using the I/O module.
7. The I/O module keeps the data temporarily in buffers that are coming in rapid bursts from main memory. This data is sent to the peripheral device at its data rate.
8. The I/O module also reports any detected errors to the CPU. While taking printouts, if paper is jammed in the print out machine then I/O module detects paper jam error and reports to the processor. Data transmission error detected using parity checkers.

The interfacing of processor with peripheral devices can be performed in any one of the following three methods:

1. **Memory/(I/O) mapped I/O:** When an I/O device is mapped into memory, the address space used by both the memory and the I/O device shares the same. This particular type of I/O is called "memory-mapped I/O". When an I/O device is mapped into I/O space, the address space for the I/O device is distinct from the address space for memory devices. This method is called "I/O-mapped I/O".
2. **Programmed I/O:** In programmed I/O, the CPU runs a programme to take complete control over I/O operation. The CPU and I/O module communicate via control, test, read, and write commands. The CPU senses device status through I/O module, and performs data transmission.

It waits until the I/O operation is completed before transmitting another instruction to the I/O module.

The control command turns on and instructs the specified task to the peripheral device. The test command checks the status of an I/O module and its peripherals. Data from the peripheral region may be stored in the I/O module's internal buffer. When the CPU needs information to be put on the data bus, it issues a read command to the I/O module. The write command instructs the I/O module to send information to a peripheral.

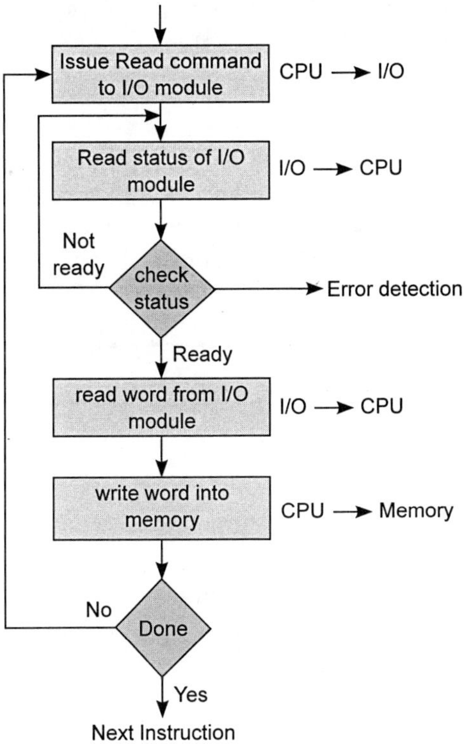

Fig. 5.11: Flowchart of programmed I/O

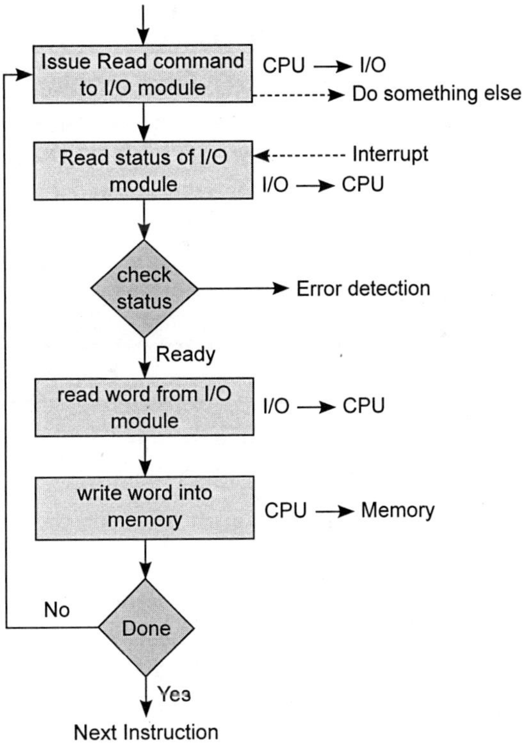

Fig. 5.12: Interrupt driven I/O flow

In Fig. 5.11, a flowchart demonstrates programmed I/O procedures. The I/O module receives a read command from the CPU and then sends peripheral status to the processor. If the I/O is ready for data transmission, the I/O module sends 8 or 16 bits of data to the CPU. The CPU sends data to memory. The CPU periodically checks the I/O module until the connected peripheral device sends data.

3. **Interrupt driven I/O:** The CPU issues read command to the I/O module and CPU does some other work during interrupt driven I/O. Whenever an I/O module connected peripheral device is ready for the operation then peripheral device sends an interrupt signal to the I/O module, the I/O sends it to the processor [6].

5.4.3 Interfacing keyboard and display devices

The 8279 integrated circuit is a keyboard/display controller designed by Intel specifically for integrating keyboard and display devices with 8085/8086/8088 microprocessors.

1. **Keyboard:** The keyboard features 64 keys, eight return lines, numbered RL0 through RL7, as well as shift and control/strobe as additional inputs. A keyboard matrix's columns are formed by the return lines. The keys are debounced automatically. The keyboard has 2 key lockout and N key rollover modes. In addition, the keyboard features an 8x8 First-In First-Out (FIFO) RAM.

   In scan keyboard mode, the FIFO can store up to eight key codes as well as status of the shift and control keys. When a FIFO entry is detected, the 8279 generates an interrupt signal. When the keyboard is in sensor matrix mode, the status of 64 switches is saved in FIFO RAM. The 8279 raises the IRQ (Interrupt Request) to interrupt the processor if the state of any of the switches changes.

For interfacing of 8279 controller with keyboard and display

2. **Display:** The output lines on the display are separated into A0 to A3 and B0 to B3. The output lines are used with scan lines either as eight lines or as two groups of four lines for a multiplexed display. For example, each LED cathode in a 7-segment display is connected to the same terminal. The display part includes 16 × 8 display RAM. The CPU has the capability to read and write to any location in the display RAM.

For block diagram of 8279 controller

UNIT SUMMARY

- Interface is the communication path between two components. Interfacing is of two types, memory interfacing and IO (input-output) interfacing.
- In memory interfacing, during instruction execution, processors communicate with memory for read and write operations.
- In IO interfacing, processors communicate with IO devices through IO modules.
- Memory is classified into registers, cache, random access memory (primary memory), read only memory and secondary memory.
- Caches are classified into two types: "write-through" caches and "writeback" caches. The "write-through" cache simultaneously modifies the cache and main memory locations.
- In writeback cache, only the cache location is updated and the associated flag bit is marked as updated; this bit is commonly known as the dirty or modified bit. When this block is removed, it is stored in memory. Caches that use this method are called "writeback" or "copying back" caches.
- RAM (Random-access memory) stores data and programs temporarily before they are used. The set and reset logic is used to store the data in memory cells.
- SRAM is used to design the cache memory. Each SRAM cell circuit requires six transistors. In SRAM, the data does not need to be refreshed periodically.
- A DRAM is also known as primary or main memory. Each DRAM memory cell is made up of only one transistor and a capacitor. These memory cells are automatically refreshed at regular intervals.
- ROM (Read only memory) is a non-volatile memory and data stored permanently. This memory holds system programs.

- In secondary memory, data can be allocated in contiguous memory blocks and data can be deleted from contiguous memory blocks. It is non-volatile memory, data can be stored permanently.
- Principle of locality of reference states that many instructions in specific areas of the programme are executed repeatedly over time.
- Blocks of main memory can be mapped to cache memory through direct, fully associative, and set-associative mapping.
- Overall, associative mapping outperforms all others, but its implementation is expensive. Therefore, set-associative mapping is preferred in common practices.
- The interfacing of processors with peripheral devices can be performed in three ways: memory/(I/O) mapped I/O, programmed I/O, interrupt-driven I/O.
- The 8279 integrated circuit is a keyboard/display controller designed by Intel specifically for integrating keyboard and display devices with 8085/8086/8088 microprocessors.

EXERCISES

Multiple Choice Questions

1. What is RAM?

(a) Read Access Memory (b) Random Aided Memory
(c) Read Analog Memory (d) Random Access Memory

2. Which of the following memory devices is very much similar, mainly in terms of speed, to the cache memory?

(a) SRAM (b) DRAM (c) EEPROM (d) Flash Memory

3. Which of the following is a static, non volatile, and permanent memory in a computer?

(a) CD ROM (b) CPU (c) ROM (d) RAM

4. Digital camera uses __________ memory.

(a) Flash (b) Main (c) Cache (d) Virtual

5. Identify the smallest and highest storage unit?

(a) GB and TB (b) GB and MB (c) MB and TB (d) KB and TB

6. __________ is not a type of secondary memory?

(a) Solid State Drive (b) Hard Disk (c) RAM (d) USB pen drive

7. Identify false statements:

1. Programmable read only memory is written once and programmed using a special PROM programmer.
2. EPROM memory can be programmed and erased by ultraviolet light.
3. EEPROM erases data using an electrical voltage.
4. In flash memory, data can be rewritten.

(a) 1, 2, 3, and 4 (b) 1, 2, and 3 (c) 1 and 2 (d) none of these

8. The personal computer main memory consists of __________?
   (a) both RAM and ROM
   (b) Cache memory
   (c) ROM only
   (d) RAM only

9. __________ types of RAM are available?
   (a) Four (b) Three (c) Two (d) Five

10. The boot sector files of the system are stored in __________?
   (a) Cache
   (b) Read Only Memory
   (c) Random Access Memory
   (d) Register

11. The devices and memory are interfaced using separate address space for __________ I/O.
   (a) Programmed (b) Interrupt driven (c) memory mapped (d) I/O mapped

12. The __________ integrated circuit is a keyboard/display controller designed by Intel.
   (a) 8085 (b) 8086 (c) 8088 (d) 8279

13. The 8255 IC features __________ input/output pins to increase the microprocessor capacity.
   (a) 12 (b) 24 (c) 48 (d) 64

14. The default rotational latency is __________ times of the rotation time.
   (a) 1/2 (b) 1/4 (c) 2 (d) 4

15. Which is not a mode of operation for 8255?
   (a) I/O mode (b) BSR mode (c) MSB mode (d) mode 0

ANSWERS															
1.	(d)	2.	(a)	3.	(c)	4.	(a)	5.	(d)	6.	(c)	7.	(d)	8.	(a)
9.	(c)	10.	(b)	11.	(d)	12.	(d)	13.	(b)	14.	(a)	15.	(c)		

Short and Long Answer Type Questions

Category-I

1. Why does information stored in dynamic RAM need to be refreshed periodically?
2. How is interfacing with the keyboard different from interfacing with display?
3. How do access time, memory cost, and capacity vary for different memory types?
4. Compare the advantages/disadvantages of set-associative mapping, associative mapping, and direct mapping.
5. Each cache memory mapping approach treats main memory addresses as fields. Specify such fields.
6. How many transistors are used in SRAM and DRAM memory?
7. Compare programmed and memory mapped I/O.
8. What is the difference between RAM and ROM?
9. Why are computer memory systems built as hierarchies?

10. Why do DRAMs have a larger storage capacity than SRAMs?
11. What relation exists between cache capacity and hit rate?
12. Why does increasing the associativity of a cache generally increase its hit rate?
13. What is the locality of reference?
14. Describe two distinctions between spatial locality and temporal locality?
15. What is the difference between write through and writeback cache?

Category-II

16. Describe how various memory technologies are used for different applications. How does ROM differ from flash memory technology, PROM, EPROM, and EEPROM?
17. List the differences between SRAM and DRAM technologies.
18. Why does increasing the line length of a cache
    - (i) often increase its hit rate?
    - (ii) sometimes reduce the performance of the system containing the cache, even if the hit rate of the cache increases?
    - (iii) could decrease the hit rate?
19. What is the difference between memory interfacing and IO interfacing? Explain the procedures involved in transferring data from external devices to the CPU.
20. Describe in detail how to interact with the keyboard and display devices.
21. Describe the direct, associative, and set-associative mapping methods for mapping memory blocks into cache memory.

Numerical Problems

22. The 128 blocks of a set-associative memory are divided into four block sets. Each of the 16,384 blocks in the main memory comprises 256 eight-bit words. How many bits are required for
    (i) main memory addressing? (ii) the "TAG", "SET", and "WORD" fields?
    [**Ans:** (i) 22 bits (ii) TAG = 9 bits, SET = 5 bits, WORD = 8 bits]
23. If a cache is 2-way, 4-way, or 8-way set-associative, and its capacity is 16 KB, how many sets does it contain if its line length or block size is 128 bytes? [**Ans:** (i) 64 (ii) 32 (iii) 16]
24. A RAM chip with an 8-bit width may store 1024 words (1K × 8). To convert a 1K × 8 RAM to a 16K × 16 RAM, how many 2 × 4 decoders with an enable line are required? [**Ans:** 5]
25. A system has 1 GB main memory and uses 32-bit memory addresses. It has an 8M-byte cache organized in the block-set-associative manner, with 4 blocks per set and 64 bytes per block. What are the fields of the memory address? [**Ans:** Tag = 11, Set = 15, Word = 6]
26. A main memory consisting of 64K 32-bit words. It also has a 2K word direct-mapped cache with 16 words per block. Suppose CPU generates the 16-bit Hexadecimal address ABCD to access a 32-bit word, Specify the cache block number in decimal to which this word maps [**Ans:** 60]

27. A disk has 10 data recording surfaces, each with 4096 tracks. If tracks are divided into 128 sectors and each sector contains 256 bytes serially recorded, what is the total capacity of the disk?

[**Ans:** Disk capacity = $10 \times 4096 \times 128 \times 256$]

PRACTICAL

Aim: In Gem5 simulator, simulate two instruction set architectures (ISA) such as ×86 and ALPHA. Compare the power consumption and performance of each ISA. Change the configuration parameters of the various cache and DRAM memory models and determine how the number of hits and misses affects the power consumption and performance of the system.

Tools: Gem5 Simulator

Theory: The gem5 simulator is composed of the M5 and GEMS simulators. M5 has different ISAs, different CPU models, and a simulation system that can be changed. GEMS is a flexible memory system with a number of cache coherence methods and interconnection models. Gem5 works with ARM, ALPHA, MIPS, Power, SPARC, and x86, which are all commercial ISAs.

Installation steps of gem5 simulator

Procedure: Gem5 is a widely used cycle-accurate computer architecture simulator. It is an open-source project that enables researchers and developers to explore various computer architectures and system-level designs by simulating them on a software platform.

The installation steps for Gem5 can vary depending on the operating system and the specific version of Gem5 to install. Here are the steps to install gem5 on Ubuntu 22.04:

For gem5 tutorial

STEP 1: Install the dependencies required for building gem5 by running the following command:

To learn gem5 parameterized options

```
sonal@sonal-virtual-machine: ~/gem5
sonal@sonal-virtual-machine:  $ sudo apt install build-essential git m4 scons zlib1g
 zlib1g-dev libprotobuf-dev protobuf-compiler libprotoc-dev libgoogle-perftools-dev  pyt
hon3-dev python-is-python3 libboost-all-dev pkg-config
```

STEP 2: Clone the gem5 repository from GitHub by running the following command:

```
sonal@sonal-virtual-machine: ~/gem5
sonal@sonal-virtual-machine:  $ git clone https://gem5.googlesource.com/public/gem5
```

STEP 3: Enter in the gem5 directory by running the following command:

```
sonal@sonal-virtual-machine: ~/gem5
sonal@sonal-virtual-machine:  $ cd gem5/
```

STEP 4: Build gem5 by running the following command:

```
sonal@sonal-virtual-machine: ~/gem5
sonal@sonal-virtual-machine:~/gem5$ scons build/NULL/gem5.debug PROTOCOL=Garnet_standalone
--linker=gold
```

STEP 5: You can test the installation by running command :

```
sonal@sonal-virtual-machine: ~/gem5
sonal@sonal-virtual-machine:  $ ./build/NULL/gem5.debug configs/example/garnet_synth_traffic.py --
num-cpus=16 --num-dirs=16 --network=garnet --topology=Mesh_XY --mesh-rows=4 --caches --l2cache --ruby
--sim-cycles=10000 --synthetic=uniform_random --injectionrate=0.1
```

The following command line options can be used to explore various cache memory configurations:

```
  --caches
  --l2cache
  --num-dirs NUM_DIRS
  --num-l2caches NUM_L2CACHES
  --num-l3caches NUM_L3CACHES
  --l1d_size L1D_SIZE
  --l1i_size L1I_SIZE
  --l2_size L2_SIZE
  --l3_size L3_SIZE
  --l1d_assoc L1D_ASSOC
  --l1i_assoc L1I_ASSOC
  --l2_assoc L2_ASSOC
  --l3_assoc L3_ASSOC
  --cacheline_size CACHELINE_SIZE
  --ruby
  -m TICKS, --abs-max-tick TICKS
```

KNOW MORE

Innovations by Indian: Madhav Desai and his team have developed the AJIT processor at IIT Bombay with funding support from the Ministry of Electronics and Information Technology (MeitY).

AJIT is a medium-sized processor, which is different from Intel's Xeon and other laptop processors. It can be used in a set-top box, as a traffic light driver, as a control panel for automation systems, or even in robotic systems. When AJIT is made in large quantities, the price will be too low. It can run one command per clock cycle and can run at clock speeds between 70 and 120MHz, which is about the same as its competitors in the market [7].

Importance of Meditation in Modern Life Style: Meditation significantly impacts Hypothalamus-Pituitary-Adrenal (HPA) Axis, a brain-body circuit that plays an important role in body's response to stress [8]. Meditation boosts energy levels and increases the immune system, allowing the body to fight diseases. It causes the relaxation response and other psychophysiological processes to occur. The mind has extraordinary control over the body. The mental state of a person can affect physiological functions such as pulse rate, blood pressure, and production of biochemical molecules, human hormones, and neurotransmitters. Meditation, in conjunction with other healthy-living practices, has the potential to be a drug-free treatment for stress-related diseases and depressive mood disorders [9, 10].

Meditation is a form of spiritual and mental practice. It aids in connecting with love, happiness, and peace. When meditating, one experiences profound relaxation. Meditation has many benefits, including a calm mind, increased focus and self-control, high concentration power, increased productivity, self-confidence, self-awareness, and compassion. It also heals the mind and body and connects to an inner source of energy.

Meditation can be traced back to ancient India. Each year, an increasing number of scientists publish research on the health advantages of meditation. As more research is published, more individuals are persuaded to meditate. The oldest references to meditation are found in Indian texts from around 1500 B.C. However, India's Vedic texts assert that meditation has existed since the start of humanity. In addition to India, numerous ancient societies saw meditation as a potent tool for spiritual growth.

Meditation can help you maintain physical, mental, and emotional health. Meditation practice is simple to add into your regular routine. Through consistent meditation practice, you will experience a profound internal change that will be visible to others around you, as they can feel the positive energy you radiate.

Meditation techniques are available in a wide variety today. Choose the option that best matches your personality and interests. You can ease into a regular meditation practice without committing to a strict schedule right away. Set aside some time and a quiet place to give meditation a try. Once you have finished, you want to do it next time. When meditating, it is helpful to set a timer and remove as many potential interruptions as possible. Everyone has the innate ability to meditate, just like everyone has the innate ability to walk. It is a matter of practice. Meditation and mindful exercise can help you feel peaceful and assertive energy in your life.

REFERENCES AND SUGGESTED READINGS

1. NPTEL Course by Prof. Indranil Sengupta and Prof. Kamalika Datta, Computer Architecture and Organization, IIT Kharagpur, 2017. https://archive.nptel.ac.in/courses/106/105/106105163/ (last accessed: Jan 07, 2023)
2. Nicholas Carter, Computer Architecture, Schaum's Outline, 2002.
3. NPTEL Course by Prof. Madhu Mutyam, Computer Architecture, IIT Madras, 2015. https://archive.nptel.ac.in/courses/106/106/106106134/ (last accessed: Jan 07, 2023)
4. Carl Hamacher, Zvonko Vranesic, Safwat Zaky, and Naraig Manjikian, Computer organization and embedded systems. McGraw-Hill Higher Education, 2011.
5. M. Morris Mano, Computer system architecture. Prentice-Hall, Inc., Third edition. https://poojavaishnav.files.wordpress.com/2015/05/mano-m-m-computer-system-architecture.pdf (last accessed: Jan 07, 2023)
6. William Stallings, Computer Organization and Architecture Designing for Performance, 10th edition, 2016.
7. Welcome AJIT, a 'Made in India' Microprocessor, https://www.iitb.ac.in/en/research-highlight/welcome-ajit-%E2%80%98made-india%E2%80%99-microprocessor (last accessed: Jan 07, 2023)
8. Meditation's Impact on Neurochemicals, https://sahajaonline.com/science-health/mental-health-well-being/neurochemicals/evidence-of-meditations-impact-on-neurotransmitters-neurohormones/ (last accessed: Jan 07, 2023)
9. William C. Daube and Charles E. Jakobsche, Biochemical Effects of Meditation: A Literature Review. Scholarly Undergraduate Research Journal at Clark: Vol. 1, Article 10, 2015. https://commons.clarku.edu/surj/vol1/iss1/10 (last accessed: Dec 30, 2022)
10. Adam Koncz, Zsolt Demetrovics & Zsofia K. Takacs, Meditation interventions efficiently reduce cortisol levels of at-risk samples: a meta-analysis. Health Psychology Review, 15:1, 56-84, 2021. DOI: 10.1080/17437199.2020.1760727.

REFERENCES FOR FURTHER LEARNING

The concepts of computer system organization will become clearer upon solving the examples and problems provided in each unit. Practice the Unit-IV examples and reference links to learn Assembly Programming. At the end of each chapter, there are links for suggested reading and NPTEL courses. Additional resources for advanced study and numerical problem solving are as follows:

1. Carl Hamacher, Computer organization and embedded systems. McGraw Hill Publication, 2002. http://103.62.146.201:8081/jspui/bitstream/1/9025/1/bok.pdf (last accessed: May 30, 2023)
2. Nicholas Carter, Computer Architecture. Schaum's Outline, 2002.
3. NPTEL Course by Prof. Smruti Ranjan Sarangi, Advanced Computer Architecture, IIT Delhi, 2021. https://archive.nptel.ac.in/courses/106/102/106102229/ (last accessed: Jan 07, 2023)
4. NPTEL Course by Prof. V. Kamakoti, Computer Organization and Architecture, IIT Madras, 2017. https://archive.nptel.ac.in/courses/106/106/106106166/ (last accessed: Jan 07, 2023)
5. Muhammed Yazar Y, Introduction to NASM. https://usermanual.wiki/Document/NASM20Manual.1164426225/view (last accessed: May 15, 2023)

As supplemental information, the author is developing video lectures on the book's few topics of the chapters, relevant numerical problems, and practical. The video links are available on the author's website ***https://nitrr.ac.in/viewdetails.php?q=cse.syadav***

CO AND PO ATTAINMENT TABLE

Course outcomes (COs) for this course can be mapped with the programme outcomes (POs) after the completion of the course and a correlation can be made for the attainment of POs to analyze the gap. After proper analysis of the gap in the attainment of POs necessary measures can be taken to overcome the gaps.

Table for CO and PO attainment

Course Outcomes	Attainment of Programme Outcomes (1- Weak Correlation; 2- Medium Correlation; 3- Strong Correlation)						
	PO-1	PO-2	PO-3	PO-4	PO-5	PO-6	PO-7
CO-1							
CO-2							
CO-3							
CO-4							
CO-5							

The data filled in the above table can be used for gap analysis.

INDEX

A

Addressing modes 103, 104, 107, 109, 110
Address sequencing 47
Arithmetic and logic unit (ALU) 11
Arithmetic Instructions 115, 143, 144
Arithmetic logic shift unit 28
Architecture of 8086 microprocessor 111
Arithmetic pipeline 71
Array Processors 83, 84
Assembler 129, 130, 141
Assembler directives 138
Assembly language programs 131

B

Branch Instructions 79, 80, 148
Bus and memory transfers 26
Bus structures 12

C

Cache memory 6, 7, 167
Cache Memory Mapping Techniques 168
Central processing unit 97, 165
Computer Arithmetic 54
  Addition 54
  Subtraction 54
  Multiplication 57, 61
  Division 61
Control memory 47, 49, 52
Control unit 47, 49, 53, 84, 115

D

Data Representation 15
  Fixed point 15
  Floating point 20
Digital Computers 3, 11, 24

E

Error detection code 22, 23
Evaluation of Arithmetic Expressions 150

F

Fixed point representation 66
Floating point arithmetic 67, 69

H

Hardwired control unit 50, 51, 53
Hazard 74, 75, 76, 79

I

Instruction format 101, 102
Instruction pipeline 73, 82
Instruction set architecture 100, 102, 129, 161
  CISC Characteristics 100
  RISC Characteristics 101
Interconnection 9, 10
Interfacing keyboard and display devices 182
Interfacing to Processor 181

L

Locality of reference 168
Logical Instructions 146

M

Memory and I/O Interfacing 165
Memory management unit (MMU) 175
Memory-mapped I/O 181
Memory types and characteristics 166
Micro-operations 3, 24, 28, 47, 50
  Arithmetic 29
  Logic 30, 31, 33
  Shift 33, 34, 35
Microprocessor 100, 111
  8085 99
  8086 111
Microprogrammed control 47, 52, 53, 102

O

Overflow detection 18, 20
Operational modes of 8255 179
Output Unit 11

P

Procedures and macros 139, 141
Programmable peripheral interface 179
Programmed I/O 181, 182

R

Random access memory (RAM) 167
Read Only Memory (ROM) 176
Register Transfer 24, 25, 26
RISC pipeline 82, 101

S

Secondary memory 177
Sorting 153
String Manipulation 151

V

Vector processing 83
Von-Neumann architecture 11, 12